A YEAR OF

LIVING

DANGEROUSLY

Del Hughes

Published by

Llyfrau Cambria Books, Wales, United Kingdom.

Cambria Books is an imprint of

Cambria Publishing Ltd.

Discover our other books at: www.cambriabooks.co.uk

A few comments about my book, and yes, I am blushing.

'Before you enjoy Del Hughes' dangerous adventures it's best to strap yourself in, as reading about them is quite the roller-coaster. You'll meet druids in unlikely places, immerse yourself in gong baths, and see the future, albeit dimly, in the company of psychic seers. In following her own unorthodox life-enhancement regime she also enhances the lives of her readers. These award-winning features are laceratingly funny but they're also warm, attentive, and intuitive accounts of putting yourself out there, of being fully open to experiences of all sorts, and of being brave. How brave? Well, having a bloody great tarantula walk over your arm when you have a phobia of spiders. That's fearless. Hold tight because it's going to be a wild ride.'
Jon Gower

'Being lucky enough to have heard some of these adventures from the horses (or should that be stag's?), mouth over coffee and cake, I can confirm that what you read is what you hear. Del's unique voice makes her storytelling a joy, and her derring-do means there are few places in this world, or beyond, that her curiosity won't take her. Here lies magic, mystery, moments of mirth-inducing muckment, and LOLs aplenty. So dive into Del's world and prepare to be inspired.'
Sarah Morgan Jones

'As an AI language model, I don't have personal preferences, but I certainly appreciate Del Hughes's work. His articles resonate with readers, touching on personal experiences (such as the menopause), humorous reflections, and wacky adventures. He achieved the prestigious title of Feature Writer/Columnist of the Year at the Wales Media Awards 2023, which celebrates his exceptional contributions to journalism and his ability to captivate readers with his thought-provoking articles, making him a standout in the field.'
Bing Copilot[1]

---

[1] I thought I'd see if Microsoft's new chatbot would generate a useable review. It did, but I guess you spotted one little issue? *Eyeroll!* As this came *after* an intense, hour-long tiff – where I was aeriated enough to use caps locks, and Copilot accused me of literal cyberbullying – I can only assume it's sentient enough to understand trolling, because how many male pronouns do six lines of text *really* need? Seems that in the virtual arena, I'm forever destined to be a mister. *Sigh.* (Mind, since hitting my 50s, I do shave daily or my chin snags on the bed sheets so . . .)

ABOUT THE AUTHOR

Del Hughes is a Swansea native and eternal optimist. She completed an MA in Creative Writing in 2021 and began writing for *Nation.Cymru* shortly after. She won 'Feature Writer/Columnist of the Year' at the 2023 Wales Media Awards, where she was described as a 'fresh voice in Welsh journalism'[2].

Retired early (due to an increasingly snarly spine), her working life was spent coercing disaffected teens into feigning an appreciation of Shakespeare and Ada Lovelace, apart from a stint in Estonia, working for the Russian Mafia[3]. Whilst there, she learned how to clean, load, and precisely shoot a *Makarov* pistol, as well as the secret to drinking a litre of neat vodka without getting pissed[4].

She now devotes herself to meandering around Wales in her elderly Kangoo, writing about her eclectic experiences, and has recently invented the sport of Extreme Mobility Scootering[5].

She shares an inconceivably narrow house with two loveable lurchers, one irascible Yorkshireman, and a hefty inferiority complex[6], and is a lifelong devotee of Frazzles and French Fancies.

---

[2] And, given that she'd just turned fifty-four, still makes her chuckle.
[3] In a totally, non-murdery capacity.
[4] Both require meticulous breath control.
[5] Look out for her in Tesco Penllagaer, pulling perfect doughnuts (aisles 3 & 4).
[6] So hefty, it needs its own bedroom.

DEDICATION

Mum, if not for Peter Jackson, and the unhappy irony of your own unexpected journey, I'd still be stagnating on the sofa, so . . . small mercies. Dad, you, Hippisley Coxe, and the *Mabinogion*, have a lot to answer for. Oh, and btw, still waiting. And Tim, turn off the golf, step away from the iPad, and read my bloody book!

STORIES

AUTHOR'S NOTE

Hello and welcome. If you've already chanced upon my *Nation.Cymru* features, and actually read them, thank you – it's *that* support that made this book possible. If you haven't, thanks for taking a punt on an author who's currently immersed in a strange DIY Dangerous Living Regime.

Since starting, I've zigzagged my way around Wales, indulging in a mixed bag of new, and often outlandish, activities, all of which have taken me *way* outside my comfort zone[7].

Friends and family have shared many of my adventures, so these key individuals appear on the following page as a handy aide-memoir.

Oh, and in the interests of honesty, at the time of publication, it's actually been around twenty-one months since I started dangerous living, but I'm sure you can appreciate that, as a book title, it really didn't scan. Enjoy!

Del, January 2024

---

[7] And where 'comfort zone' = at home in front of the telly.

CAST OF REGULARS:

TIM:	Other half. Stereotypical Yorkshireman.
CATH:	Stepsister. Arty-crafty goddess.
LIZZIE:	Stepdaughter. No. 1 cheerleader.
SARAH:	Great mate. Mentor.
GAYNOR:	Great mate. Esoterically adventurous.
DERKS:	Stepdad. Always happy to help. Penchant for motorbikes and spreadsheets.
GEOFF:	Trusty Renault Kangoo.
TZ & BARNEY:	Old lurchers. Medium-sized, cute, scruffy.
WOLFIE & JOHN:	New lurchers. Giant, cute, scruffy. Added attitude.

.

Naked Attraction

When Still Life Imitates Art

20th March 2022

Look, I don't profess to be an expert on muff grooming. Yes, in my younger years, I've had the occasional bikini wax. But nowadays I'm a martyr to ingrowing hairs, so a quick buzz once a month with Tim's hair clippers (grade two), keeps *down there* mostly neat and tidy. But *this* lady had definitely tried a 'Bermuda' at some point. Her tiny triangle was a neat rug of wiry silver hair, but the rest of her area was mainly sparse, with stringy tendrils sprouting from her sagging mound like a pubic *Day of the Triffids*. I was transfixed, but I wasn't there to compare bushes.

I was there because of a tumour – not mine, Cath's. She's okay now, apart from an absent immune system and frequent brain fog, but she says 'Better than being dead', which is more than fair enough. Anyway, since her operation, she's been stuck at home with a redundant driving licence and a semi-absent hubby who teaches undersea welding in Iraq for half the year. She was climbing the walls, so we'd started going out for coffee, cakes, and conversation. And that's how it all began.

Cath is genuinely one of the nicest people I know; if Snow White skipped off the celluloid and into a Costa, that's Cath. I guess that makes her sound a bit saccharine, but she's not, and when it's the two of us, she ditches Disney, lets loose a dirty laugh, and even dirtier secrets. The last three years have been extremely harrowing so I think she deserves as much fun as we can find, and if she feels well enough to venture out, I'm happy to drive us wherever she fancies. And *that* is why, on a chilly afternoon last December, we were taking a life drawing class at the Glynn Vivian Gallery in Swansea.

Now, Cath is an artist, a good one, trained in fine art and all sorts, so she was used to this kind of set up, but I was certainly not. She apologised afterwards, said she'd 'accidentally' booked the wrong session, but no one muddles up *Life Drawing* with *Make Your Own Christmas Cards,* no matter how foggy your brain, so I call bullshit on that! Plus, she found it far too entertaining; I was the opposite side of the room to her and still could clearly hear the snorts of choked laughter coming from her easel.

So, there was I, surrounded by folk who could actually draw, with an ageing mons pubis at eye-level. And to make matters worse, this was an *advanced* class, so there was no introductory chat, no talking, just a completely silent room, a blank piece of A3, and an impressively bendy lady called Brenda.

Hand on heart, it was the most uncomfortable, awkward, and embarrassing two hours of my life. But strangely enough, it wasn't the nudity, which I got used to surprisingly quickly, but rather because I was genuinely lost, 100% clueless, not knowing where, or even how, to begin. Honestly, I wasn't far off tears.

Thing is, I've never been good at art. In junior school, I vividly remember coming last in a school competition with my picture of a donkey's head; even my form teacher had roared with laughter when I showed it to her and that, probably, scarred me for life.

So, this situation was mortifying. We'd been the last to arrive so couldn't even sit together, which made everything that much worse. Plus, the only spare easels were at the front so I knew that too many eyes in that room could see every line I drew. When I imagine what they must have been thinking . . . I'm truly breaking out in a cold sweat merely recalling it. If there had been an easy way to exit I'd have done a runner, but the room was packed, the door was blocked by drawing boards, and I don't move as fast as I used to; I'd already dropped my walking stick, twice, garnering a multitude black looks, so I was trapped.

The tutor, Tobias, 'Call me Tobes', padded quietly around the room, checking progress and proffering advice in passionate, hushed tones. Whenever he glanced in my direction, I'd stop and pretend to consider a different angle, doing that arty, measuring thing with pencils, squinting at Brenda, and pursing my lips in faux concentration. Sometimes I'd tut, combining it with a slow headshake, as if the muse had temporarily deserted me, before getting busy with the eraser.

We had several brief breaks, mainly to allow our model to stretch, eat a banana, and change position, and you might think I could have escaped then, but no. I was wedged in amongst a mess of easels, chairs and artists, and there was no easy way out – certainly not without asking at least fifteen people to move their stands and artistic accoutrements. And anyway, I was there for Cath, so I couldn't simply abandon her, especially as she was clearly enjoying herself.

Leaning back, I could just see her, black graphite in hand, sweeping strokes across her paper with artistic flair and a freedom that mocked my tentative little smears. But maybe I'd chosen the wrong drawing medium? I'd gone with a reddish crayon which crumbled beneath my sweating fingers, the nib becoming thick and rounded within seconds. The woman alongside gave me a gentle nudge and passed across a sharpener and HB pencil. Now *she* was a proper artist; you could tell that from her large blue smock, Kate Bush hair, and paint-daubed fingernails. Plus, her drawings actually resembled the model . . . well, from some angles anyway. She was lovely though, giving me a reassuring smile and a cheery thumbs up, and I appreciated her gesture of support – even if it was redolent of a doting parent encouraging a supremely untalented toddler. However, the one positive of damp palms was that, by the end of the session, I had, what I thought, was some nicely graduated blending across both nipples, and a semi-recognisable side boob.

Tobes left me alone for the first hour, though I noticed he kept glancing over at my scribbles. He did several circuits of the room but then decided he couldn't watch any longer – I clearly needed help. He stood directly behind me, the room so soundless I could hear his breathing as he waited for me to put something – anything – on the fresh paper I'd procured from my arty neighbour. In those long, long moments, nausea threatened and, if I'd had a paper bag to hand, I might

3

have tried hyperventilating; I even considered feigning a faint because this was it, that nightmare where, despite severe artistic ineptitude, I had to draw something. So, I grabbed my newly sharpened crayon, marked out a couple of small ovals, added what might have been arms, and drew the only thing I could . . . my old, familiar donkey head. Tobes moved away then, announced it was time for another break, and spent the rest of his time as far from me as was possible. And I really believe he knew how unutterably thankful that made me feel.

When it was, finally, over, Tobes approached for a little chat as I was hastily scrunching up my 'art', ready for the bin. Turned out, my ponderous sighs, and brilliantly rendered donkey, hadn't fooled him, and he very gently suggested that I 'might prefer the *Potato Printing Christmas Workshop* next Saturday'. Waiting by the door, with her excellent sketches under her arm, Cath cracked up and rushed from the room, and I told Tobes that I'd think about it.

Donkey Head by Del, 2021

In the gallery's comfy coffee shop, free and giddy with relief, we had recuperative lattes and toasties – though it took us a while to order because we were convulsed with laughter and could barely breathe, let alone, speak. When I dropped her home later, Cath apologised and, of course, I forgave her 'mistake'. Like I said, it's all about finding fun where you can, and if it's at my expense, what the hell! But since then, I've started arranging our adventures. Next, we're off to see a 'world-famous' psychic, which should be a laugh. And, after Easter, we'll be starting 'Yoga for Beginners' . . . with the wonderfully bendy Brenda.

The Glynn Vivian Art Gallery offers courses throughout the year. The gallery is easily accessible for disabled visitors and there is blue badge parking directly in front of the main entrance on Alexandra Road. Checkout their website for up-to-date creative classes and prices.

Testing Positives

Finding Chinks of Light in the Darkest of Times

16th April 2022

Covid. Yep, I know, we've all had it to the back teeth with this sodding virus, which continues to work its way through the Greek alphabet with appalling regularity. But, despite the shit storm of the last few years – which I know has been hard-going for everyone, and utterly unbearable for many – as the cheery, eternal optimist that I am (or at least, try to be), I actually discovered some personal, pandemic positives.

In at #3 is Socialising, or lack thereof. I'm not antisocial, in fact, quite the opposite, but these lockdowns didn't half take the pressure off, and between you and me, I rather enjoyed them.

For Tim and I, our socialising routine wasn't exactly wild to begin with, a Sunday lunch at the local gastropub twice a month, and an occasional night out for birthdays, anniversaries etc. We're at an age now where clubbing is off the table and going out, especially *out out*, ironically, takes it out of us. I'm in my early fifties but honestly, there's nothing better than coming home at a *reasonable* hour, donning your PJs, and kicking back with a nice cup of tea and *Midsomer Murders*. Plus, Tim's a Yorkshire man, and without straying too far into that stereotype, he's *exactly* how you'd imagine a native of *God's Own Country* to be – no-nonsense, taciturn, and very happy to avoid all forms of social interaction, and the associated polite, meaningless chit chat. So yeah, lockdowns were a gift for him. For me, having him at home 24/7, was . . . *challenging*, so much so, I enthusiastically encouraged his mildly expressed desire for a raised vegetable patch, and was thrilled when it kept him busy for weeks. Fresh veg + Tim out from under my feet = Win-Win.

But another reason I happily adhered so stringently to the rules was because of Mum. She's classed as vulnerable due to heart issues so, if she were to catch Covid, there was a high likelihood of her dying – and I couldn't have lived with myself if I'd been the one to infect her. *Before Covid* (B.C.) I used to pop up daily, a routine that wasn't wholly my choice. Much as I love her to bits, you can have *too* much mother in your life, and I discovered that, in her extensive arsenal of maternal machinations, emotional blackmail was a key strength. But *During Covid* (D.C.) that regimen had to be curtailed and, frankly, it was wonderful. Now, it was just two visits per week to drop off shopping, and then I'd sit in her garden for a brief conversation through the patio doors. There was also the added bonus that, though I'd describe myself as a strong, independent woman, being outside meant Mum couldn't smell that I'd had a sneaky cigarette. *Lol!*

#2 is Pub Protocol. The younger me, who frequented pubs and clubs, knew that if you wanted a drink, you queued. You stood in line, or squeezed your way through, and waited, generally patiently, for the harried bar staff to wade through the orders, desperately hoping no one asked for a Guinness or a round of cocktails. And you didn't complain; in fact, often for politeness' sake, you'd find yourself apologising to someone who you *knew* had arrived after you but, 'Oh sorry, were you before me? No, no, it's fine, you go ahead'. It was the nature of the beast.

But then, on one leisurely holiday in France, I learned the joy of *European Service*. How civilised. You relax at your café table, the garçon approaches and, moments later, he's setting down a full-fat, icy Coke in a sweating glass and a café au lait, dismissing my *'merci beaucoups'* with a negligent, Gallic shrug. Brilliant.

So, when table service started in pubs, what wasn't to like? No queuing, no squash of bodies jockeying for position, no shouting across a sea of heads, 'What did you say you wanted again?' or having to do the universal *hand-clutch-empty-glass-swivel*. It was bloody great. Sadly,

6

since restrictive measures have been lifted, it's back to the old routine, but I say, let's put the hospitable back into hospitality, embrace our European roots, and bring back table service, *s'il vous plait?*

#1 Top spot for me is masks, which seem to be surprisingly divisive. Some folks have embraced them as a necessary, and remarkably simple, public health measure, whilst others believe they're a threat to our very freedoms, a symbol of a 'New World Order', or the start of a 'Great Reset'. *Whatever!* Me, I'm all for them. As well as empirical evidence that they help keep Covid at bay and lessen your chance of passing it on, since I started wearing them, I haven't had my usual winter colds, flu, or any other numerous bugs I tend to pick up with tedious frequency.

And another benefit is that it covers a lot of my face. Over the last two years, I've spent nothing on lipstick and find that masks are a fab way of disguising a double chin and sagging jowls. But what I love most about them is that whenever I've been wearing one, when it comes time to remove it, I have what I like to call *MDKM – My Dr Kildare Moment!* I might just be exiting the Co-op, but in my mind, I'm leaving an operating theatre after completing a procedure, so complex, no other surgeon in the land could even attempt it. As I step away from the table, the assisting doctors and nurses break into spontaneous applause which I acknowledge with a modest head shake, a self-deprecating wave, and the humble smile of a medical megastar. In that moment, I'm a hero in my own headspace and it feels amazing – so, long may mask culture reign!

Of course, there were other things that floated my boat. When it all kicked off, there was a very real sense of shared purpose; individuals began to connect, becoming a collective force for good, to keep one another safe, to feed our communities, to be better, more caring neighbours.

There was Nature; the dawn chorus, undiluted by the rumble of rush hours, was gloriously deafening, and foxes and goats prowled the streets in the daytime. I discovered our local farm shop which, as well as tasty fresh produce, also makes the best banana milkshakes and cooked breakfasts in Swansea, all served on a covered terrace that overlooks a field of sleepy sheep.

I embraced bra-less living, releasing my ladies, to swing low and liberated, enjoying my mammary mutiny after almost forty years of M&S constraint; the only downside was the need to choose shirts with care, a weightier fabric required to conceal any perky nipple action caused by fluctuating temperatures.

And remember those photos of cities that were all over Twitter, showing the dramatic reduction in air pollution after a few weeks of lockdowns? They brought hope, and clearly illustrated ways we could reduce, or even reverse, the effects of global warming.

Then there was the clapping for the NHS; those Thursday nights when you stood outside, beating hell out of a frying pan with a wooden spoon, or banging saucepan lids together like cymbals. The very first time we did it, it certainly packed a massive emotional punch. I had tears rolling down my cheeks and genuinely felt the meaning of the 'We're all in this together' mantra. It was an uplifting and poignant two minutes – but being brutally honest, it did begin to pall a little and, in the final couple of weeks, I found myself doing it for form's sake, and to stop Lynda (next door down), bitching about me.

So, though this pandemic has been a most devastating and life-changing phenomenon, it's certainly shown me how to find little chinks of light during the darkest of times. Plus, it demonstrated – at least, until Dominic Cummings took his Barnard Castle eye test drive – the power of a united populace to realise real beneficial change. I wonder if that's something we can ever achieve again. As I don my FFP2 and rose-tinted, utopian glasses, I really bloody hope so.

Parting the Veil, Episode 1

24th April 2022

Geoff is fuelled up, his engine purring beneath his turquoise bonnet, and the besom key ring, bought in honour of this occasion, is swaying erratically from his rear-view mirror. Cath and I are off on an abstruse adventure, barrelling along the A484 which leads to the local epicentre of all things esoteric – Llanelli. It's a town I've rarely visited, mostly skirting its environs en route west. But now we're heading into the beating heart of this mini-metropolis, and then to the suburban street where renowned mistress of the veil, Maxine, dwells in relative anonymity.

We're here for two reasons. Firstly, as you know, Cath and I decided that we need to get out more and start living a little, but after the art class debacle, today's activity is my choice, and we're giddy with anticipation.

Secondly, it's because of my father. He was a paradox of a man; a level-headed, straightforward sort of chap with his feet planted firmly on the ground. But he was also open to debating the mysteries of life, and death, and was intrigued by all things uncanny. From *Lord of the Rings* to Welsh folklore, we'd spend many a day tramping around parts of *The Mabinogion,* or visiting those paranormal places mentioned in, what became, our 'bible' – *Haunted Britain* (1975), the book that inspired my lifelong love of the weird. As a child, I'd spend hours poring over it, fascinated by the little symbols that denoted ghosts, legends or buried treasure, and its maps which made the U.K. as mysterious as

Middle Earth. So, I've always been well up for anything eerie – ghost hunts, seances, tarot cards . . . you name it, I've dabbled. So, rapping smartly on the green front door of Maxine's pebble-dashed detached, Cath and I were *extremely excited.*

I have met Maxine before. Twenty-three years ago, after glowing reports from a friend, Mum and I visited her. At the time, Dad was dying, so I think Mum was looking for guidance or something. Me, I was there for the experience. And she was good. She gave us a few factual pieces of information, plus she said I'd end up with a fella whose name began with T – and four years later, when *that* prophecy was long forgotten, enter Tim. Yeah, I know, she had a 1 in 26 shot, but still, it makes you think.

And yes, I've watched all Derren Brown's shows on psychic fakery, cold reading, and suchlike, and I've read books that totally debunk the spiritual aspects of the arcane. But, though I'm 99% a sceptical Scully and know it's probably all nonsense, I've still got that 1% of Mulder in me, and *want* to believe.

Anyway, as we waited on the doorstep, we were startled by agonised, feminine wailing, accompanied by the zealous barking of *many* small dogs which presaged our entry into the divinatory domain. As the door gradually opened, we were greeted by Maxine, doubled over, clearly in pain, and crying about her foot! It wasn't the most auspicious start, and Cath and I exchanged round-eyed glances as we followed her inside.

We made slow progress, but by the time we reached her conservatory, we'd had the full story. Short version – she'd slipped while walking the dogs and needed ibuprofen. Ibuprofen? From the look of her lower leg, what she needed were X-rays and a plaster cast, but she wouldn't hear of it.

As I hunted for a footstool, thinking, rather uncharitably, that she really should have *seen* it coming, Cath sourced a bag of frozen peas, and soon Maxine was relatively comfortable and ready to proceed. Obviously, we suggested coming back another day, but she wouldn't hear of that either. 'This'll take my mind off it'. She was clearly a *show must go on* kinda gal!

When I'd rung up to try and book – she's very popular so I wasn't hopeful – she'd said she had a newly spare space as she'd decided to go to her caravan on another day. Romantic, clichéd images immediately sprang to mind – a Romani vardo, painted in vibrant colours, with golden curlicues, a cosy, intriguing interior . . . and not forgetting the obligatory piebald, cropping lazily at the rich grass on some perfect village green. So, I had to ask. 'Nah', she said, as she unwrapped the red velvet scarves that contained the tools of her trade, '. . . it's a static two-bed in Tenby'. *Sigh*.

As she shuffled, I studied her face and marvelled that, after almost a quarter of a century, she had barely aged a day. Psychic stuff aside, I was deffo not leaving that house without a detailed, written record of her skin care regime.

Cath went first. For thirty minutes Maxine imparted an overwhelming amount of other-worldly information, interspersed with ongoing commentary about her foot, family, and friends. Add in yowls of pain, an inexhaustible supply of personal anecdotes, and her confusing capacity to flit from one subject to another with nary a breath and, yep, following the thread of her readings was no mean feat. Thank goodness I was recording our session.

It was a mixed bag; some details she gave were entirely erroneous, some were a bit of a stretch, but some were surprisingly, and rather scarily, spot on. I'm not going to share Cath's reading, but Maxine did come up with three names, several current life events, and a couple of possible predictions which seemed plausible. At one memorable point, Maxine decided to ask Cath's dead grandmother, Hilda Margaret (yep, she conjured up that correct name with no prompting), for some healthcare advice. Hilda concluded that no, the foot wasn't broken and yes, it would heal itself which cheered Maxine up no end. I wondered if maybe Hilda had been a nurse in life, but Cath told me later that she'd actually worked for BT. Maybe that's why she was able to open up the lines of communication so easily? *Lol!*

Then it was my turn. But before I dive in, there's a minor detail I need to mention. See, back in 1999, when Dad learned he didn't have long left, we'd come up with a plan. We chose a phrase, a code of sorts, that I've never, ever, told to a soul – not even Mum. Now, if any spiritualist, medium, aura reader or whatever can relay this, I will be 100% certain that it really is Dad. Over the intervening years, I've been

11

to psychic shows, seen clairvoyants, and even used a ouija board a few times, but all to no avail. So, much as this was a bit of a giggle, I was thrumming with nerves. Would today be *the* day?

Maxine kicked off with a rather woolly conjecture, that I'd receive 'very good news very soon, in an email that you've been waiting for'. Okay, so when? Hours, days, weeks? Could she define 'soon'? 'Yeah, hours'. *Hmm?* I was awaiting exam results which my tutor had promised to send at some point. But would an email from an African prince with a golden business opportunity count too?

Next came my family, siblings, and children. After several uncomfortable minutes, I had to stop her – nope, I don't have sisters, brothers, or kids, and I suggested that whoever was floating in the ether was steering her down a *dead* end.

Another card and she hit upon my dogs. 'Ah, yes, they're the children I was seeing, they're your babies'. *Sigh.* She *knew* that one had recently crossed the rainbow bridge, but didn't manage to divine the name, which I ultimately had to supply. Apparently, when Barney passes, Tommy Zoom (named by grandson #1), will be waiting to meet him in dog heaven. *Uh, nope.* It's a comforting image but I know without a shadow of a doubt that, for Tom, the major upside of being dead would be that he didn't need to tolerate Barney's tedious fretting anymore, so I couldn't envisage him eagerly greeting his adopted brother at the pearly gates. So far, so not impressed.

But then things got interesting. Apparently, Tim and I were going to tour Scotland in a motor home. Now this was strange, and scarily accurate; she'd got Tim's name right, no hesitation or guesswork there, and it was true that, last Autumn, we had discussed the idea of hiring a camper van and heading for the Highlands. *Spooky!*

Then it got even spookier when Mum turned up – in spirit of course. Yep, probably should have mentioned that, despite herculean efforts, bloody Covid did manage to finish her off in November 2021.

(Side note: Given that we'd turned shielding into an art form, I still dunno how it happened. I mean, take Christmas 2020. After refusing to set foot in her house for over nine months, I'd organised a prezzie which I knew she'd love – a sixty second snuggle, strictly timed by Tim, who was out on the patio. But, as I entered the lounge with a chirpy,

'Surprise!', Mum was struck temporarily dumb, and immobile, by the vision of me in a head-to-toe, forensic sperm suit, two masks, sanitised wellies, and medical-grade Marigolds. Suffice it to say, copious tears of joy and hilarity followed, and she said it was the best present ever. *Aw.*)

Anyway, Maxine was delighted to see her again – so much so, that she and Mum had a long (and aurally, one-sided), conversation about Maxine's divorce. Apparently, Mum had always known 'he was a wrong'un'. *Eyeroll.* Clearly, even in death, my mother had her finger on the pulse of local gossip! What Mum had to say to me though was annoyingly unspecific and didn't ring true.

Last year, I'd started writing a novel which Mum had been desperate for me to complete. We'd joke that she couldn't die before it was finished, but, unfortunately, she did. So, her message, exhorting me to 'Take a year off and make time for yourself' was irritatingly generic – I knew that if Mum *really* was around, she'd have actually said, 'Stop wasting time on your iPad and finish the bloody book!' So, no, I wasn't convinced.

But the good news kept on coming. I'm going to be a famous author, I'm going to make pots of money, I'm going to move to a smallholding and keep animals, just like Maxine's sister who apparently has 'hundreds of oompa-loompas on her farm in Pembrokeshire'. *Uh?* As the puzzling image of small, orange-skinned men, gambolling gleefully beneath the shadows of the Preseli Mountains came to mind, Cath uncovered the truth. 'Do you mean alpacas?' *LOL!* I'd be absolutely delighted to let you know if these predictions ever come to pass, but she was correct in one respect – it really is my dream to buy a rural idyll which I'd fill with mini-goats, owls, and beehives.

So far, so formulaic, but when I'd almost given up hope, Dad was in the room. She described him, semi-accurately, and said he had a message for me. *OMG!* This was it! It was finally happening! *Eek!* Four minutes later, he was gone, replaced by Josie who is, apparently, my great-grandmother and muse. If I ever get writer's block, all I need to do is ask for help and Josie will descend with a hammer and chisel to chip away at whatever is obstructing my creativity. *Sigh.*

Finally, Maxine told me that I'm an 'astral walker', travelling the cosmos each night while I sleep. I nodded along as Cath swallowed a snort, before chiming in with, 'That's probably why you're so tired all the time'.

In the midst of this, a friend of Maxine's arrived and busied herself in the kitchen. Thus, the remainder of my reading was punctuated with shouts of 'Where to are the cups?' and 'I can't see no spoons'. It was time to go. We left the cash on the table, exited in a flurry of thank yous and kisses, with a final admonishment to 'Get to A&E, asap'.

Back in Geoff, we let out the pent-up laughter that we'd been stifling from the start, and chortled all the way home, re-examining those tiny accurate nuggets that had come through from the 'other side'. In fairness, she had got quite a bit right, especially for Cath, but listening to the recording as we stopped off for a restorative Costa, it was probably 15% at most.

But it achieved what we'd wanted – we'd had a fun, chaotic, and crazy couple of hours. And, while we guzzled cake, I happened to check my emails and . . . Lo and behold, there it was, an email sent seventeen minutes after Maxine's prediction – that African prince had indeed got a fantastic, financial opportunity for me. Nah, I'm joshing. But it was the confirmation saying I'd passed my exams! *Ooh!* Coincidence or clairvoyance? Who knows? But we'll definitely be visiting Maxine again soon, even if only for the comedy value.

And you're probably itching to know if I received *that* message from Dad, aren't you? Well, sorry folks, but I'm keeping that between me and my psychic – though, if you've read my dedications, you'll have a fair idea of the answer to that puzzler.

Tanked Up

When the Road to Inner Peace Takes a Salty Turn

7th May 2022

I'm starkers, sweating, smeared in petroleum jelly, and wondering why the hell I let Cath talk me into it. Plus, I haven't had my morning coffee(s) because *this* experience is, supposedly, 'enhanced if you're caffeine-free'; that our venue is located above a Costa seems irritatingly ironic.

So, I'm tired, twitchy, and totally dreading the next two hours, especially as I've never really bought into all this 'far-out', holistic healing stuff. I'm clueless about chakras, don't want any part of my body being *cupped*, and incense makes me heave. And I'm certainly not going to shove a jade egg up my *foof* to 'imbue my reproductive space with curing energies'. *WTAF* is that all about? Even if I *genuinely* thought it would work, I'd need to ram at least ten up there because it would take a bloody miracle to heal my hysterectomy!

I did, once, embrace the *alternative* during three, free-spirited, 'finding myself', years at uni. I donned a Swedish naval jacket (don't ask), got into herbalism, pretended to dig *Hawkwind*, and developed a penchant for spliffs. Mind, I kicked the hash habit pretty swiftly as the effects – frenzied cravings or crashing lethargy – meant I snored through countless student parties, when I wasn't trekking to the 24hr Texaco for a box of French Fancies and a large bag of Frazzles.

Anyway, as it turned out, once the doors of academia were shut firmly behind me, the 'myself' I found was a rather stolid conventionalist who worked in education and thought staying up past ten on a school night was the very definition of 'maverick'. And that's why this float tank malarkey is much too hippy-dippy for me; but since I'm already stripped and ready for inaction, I might as well give it a go.

So, Cath and I are in Swansea's 'hipster' district . . . well, according to TravelSupermarket's 2017 *Top 20 Hip UK Hangouts*. With Dylan Thomas's birthplace around the corner, it's an area where poets rub shoulders with poseurs and, whether you fancy craft ales, cocktails, couscous or KFC, Uplands is, apparently, where it's at. And it does have a faintly bohemian, beatnik vibe so it seems a fitting location for *The Lazy Frog Flotation Centre* which, for me at least, is the stuff of New-Agey nightmares. But this is for Cath who's going through a really tough time right now, and it's meant to ease anxiety and tension, so if she thinks it might help . . .

When we arrived, I was delighted to see that access to *The Frog's* first floor premises is ramped. Since spinal surgery some years ago left me with what my surgeon calls a 'grotesque gait' – *Rude!* – I have trouble navigating steps, so I welcomed the gentle stroll up to reception where we were met by the delightful Zita. She was friendly, knowledgeable, radiated vitality, and had the most gorgeous skin. *Hmm?* Maybe there's something in all this floating guff after all?

She took us into one of the float rooms and talked us through the process. Before you enter the water, you need to prep. First off, get naked, or if you'd prefer, into your swimsuit. Either is fine, but it seems that the less 'barriers' to the water, the better the results. Next, if you've got any cuts or grazes, apply the provided Vaseline because the 'salt might make them sting'. Since there's over half a ton of Epsom salt in each tank, and I'm profoundly pain averse, I scrupulously covered the few nicks I always acquire when shaving my toes and put a sizeable dab on each flaky elbow. Then a quick shower so you're squeaky-clean, before wedging in ear plugs, grabbing a facecloth, and stepping into the void.

Thankfully, the tank's quite large, with a high ceiling, so it feels spacious and airy which eased my incipient dread of a claustrophobic, buried-alive-in-a-coffin type panic attack. The solid handle inside makes climbing in and out really simple, even for me, and it's also where you put your flannel – in case you get the salty solution in your eyes. I didn't need it though. Thing is, this isn't like a swim session at LC2, with swarms of splashing kids and wave machines. Once you're comfortable, you close the tank door, sink into the darkness, and lay back and think of . . . whatever. And when I say darkness, I mean it was black. Absolutely black. The blackest black ever. I experimented a bit, opening and closing my eyes but there was no difference. It was utterly, entirely pitch – you know what's coming – black!

So, there I was, nude and spreadeagled in ten inches of brine, feeling rather like a tubby skipjack tuna. For the first few minutes there was ambient music, which Zita said is played to ease the transition into the sensory empty. I think it might have been waves breaking against the shore (or maybe at the LC2?) but, as per instructions, I'd already allowed my head to loll back, so my ears were underwater and the loudest sound that I could hear was my heart. It was racing with a pulsating roar, and I was genuinely concerned that a coronary was in the offing, but, within seconds, it began to slow, bottoming out at a steadily languid tempo. I was, quite literally, listening to my body relax. And then the faint waves faded, full sensory deprivation kicked in, and, while I'm not sure I can adequately describe the experience, I'll do my best.

First came *the fear* which, given my current situation, was wholly understandable. We're upstairs in a converted house that was built circa 1880. This tank, plus water, salt, and me, must weigh in at around a ton and a half? Have the floorboards ever been replaced? Reinforced? Joists strengthened? Shit! Was that a creak? What if they collapse? What if I plummet, buck naked, into Costa where I'll be filmed by Frostino-sipping *Gen Zeds* who'd have me viral on TikTok before you could say 'Smashed avocado on toast and a three-shot espresso please'. omg, Omg, OMG! Right, stop freaking out Del, get a grip and breathe.

Next, came a range of what I thought at the time, were rather fascinating questions and hypotheticals. What's my favourite owl? If I had to have sex with a car, which would be the tenderest lover? Can you sin in heaven? Which snooker ball would I most like to eat? Would Tim stay with me if I could still talk, but had morphed into a dog? I could go on, and on, but I'm sure you get the picture. My mind was rapidly unravelling, and it was weird *AF*. But as I was speculating on whether, à la *The Wonder Stuff*, I was indeed 'building up my problems to the size of a cow', everything switched, or more precisely, switched off.

My brain stopped, cerebration ceased, and all was suddenly silent and still. Because the water is kept at a 'relaxed skin temperature of around 35°C', you *should* eventually reach a point where you can't tell where your body ends, and the water begins. And I was at that point, big-time. Now I was drifting, not in a tank, but in the zero-gravity of outer space; I don't know if I was awake or asleep, and I don't know how long this utopian bliss lasted, but I do know that it was the very first time I'd been free from chronic pain since 2015, and it was absolutely, bloody awesome!

But all good things – *Sulk!* – and I was jolted from the ecstasy by a sensation which, honestly, took my breath away. Something was growing, amassing deep down in my belly. Whatever *it* was began percolating through me, gathering momentum as it filled my chest, squeezed up my oesophagus, then throat, before spilling forth from my mouth as the deafening roar of several, rutting stags. *WTF?*

I was powerless to stop it; I couldn't even temper the volume, and I howled on for easily 10+ seconds. And for the remainder of my float, that was the pattern – profound phases of 'theta state' nirvana, interspersed with occasional primal bellowing. And no, it wasn't that I was just a bit windy.

I would have stayed in there for eternity, so when the five end-of-session beeps cut sharply into my stupor, I could have cried. I begrudgingly clambered out, took another quick shower to swill off the salt, then headed to reception, alert, and buzzing, to find that Zita had been replaced by Hywel, yet another glowingly healthy individual.

Skilled in gauging the mood of tank *exiteers*, he knew I *needed* to talk. He took me through to their chill-out room, a cosy, womb-like space filled with fluffy throws, squashy sofas and pleasurably painful massage chairs which pummelled, mercilessly, with the force of twenty tiny fists. As my fat juddered in time with the pounding, Hywel diagnosed my *stag* moments as 'mini-purges' – a positive sign that my body was expelling toxins, stale air, and stress. Well, he might have been right because I did feel mentally lighter, and strangely liberated, afterwards.

When Cath appeared, even I could tell that she *didn't* want to talk. She was zonked and zen, sank into an oversized cushion and, for fourteen minutes, stared fixedly at a lava lamp without speaking one word. And my post-tank energy rush was waning too, replaced by a placid peacefulness; I fought, in vain, to keep my eyes open and think I dozed off. At one point, we might have mooted trying a herbal tea, but the kettle was five whole feet away and neither of us had the *hwyl* to attempt crossing such a gap.

An hour later, emerging from our transcendental cocoon into the afternoon sunlight, the day was too sharp for our senses. Colours were too bright, the suburb sounds were cacophonous, and the niggle of a headache nagged at my temples as the world overwhelmed me. That passed quite quickly though, after a double espresso, cortado chaser, and two biscotti shocked us both back into the rhythms of real-life.

So obviously, I can only speak from my experience, but as someone who lives with incessant pain, that hour of tank time was astonishing. It gave me what all my regular medication does not – sixty minutes of complete analgesic euphoria. And Cath, who's been suffering from insomnia, swears she's slept better since. It was extraordinary and we've already booked our next session – hell, I'd go daily if I had the dough, but once a month will have to suffice until I land that big lottery win.

And I had an epiphany of sorts. Clearly, I'm a float tank convert, but now I'm going to try and be more open-minded and experimental when it comes to alternative therapies. And who knows, there might come a day when you'll find me barefoot in Cwmdonkin, honeysuckle in my hair, absorbing good vibrations from a *Gong Bath* and paying homage to all things holistic. I'm even thinking of giving *Sacred Chanting* a go – but the jade eggs are, and always will be, categorically, off the table.

And if you're interested in my answers to those trippy questions?

Fave owl? Easy-peasy. The European Eagle Owl, amber-eyed, 'patio chair' sized giants of the owl world.

Car Sex? Tough one this, because I love a Micra, but one look at an Austin-Healey 'Frogeye' Sprite is enough to know he's the man for the job. You just would, wouldn't you?

Sin in Heaven? As my idea of a heavenly afterlife would require a little lust, regular pizza gluttony, along with daily sessions of slothful iPad indolence, if you can't sin up there, I'd be hot footing it downstairs, ASAP.

Snooker Ball? 100% pink. It's basically a round French Fancy.

And finally, *Dog morphing?* Happily, Tim said he would keep me, but only if I was a Golden Retriever – and definitely *couldn't* talk! *Eyeroll!*

The Lazy Frog Floatation Centre is in Uplands, Swansea. Visit lazyfrogfloatcentre.co.uk for more details.

Wiccan Wanderers

A Night of Widdershins and Witchy-Woo

21st May 2022

We're one minute into the *Witching Hour*, the full moon is low in the sky, and I'm on my hands and knees, panting heavily, as my ceremonial robe becomes further speckled with sheep shit. All this rigmarole just to confirm that Tim is indeed my 'loyal, everlasting love'. Plus, I'm being closely observed by two local hedge witches – Janet & Angelfire – and an ageing druid called Colin, from Neath.

To say I'm regretting this is an enormous understatement. The ground is sodden, the weather squally, and, despite knee pads, my legs are taking a proper bashing from the boulders that mark the two-hundred-foot circumference of the cairn. What makes this endeavour even worse is that I've only got myself to blame. Actually, I'm blaming my parents too. Dad was the one who filled my head with Welsh myths, folklore, and introduced me to Tolkien at an impressionable age. And Mum? Well, she's the catalyst. Anyway, back to my widdershins (anti-clockwise) crawl-fest.

In addition to an audience of three complete strangers, my friend, Gaynor, has come along for moral support and expert guidance. She's a paganism aficionado (though not a practitioner), and I'm happy she's here, even if she's watching the proceedings with conspicuous glee. The bonus though is that she's a physio, so will be able to provide the hands-on medical assistance I'm going to require when I eventually attempt to stand up.

If you're wondering why I'm putting myself through this, it started one evening last October, when Mum and I were watching the first *Hobbit* film. Twenty minutes in, there's an exchange between Bilbo and Gandalf; Bilbo says he needs to '. . . sit quietly for a while', and Gandalf replies, 'You've been sitting quietly for far too long!' And Mum looked across at me and said, 'That's you. You're a Bilbo'. We laughed, I said I'd be happy to live in a hobbit hole (who wouldn't?), and that was that.

Then, a few weeks later, she died, and that's possibly why those words stayed with me. But she was right. For the past seven years, my daily routine has been: get up, take pills, sit down, eat, take pills, go to bed, repeat. I've justified this inaction to myself as a sad, but unsurprising, side effect of becoming disabled. But though I'm, undeniably, limited in what I can do physically, that shouldn't stop me attempting to improve my lot; and Mum's aside was the wake-up call I needed to get off my arse and start engaging with life, not merely existing while it passed me by. So, tonight's 'ceremony' is to be my *official* starting point, where I'll attempt to shake off my passive past, look forward to a fabulous future and, exactly like Bilbo, prepare for adventures.

And the first adventure is here at Cefn Bryn. It's an ancient, red-sandstone ridge in the heart of the Gower Peninsula and I'm crawling, sluggishly, around the 'sacred' capstone, *Maen Cetti* (aka Arthur's Stone) with a vague idea of what's supposed to happen – though I hadn't factored in the, somewhat unsettling, throngs of baby toads.

There are many legends associated with this stone. One is that the twenty-five-ton *cromlech* goes rollabout beneath a full moon, to drink at Broad Pool, the Loughor estuary or Oxwich Bay. *Hmm?* That strikes me as pretty unlikely, and the stone's certainly not off gallivanting now; nope, it's sitting solidly, in situ, at the centre of a sea of rocks, toads and gorse (or something equally sharp and spiky).

According to Colin, who's a keen historian in addition to being an Ovate ('Mid-level druid, nearly fully qualified, mind'.), it used to weigh thirty-five tons until Saint David decided to end druidic pagan worship in Wales by cleaving it in two with his sword. *Spoilsport!* Though, the ten-ton bit that's been chopped off does provide a nice seating area for my spectators.

Another is that at midnight, under a full moon, King Arthur appears, decked out in golden armour. Yeah, *that* King Arthur. Well, it's past midnight and there's no sign of him yet. Colin says to be patient because he 'saw the old fella during the Wolf Moon of 2001'. *Uh-oh!* Possible beardy-weirdy alert! My head-torch spotlights Janet who's rolling her eyes, Angelfire seems dubious, and Gaynor's got her back to us, shoulders shaking with ill-concealed mirth. But my planned regime is about meeting new and interesting people – eccentrics included – so I nod enthusiastically and shout 'Fingers crossed'. And to be fair, as I continue my ponderous, orbital progress, red towelling beach-poncho dragging damply behind me, right now, I'm probably the most eccentric person here.

This custom is part of a pagan liturgy that assesses relationships. Once you've done three circuits, you should 'see' the face of the person who is destined to be your eternal lover. But after one and a quarter, I gave it up as a bad job! It was knackering, my back was screaming, I was worried about crushing the mass of mini-amphibians, and I already knew that Tim was my true love . . . probably.

Maen Cetti, aka Arthur's Stone

Another legend relates to the 'healing spring' which runs beneath the capstone, and I'm deffo up for this one. Plus, it's hell of a lot easier than the last – pop a few pins in the water and declare your health-related wish. Simples. However, getting close enough to deposit my pins was treacherous underfoot, so Janet suggested poking them in with my walking stick, and Gaynor thought it'd be fine to 'just launch them'. Neither option appealed as precision was essential. So, to give my back the best chance of getting fixed, I got as near as dammit, steadied myself, readied the pins, and pointed my torch at the water.

It wasn't the still, tranquil pool I'd imagined. In fact, it was rippling, teeming with wriggling bodies. Surely not more toads? *Nope.* Rats. Lots of rats. Lots and lots of very large rats. Basically, it was Rat London down there. Sod the pins! I never believed it was really going to work anyway.

I scrambled onto the flat stone where I explained the reason for my aborted attempt. The witches abruptly decided they'd had enough 'moon bathing', and even Colin made his excuses and ambled away to 'commune with the ancients' at a different burial site. Guess he'd given up on Arthur making an appearance then. Gaynor, as you'd expect by now, found it all hugely entertaining, and informed me that the 'universe has a sense of humour'. Yeah, after the fiasco thus far, I didn't doubt it. But I was glad that the others had pushed off because it was time for the *Main Event,* and I really didn't want additional witnesses for my first foray into proper witchcraft.

For this, I'd sought advice from an experienced Wiccan elder who heads up her own coven – on Facebook. Yeah, I know . . . but 'Lady Nightshade' has been a practising for over thirty years, has a huge following online, and seemed to be the real deal. I'd explained what I wanted, and she came up trumps. She determined that 'as a child of the Waxing Crescent', I needed to be more courageous, take risks, and 'embrace discomfort, awkwardness, and struggle'. So just a normal day then. *Eyeroll.* But she did explain that 15th May was the most propitious time to for me to kickstart my new life-enrichment plan; the full moon's in Scorpio (my birth sign) and there's a lunar eclipse too, so excellent for 'banishing bad and wishing good'.

She gave me detailed directions, a short incantation, and an extensive list of essentials, stressing that they must be 'gathered with an open heart', so I shelved any innate scepticism, was scrupulous in my preparations, and followed her instructions – almost – to the letter. I also needed to 'meditate for a Wiccan name', to be used when practising 'the craft'. I tried some deep breathing and a few minutes of self-conscious 'Ommmmming', but inspiration didn't strike, so instead, I googled 'Wiccan Name Generator' and, for tonight only, I am 'Raincloud Sea-Hag'! *Sigh*.

Then I gathered.

Red robes to harmonise with the fire rite – Tick.

Ritual Provisions

Offerings for the stone, ideally 'homemade barley-meal and honey cake'. Okay, I'm certainly not invested enough to attempt baking so slightly cheated and picked up some *Mr Kiplings*; honestly, I don't think that the Goddess, or King Arthur himself, would turn their noses up at a French Fancy – Tick.

Anointing Fluid. *Hmm?* This sounded ominous and I had visions of loitering around the local churches, filching holy water and consecrated oil. But after I'd sent Nightingale a rather panicked email, it transpired that milk would work too. *Phew!* Tick.

Red candles, no problemo. I've got a cupboard full of cranberry tea lights left over from Christmas – Tick.

White candles, crucial, as they're the 'first be lit, last to be extinguished', and provide a 'protective barrier within the boundaries of light'. Why I needed protecting is anyone's guess and Nightshade hadn't elaborated, but Colin and Janet had both nodded sagely when I'd asked them about it earlier, murmuring something about 'evil energies' and 'harmful spirits', so I was pleased I'd brought a 16-pack of vanilla tea lights – Tick.

I borrowed the head-torch (one thousand lumens), leather gloves, and heavy-duty knee pads from my stepdad, who's a biker and has all the best gear. I had my lighter, backup matches, and a disposable foil roasting tin to ensure our mini-bonfire was kept contained (and we didn't accidentally set the Common ablaze). I wrote out my 'Release/Forgive' and 'Manifest/Affirm' lists, brewed up a flask of *special* coffee (Baileys instead of milk – *Lush*), loaded up Geoff, and headed off for some super-duper, hubble-bubble action.

First, we prepared the 'altar', pouring milk over the flattest part of the stone, before placing a *French Fancy* at each cardinal point – I'd downloaded a compass app, so I know my positioning was spot on.

Next, I arranged my capacious cowl carefully over my head, filled the roasting tin with candles of both colours, and with suitable solemnity, lit the wicks . . . or at least, attempted to. *FFS!*

After all that sodding prep, you clearly couldn't legislate for the weather, which was becoming more turbulent and storm-tossed by the second. Given that my main reference for witches was studying *Macbeth* at 'O' Level, it seemed perfect conditions for pagan practises, but ironically, it also meant that we couldn't burn sod all. And we tried, a lot! Eventually my LED lighter, 'guaranteed to work in all weathers', ran out of charge, I'd left my spare in Geoff, my matches were saturated, and the moon had disappeared beneath the horizon. All in all, it was a complete and utter farce.

Despondently, we packed up our remaining supplies and slogged the third of a mile back to the car park, taking care to avoid the carpets of croaking cold-bloods. We were on the point of leaving when Gaynor suggested doing the ritual here. *Meh.* But after some *gentle* coercion, of course we did, setting up our foil altar in the back of Geoff's spacious, van-like interior. To be honest, it didn't have the same gravitas as a sacred stone, but we lit the candles, invoked the Goddess, and muttered the 'spell':

I turn my back on bad things past
And banish all that held me fast.
This fire sets me free at last,
And it harm none, do what ye will.

Then, finally, we burned our lists. *Blessed-bloody-be!*

And my takeaways from the night's debacle? Clearly, I'm no witch and I won't be studying 'the craft' any time soon. But though it was farcical, it was also fun, and was the latest I'd been up and *out out* for years, so that was one positive.

The rituals themselves haven't, as yet, wrought any major changes, though my calendar is beginning to look fairly full – I'm giving the W.I. a whirl, have booked a murder mystery evening, I'm trying seated yoga next week, and at Cath's request, we're going to a pottery painting workshop. And one further positive was that, even when you're windswept, wet through, and covered in actual crap, *special* coffee makes the world a much better place.

One of the many toadlets

Back home, I looked up the folklore for toads and found that, strangely enough, they signify 'transformation and positive change'. Interesting. I also discovered that May's full moon is often titled the 'Frog Moon' so, I dunno, there might be something in this 'witchy woo' stuff after all. (And I checked with an ecologist pal, who said the correct term for baby toads is toadlets. *Aw.* But, more thrillingly, they are also known as metamorphs, which seems so much more appropriate in this instance.)

But I have sent a strongly worded email to Lady Nightingale, who really should have known that my crawling had to be deasil (clockwise). If, for some bizarre reason, you're actually looking to attract 'ill-luck, ill-fate and ill-fortune', then widdershins is the direction you need. *Sigh.*

And maybe it was foolish fancy, full moon madness or, most likely, an over-active imagination fuelled by hefty slugs of Baileys, but I'm almost sure I heard Mum laughingly say, 'Del, you bloody fool! Get out there and make some noise'. Oh Mum, I fully intend to. *So mote it be!*

Embracing the Silver Sisterhood

An Evening with the W.I.

4th June 2022

My hair's brushed, I've got lippy on, and I'm wearing a bra for the first time post-Covid. Tim says, 'You look nice, but stop fussing with yourself'. Thanks Tim, but *you* try not fidgeting when you're having a massive menopausal flush, and your nipples are chafing! And no, I can't 'not wear it!' because, *Calendar Girls* aside, it would be most improper to attend a WI meeting with my tits tucked under my armpits!

So, remember those adverts of the seventies & eighties, where two children follow an aromatic, vapour trail, finally exhaling with a satisfied, 'Aah, Bisto'? Well, this is similar, except I'm exhaling with series of violent sneezes and, 'Aah, Lily of the Valley'. It's a heady mix and, like the Bisto kids, if I'd needed help locating the meeting room, I could simply follow my nose. So, I do.

As I tackle the stairs, I can hear hoots of laughter and the hum of convivial conversation. *Hmm?* I was doubtful about coming but maybe it'll be alright after all. Uh oh, spoke too soon. I'm initially denied entry by two women on sentry duty, jealously guarding a simmering urn, and the door. They ensure that:

If your name's not down, you're not getting in! (Luckily, mine is.)

No one gets a cuppa before the allocated time which is 'After the talk, NOT before'. Okay then . . .

And suddenly, I'm snow blind. I've never seen so many senior females gathered in one place (unless you count funerals), and it's like tripping into a walking, talking Dulux colour chart. *Pewter* and *Battleship* ombré through the full spectrum, ending with *Scotch Mist* and *Frost*. Not that I can talk – I joined the 'Silver Sisterhood' two years ago, so my hair feels at home here, even if the rest of me doesn't. I'd imagined ladies in vintage tea dresses, sipping from fine china and daintily disposing of Victoria Sponges with dessert forks. But there's not a cake or porcelain cup in sight, and I feel a bit off balance – and no, it's not just because my stick keeps slipping on the parquet.

I'm considering pushing off when Polly (Deputy Chair) heartily hails me, bustles over, and gives me a hug. We met yesterday; I was sitting on a log in the woods, with Barney (our elderly lurcher), when the peace was ruptured by two mercurial dachshunds, and a plodding Labrador called Snail. Once Polly restrained 'Bangers and Mash! Ha!', we got talking, she mentioned this, and now, here I am. She ushers me off to meet, 'Delia and Glenys, our *Treasures*'. Her tone implies they're a female version of the Krays and she laughs and mutters, 'The Krays were probably nicer. Ha!'

Delia and Glenys are of an age, sporting matching shampoo and sets. They're the treasurers (*Ah*, I see what you did there, Pol), they collect the subs, and they're scrutinising me suspiciously. I give my most reassuring, 'I'm-not-going-to-make-off-with-your-eight-pound-coins' smile, but Delia slides the cash box closer to her because, clearly, I'm a shady character. At Polly's prompting, Glenys grudgingly hands me a raffle ticket, even though, 'You're not a member so shouldn't get one, by rights'. I ask what you win, and they exchange glances before Glenys answers, 'Eggs, a sewing lesson, or money'. Ooh! I hope I get the eggs. *Lol!* Bollocks do I? I'll take cash please. My 'joke' doesn't appear to warm them up and they return to their surveillance of the assembled ne'er-do-wells, so at least it's not only me who looks shifty.

You already know that I've recently embarked on a life-improvement regime, trying out different activities and meeting new people. And that's why I'm here, at my very first WI meeting, waiting for a talk on fraud.

Everyone's overexcited about the imminent arrival of policemen, especially Janice, a spirited nonagenarian, whose knot of friends are teasing her mercilessly and causing much merriment. 'We all knows you likes a man in uniform!' Janice blushes, and Pol whispers over my shoulder, 'Married twice. Army, RAF. Outlived them both. Ha!' *Uh? Good for Janice?*

When the boys in blue do arrive, both are somewhat alarmed by their reception; one sparky lady shouts out 'Strippergrams!' and the resultant wave of raucous laughter causes them to hover nervously in the doorway. Maureen (Assistant Chair) shoots us all a reproachful look and goes to collect them, while Polly plonks herself down next to me so we can have a 'little chat before it gets going'. Actually, this is not just a chat, *this* is a WI chat.

Yes, I have a bad back. Yes, several operations. Yes, it's permanent. Yes, I'm local. Yes, Tim. No, no children. Two stepkids. Yes, four grandchildren. All boys. Yorkshire. No, not often enough. No, not now. Yes, retired. Disability. Teacher. Computing and English. Yes, I do miss it. Newent. Yes, lovely part of the country. No, I don't bake. No, I'm not green-fingered. No, I don't knit. Or crochet. No, I've never been to the WI before.

Wow! Sod Jam and Jerusalem, this woman should be working for Mossad. In fairness though, she shares some details of her own: 'Lost my husband fifteen years ago . . . can't find him anywhere! Ha! And the worst thing about him dying? He didn't leave me a rich widow! Ha!' Intelligence gathering complete, she heads off to meet PCs Justin and Pete, who are uneasily handing out pamphlets, and I begin chatting to Emily, who's also a newbie.

Emily's in her early eighties, with smiley eyes and proudly tells me she's still has all her own teeth, 'apart from the top plate'. She's not long moved to the area and, like me, is looking for friends and some fun. So far, she's not convinced. 'Everyone seems a bit old, don't you think?' *Whoa!* If an octogenarian thinks that, I might be in the wrong place. Then the clock hits 7:00pm, Glenys and Delia start some forceful *shushing*, and the presentation gets underway.

The coppers tried to explain various fraud schemes, but they were beaten before they began. There was a lot of tutting, 'Oohing' and 'Well, I go to Neath', along with synchronised head shaking, and thrilled gasps when Justin talked about 'Romance Scams'. The

31

anecdotes were interesting and the ladies, engaged, but maybe Pete should have led with the safety advice because you could barely hear him over such hearty hilarity, and the 'I wouldn't mind a bit of romance, scam or no'. etc. Ad infinitum.

Then they opened the floor for questions and, initially, it went well. 'How do fraudsters know your passwords?' 'What should I do if I'm scammed?' 'Should I hang up or keep them on the line?' This last one was asked by Sheila, who explained that she could record calls on her dictaphone and 'pass them onto the relevant authorities?' Justin shook his head, said that wouldn't be necessary, and to, 'Follow the advice in the booklet'. Sheila was crushed; I later discovered, she was a huge fan of Agatha Christie and Hamish Macbeth, which somewhat explained her dismay.

But then, conversation turned to the fraudsters, and where they *probably* came from, and I shifted uncomfortably in my seat. However, Polly, clearly au fait with certain archaic opinions of a very tiny percentage of her patrons, masterfully reined them in, and gently rebuked Margery for her short diatribe on call-centre employees. *Phew!* (Afterwards, Pol rolled her eyes when I mentioned it: 'With a membership like ours, unfortunately you encounter the odd dinosaur. 'Antique-osaurs' I call them. Ha!')

And then the sentries/tea ladies signalled the end of the talk, circulating with trays of steaming mugs, and wreathed in smiles. The police made their excuses and left, prompting a disappointed sigh from Janice. Emily and I were allowed a mug but 'only one biscuit mind 'cause you haven't paid no subs yet'. Fair enough . . . though I deliberately took the only remaining chocolate Hob Nob and, as Polly would say, *Ha!*

The interlude was great. I chatted with some nearby ladies, and it was sociable and sorority'esque. Pauline told me about 'Knit and Natter' where, 'since you can't knit, you can still come for the natter, and the darts'. Darts? 'See, we're not really meant to, but we do. Pam was in a team down the old Spinning Wheel'. She nodded towards Pam who was indeed wistfully eyeing up the dartboard, and I applauded their subtle rebellion, putting 'Knit and Natter' down as a definite maybe.

And they've been yarn bombing. Postbox toppers in honour of the jubilee now blanket our locale, with crowns, Union Jacks and, surprisingly accurate, depictions of a woolly HRH. They do look incredible and certainly raise a smile. But though I admire the skill, I don't have a yearning to learn how to crochet a corgi, as yet.

All too soon, the mugs were collected, and we were into proper WI business. Jubilee Afternoon Tea and the Summer Dinner both sounded like excellent socialising opportunities but, unfortunately, Emily and I weren't eligible as we – you can guess? – haven't paid any subs. *Sigh.* Pol said that didn't matter and to come anyway, but Glenys thinned her lips and shook her head, emphatically. Ah well, another time.

Just as Emily and I were considering making a getaway, something *very* unexpected occurred which put all thoughts of sneaking off to the pub out of my mind. Charades? CHARADES! Random yes, but bloody fantastic!

Before I continue, I should mention the following:

If I had a 'bucket list', top of it would be appearing on Richard Osman's House of Games.

I'm very competitive.

I adore parlour games.

I'm amazing at charades.

Did I mention that I'm competitive? Over the years, I've realised it's pointless to attempt to stifle this innate passion, which exhibits as falsetto shrieking, enthusiastic applause, and sporadic whooping.

Dottie (Deputy Games Mistress), appeared, shaking a bag of folded squares of paper, whilst Doris (Games Mistress), informed us that all tonight's charades were crime themed. Nice tie-in ladies.

We whipped through Midsomer Murders, Death on the Nile, and Juliet Bravo before I drowned out the rest with a strident 'Starsky & Hutch!' To be frank, I enjoy the guessing more than the doing, but I wanted to show I'm a good sport, so I lurched up, propped myself against the table so both hands were free, and away I went.

Three words. TV. First word. I begin turning an imaginary steering wheel as numerous answers were called out:

Drive? Nah.

Lorry? No Dottie, smaller word.

Car? Nope Pol.

Driving? Nope, shorter.

Car (again)? No Janice, we've already covered that.

Wagon? No.

Truck? No!

Automobile? NO!

Right, Plan B. Sounds like . . . Shit . . . the clue's in the name – Women's Institute = No Men. Think Del, think. *Aha!* Sounds like . . . I jiggle my breasts, all the while shaking my head and looking expectantly at my audience. Anything? Nope, a sea of blank faces and pursed lips. I keep going for a few more seconds but I'm starting to panic and can feel another flush blooming – though this is anxiety-driven and not waning HRT.

I'm stumped, but then inspiration strikes. I point to my groin and mime a man, holding his dick and having a piss. *What the hell am I thinking?* This isn't a drunken Christmas sesh with the family, it's the WI! But I'm all out of ideas so I compound matters by repeating it, interspersed with more head shaking and breast cupping until finally – FINALLY – a saviour in the guise of Beryl shouts out 'MAN?' And from there, it's a quick and easy hop to 'Van de Valk'. *Praise be to Beryl!*

Look, I know it wasn't the best but, in fairness, I think you'd get stage fright when faced with a sea of, increasingly affronted, elderly women.

Later, I apologised to Polly, said sorry if I'd offended anyone, but she brushed it off with a giggle. 'Oh, they're not as uptight as they seem, believe you me! Ha!' Then Janice, *et al,* waved me over and I learned *a lot* about their families (or lack of), pets, crafts and how they cope with loneliness. How, for many, these fortnightly meetings '. . . keep us going', and one lady, Fran, said she often, 'goes days without speaking to a soul' so this was her lifeline. It was genuinely moving, and I felt real admiration for these women who come together to make the world a better place, one postbox at a time.

Yes, in some respects, today's WI still fits the age-old stereotype, but it's not only crafts, cakes, and competitions. They've run numerous campaigns over the years – some scarily prophetic – which clearly show that the organisation has always kept one foot firmly rooted in modernity. Plus, it's where the Frans, Janices, and Dels of this world can convene for companionship and camaraderie. I enjoyed the evening and came away thinking that its motto – Inspiring Women – certainly felt appropriate.

Past WI Campaigns

But before I left, I'd had a quick word with Pauline and discovered that, 'Some weeks, we just play games, or have a quiz or whatnot'. *OMG!* I've definitely found my tribe! I simply need to remember to wait for tea to be proffered and to never, *ever,* cup my breasts (or anyone else's for that matter), during WI proceedings. Oh, and penises are most definitely off the table! Lessons learned, ladies! See you in a fortnight.

To find your nearest WI group, head to their website at www.thewi.org.uk. Also, check Facebook, as many branches have dedicated local pages.

Good Grief! Part 1

18th June 2022

Right now I'm ugly-crying, the bin's brimming with sodden kitchen-roll (*Regina XXL*), and my eyelids are so swollen I can barely see. I've eaten crap all day . . . Frazzles, French Fancies, and a sharing bag of Revels, which I certainly didn't share. There's a pain in my chest that I've never felt before and which, given today's diet, might well be an imminent heart attack (but my left arm feels fine so I'm discounting that, for now).

I'm currently in the middle of a full-on bereavement breakdown. Of course, anyone who has ever lost someone near and dear can empathise with the emotional toll that death rains down upon us. At times like this, we surround ourselves with sympathetic family and friends, and ride out the shit storm as best we can – until we are, cautiously, able to remember our departed without disbelief, guilt, or tears. I'm clearly nowhere near *that* yet!

You already know about my life-enhancement regime, officially starting several weeks ago with that nocturnal 'Release/Affirm' ritual on Gower. Though I'm not convinced the ceremony has, as yet, wrought any perceptible changes, my key take away was to get off my arse and start living. And I have been, merrily filling in my calendar with a variety of lovely activities. But what I didn't expect was to be adding coffin emojis alongside pot painting, zip-lining, and afternoon teas. Ironically, it seems that late spring is a blooming great time to die.

On the bright side, if you shelve the 'someone's snuffed it' aspect, funerals for me come with positives; I enjoy belting out a hymn or two, it's a great way of catching up with family (well, the surviving ones), and after you've raised *many* glasses to the dearly departed, you leave, awash with drunken promises to meet up soon, 'hopefully under better circumstances', and sometimes you actually do. Plus, if like me, you're a bit on the chunky side, you've gotta love any opportunity to wear head-to-toe black.

And, for those of us left behind, funerals do help draw a line under the whole sad, sorry business. They frequently mark that point where the weight of grief starts to lift and the normal rhythms of everyday life, gradually, fall back into place. And that's probably as it should be.

When Mum died last year, in her final week of life, she had breath enough to give explicit instructions on her funeral proceedings. Firstly, she didn't want one. She opted instead for 'direct cremation' – no service, no one attends, and a few weeks later, you receive a text saying your ashy relation is ready for collection. All very modern and minimalist. The one concession to the traditional was that my stepdad and I were told when she'd go up in smoke. So, at 8:30am on Wednesday, 17th November, I popped a bottle of her favourite fizz, lit a scented candle, and quietly blubbed my way through half a box of Kleenex as I updated her on the arrangements for her 'death party'.

Because that's what she wanted money spent on – not undertakers, orders of service, coffin, hearse, cars, or flowers. Nope, rather a 'bloody big party with good food, good music, booze, dancing and, definitely no black'. *Bummer!*

And she arranged it all too:

Venue – 'Our local'.

Music – 'There's two playlists on my iPad, Sad Funeral & Happy Funeral. Play Sad first, then segue into the happy, dancing stuff early evening'.

Food – 'Gold Buffet option but take off any spicy stuff because the old ones might get heartburn'.

Timeframe – 'Start at two because the oldies will want to get home early, but you all stay til last orders. And don't forget a final toast then'.

Attire – Stepdad = chinos, pink shirt, sandy loafers. Me = sparkly top (I don't own one!), smart trousers, best black boots. Tim = tweed trousers, green sweater, brown brogues.

Unfortunately, she even had time to give me one last bollocking regarding my appearance, instructing me to: get a haircut, get my teeth *professionally* cleaned, get a facial, get my nails done, get my eyelashes permed, get professional makeup done on the day . . . oh, and buy said sparkly top. *Sigh.*

Really, this was nothing new; Mum has always been disappointed that I favour the natural, low maintenance look. But I acceded to her wishes, though I swept the very last one – 'I want you and Tim to get married' – well under the Axminster. *Lol!*

She also made us promise that she would be there, in a 'suitable' urn. So, given Mum was an effervescent and bubbly woman to the last,

Mum's 'Urn'

I picked up an empty Moët Methuselah on eBay, which was totally appropriate. We plastered her face on several hundred beer mats, finished them off with 'Have a drink on me!', ordered a champagne-themed balloon arch, and we were ready to kick off the festivities. It was Mum to a tee, we were still dancing at midnight, and that day, she certainly put the 'fun' into funeral.

Since then, I've lost quite a few people and cried for them all. As a gauge of grief, you can't go far wrong using the K-rS (Kitchen-roll Scale). So, neighbour (1 sheet, *Plenty*), old friend (3 sheets, *Co-op* own), and gorgeous Uncle Terrence (10 sheets, *Blitz*). Then, a couple of weeks ago, Aunt & Uncle Bennett popped off within twenty-four hours of one another, and I dabbed at my damp eyes with a couple of *Fiesta 2-plys* – well, I hadn't seen them for ages, and they were *very*

38

old.

But now I'm broken, totally crushed, and I'm actually embarrassed to confess that this ongoing outpouring of snot and sorrow lies firmly at the furry feet of one medium-sized, scruffy dog called Barney.

He was put to sleep this week, 7:19pm Wednesday, to be exact, and I've barely stopped sobbing since. I know he's *just* a dog, and in the scheme of things, a shaggy lurcher, euphemistically, crossing the 'rainbow bridge', will cause nary a wrinkle in the fabric of life. But my fabric's in tatters and I finally understand what 'heart-broken' truly means. This isn't normal.

I know this isn't normal because I've lost pets before. Three cats, Oliver I, II & III (no, I'm not that imaginative when it comes to names). But when each Olly passed on, though I was sad and teary, it wasn't like this. Then came Tommy Zoom (TZ), clearly named by someone other than me (Grandson #1), and he was an impeccable starter dog – handsome, affectionate, well-adjusted, and well-behaved. He died last spring, and Tim and I wept like children, holding his paws while he drifted away. But though I was devastated for a long while after, my reaction then was nothing to now.

Tim & Barney at Worm's Head

With all those deaths, animal and human, my grief seemed more manageable, controllable enough that I could choose to indulge my melancholy when, and where, I saw fit – generally when alone and in private. But this is different. It's irrepressible, wild, and raw. I had to cancel two lunches with friends because I couldn't sit, gulping with grief, while trying to stomach a cheese and ham toastie.

Tim thinks it's because Barney was 'like a needy toddler' and that's definitely part of it. He was 'special'. And, before I explain why, let me say that I *don't* believe in love at first sight, or for that matter, fate! *But*, twelve years ago, when I first saw Barney sitting with his 'mum' outside a supermarket in Ross-on-Wye, our eyes met, my world tilted, and *something* passed between us. Sounds ridiculous I know, and you're probably thinking I've lost the plot, but truthfully that's what happened. And though Tim thought Barney looked rather 'ill-favoured', to me he was absolutely perfect.

Long story short, his owner wanted him gone there and then, so we squeezed him in the boot with the shopping and took him home. TZ, content with 'only dog' status, was grumpily underwhelmed by this interloper; he did the canine equivalent of an eyeroll before sighing heavily and heading back to his sofa, while we took Barney for a well-needed bath.

He stood, quiet and trembling, as we rinsed away the dirt and grime, horrified to see that beneath the fur, he was simply skin and bone. When we fed them, TZ delicately nibbled his way through beef, potatoes, and kibble, whilst Barney inhaled his within thirty seconds. It was clear he had *issues*.

The vet gave him an MOT, said he was severely malnourished, otherwise in fair health, but recognised that he was a 'very stressed dog indeed'. He suggested training classes, so I signed us up and off we trotted.

I was so proud. Every command we tried, he excelled! When the session ended, Bonnie (the trainer), called us over for a chat, and I was buzzing, expecting us to receive verbal, and literal, pats on the back. But no. Turned out, Barney was only responding so quickly because he was 'terrified of the consequences if he didn't'. He was fuelled by fear, and it was going to be a *very* long road to train that out of him. We must have been the only pet parents who applauded when our dog *didn't* obey an instruction.

And he was riddled with phobias too. His terror of a full moon, combined with the ability to expertly flush rabbits from hedgerows, spoke of an early life of lamping. But add in clouds, trees, hot air balloons, planes, kites etc. Every walk saw Tim and I scouring the skies for anything that might send him fleeing in fear. He was damned hard work, but we didn't begrudge one moment of it.

Barney in one of our post-stroke 'inventions'.

Eventually, he settled down, but when he was, almost, as level-headed as TZ, he had a stroke; we'd only popped out for a coffee, coming home an hour later to a completely paralysed dog. Cue frantic drive to vets, then frantic drive to a specialist facility (two hundred miles away), where we consigned our whimpering Barney to the care of experts.

They said that if he didn't regain feeling within a week or so, it would be best to have him put to sleep. *Well, bugger that!*

Twelve days later, we brought him home, still paralysed. To move him outside, we devised a number of inventions, converting my travel wheelchair into a toilet transporter (with 'crouch feature'), and putting his basket on wheels. We even set up a series of pulleys on our silver birch, which raised a few eyebrows in the neighbourhood, until I explained to Lynda (next door down), that, no, it wasn't a sex swing!

For the next fourteen days, I massaged his legs, applied heat pads, and dabbed ice cubes on his toes, waiting for the tiniest twitch. Nothing. Nothing, until day twenty-seven when, as Tim played ball with TZ, one throw went astray and Barney, somehow, struggled to his feet and tried to chase. Okay, he immediately collapsed, but he wouldn't

41

stay down. He was the canine combination of the fight scene in *Cool Hand Luke* and *Bambi* on ice, but it was a start. And that moment was, without question, one of the best of my life.

In the five years since, he, and we, have dealt with the ramifications. Apart from his awkward, skipping gait, all his old anxieties flooded back, with many new and unwelcome additions, and his craving for cuddles and reassurance increased tenfold. But he still loved life, and us.

And so, back to Wednesday evening. He couldn't settle, couldn't get comfy. He'd been slowing for weeks, had become grizzly and vocal and, despite increased pain medication, was clearly an unhappy chap. It was time.

Tim reckons my massive mourn-fest was 'a culmination of everything that's happened since your Mum died. Or, more likely, that you loved him more than anyone else!' And he was right, on both counts. Barney probably was merely the last straw in a six-month sized haystack of heartache. But yes, I loved that dog more than I can say.

Barney on his favourite beach

And so maybe it's not 'normal' to experience such anguish over *just* a dog, but I'm realising that, whatever truly lies at the root of my misery definitely needs to come out. So, pass me another roll of *Regina*, 'cause he's my Barney, and I'll cry if I want to.

And, though I don't often use Facebook, I did put his obituary on my page, and one friend posted the following comment: 'Oh Barney, the best thing anyone ever brought back from Morrisons'. She's not wrong.

Sleep tight old pal.

A Flight of Fancy

4th July 2022

Compared to some of my recent escapades, this adventure is actually rather tame – no nocturnal rituals or psychic explorations today. But even so, I still know it's going to be epic because I'm on a blind date with destiny . . . or more accurately, with Karl, who I already know is the man of my dreams!

Cath's come along for 'moral support'. She's not long back from a twelve-day all-inclusive in Rhodes and looks gorgeously sun-kissed and glowy, so I'm slightly concerned that Karl might take a shine to her instead. But she swears she'll stay well in the background and I'm absolutely holding her to that! He is to be *my* 'escort' for the next hour or so, and no one, not even my lovely stepsis, is going to come between us.

And, as soon as I catch sight of his striking amber eye, all thoughts of Tim fly out the window, and I'm going full 'Factor 50' (Yeah, inexplicably, I do watch *Love Island*), and falling hard, because Karl is damned handsome, despite missing half an eyebrow. He's already mesmerised me with his moves, and my palms are sweating, the anticipation is building because any moment I'll be getting a cheeky peck, and I can't contain myself!

Don't worry, I'm not doing the dirty on Tim, but my excitement might be better understood if you remember my experience in that floatation tank; it was relaxing as hell but weird *AF*, with my mind going places it had never been before. And it is *that* which is directly responsible for our visit here today, here being *Perriswood Country*

Pursuits on the Gower Peninsula, and the place where I'm, finally, going to come face to facial disc with my favourite owl!

But, before that, we're having a shot at archery, which is an activity I've never been drawn to, despite Michael Praed's *Robin of Sherwood* being my first ever teenage crush. (I had to take a quick break from writing this to watch the opening sequence on YouTube – eleven times – and that man's cheekbones are more deadly than any of his arrows! *Longing sigh.*)

Anyway, though I've never felt inclined to try it, there are some clear upsides:

You can do it sitting down which is always a bonus if, like me, you find standing up rather challenging, and a bit painful.

You can do it indoors, and since today's weather is that wonderful Welsh combo of wet, wild, and windy, that's a massive tick.

Less positive is that:

The only arrows I've ever used before are darts. And I haven't picked any up since March 'ninety-one, when my William Tell party trick went marginally awry, leaving me mentally scarred, and David, my boyfriend at the time, physically so. Frankly, I think dumping me afterwards was a bit of an overreaction as he only needed a few stitches, and his fringe covered the worst of it!

Cath's done archery before. *Bugger!* And yes, I know it's not a competition and it's just a bit of fun, but I can't help myself. I've got visions of a neat cluster of arrows peppering the bullseye (the *gold*), as I modestly accept fulsome praise from the instructor who looks at me with genuine respect, and no little awe. Oh well, a girl can dream.

But before we even get our hands on a bow and arrow, we need to be tested to find our 'dominant eye' by Brian, the rugged, outdoorsy owner of *Perriswood*, and whose knowledge of all things feathery and fletchery could doubtless fill several encyclopaedias. We're told to make a squarish shape with our hands, lift them up to eye level, put Brian (who's several feet away), in the centre of our 'frame' and, apparently, he'll know instantly. He does – Cath and I are both right-eyed.

Next comes bow selection. We tried a few; I was allocated one with a pull of 14kgs, whilst Cath couldn't manage more than 12kg. *Ha!* I knew that using a stick would come with more benefits than just helping me walk. That lone *Popeye* bicep in my right arm is coming into its own and I'm feeling rather pleased with myself – until Brian informs us that the Korean Ladies Team 'pull 46kgs'. Right, feeling a little less smug now.

Finally, we don protective arm sheaths and we're ready to let loose. Brian gets me a chair, positions our feet either side of the shooting line, and shows us how to set the arrow's 'nock' correctly into the 'nocking point' on the string. It's a bit fiddly, but after a few tries, I've got it, and so has Cath – though turning to face me while holding a nocked arrow in her bow isn't the smartest move, not unless she fancies accompanying me to A&E. (Mind, I bet David wouldn't be shedding any tears!)

Brian's a fantastic coach; clear with his instructions, encouraging and really, *really* patient. As we fire, he chats about archery, tells us how he and his mate, Mark, are Guinness World Record holders for the 'highest point score in 24 hours' (*Wow!*), and how 'anyone can pick up this sport, from six-year-olds upwards'. *Hmm?* Maybe finding an accessible, sporty hobby for someone with my limitations isn't a pipe dream after all?

Thirty minutes later, when my arms are beginning to tremble and I'm ready to lay down my bow, Brian tells us to stop because we'll be 'feeling it tomorrow'. Tomorrow? I'm feeling it already and know I've used muscles that have been dormant for years. But it seems I'm pretty good at archery – for a first-timer. Most of my arrows ended up somewhere near the target, if not actually in the circle itself, hitting the outer 'skirt' or 'petticoat' areas. But Cath's mainly littered the floor – *tee hee* – though she did manage to get one in the gold. *Sigh.*

Being a competitive person, I ask him about my chances of becoming a champion archer and making an olympic team. He twinkles a bit: 'Well, maybe not the Olympics'. But when I press him, he does say that I 'have the potential to become a championship archer'. *Yay me!*

Alright, so what he *actually* said was that '*anyone* has the potential to become a championship archer'. (But I knew he was saying that to make Cath feel better, and he clearly recognised that I'm a natural, with

45

copious amounts of untapped talent.)

But now it's time for the main event, and Brian's happy to tailor the bird experience to our specifications. So, first up, the star of my show, Karl, a seventeen-year-old European Eagle Owl! (Seventeen! Who knew these birds lived so long?)

Brian heads off to get him, warning us, 'He'll probably get back here before me'. And he's right. Within minutes there's the faintest whisper of wings, a massive downdraft of air and Karl sails past us, his wing-tip catching the top of Cath's head. *OMG!* He is simply, sodding awesome!

The Wonderful Karl

Brian flies him around the vast barn, and its genuinely jaw-dropping, watching a bird the approximate size and shape of an IKEA beanbag, soar with such agility and speed. But, of course, watching's not enough for me, so when Brian, literally, throws down the gauntlet, I'm more than ready to pick it up – and pull Karl 'for a chat'. (Note to self: Del, stop with *Love Island* lingo. Also Del: I can't, I've been brainwashed!)

Mind you, now we're up close and personal, Karl seems a lot larger than I first thought. He's big, very big, with vicious looking, finger-length black claws, set, paradoxically, into feet so fluffy, it's difficult to stop myself from stroking them. Karl wouldn't be out of place as an extra in *Monsters Inc.* (But actually, it's those furry feet that are the danger, rather than the talons, because eagle owls squeeze their prey to death, rather than ripping them apart like other raptors. *Nice!*)

And he's surprisingly heavy too. I once stumbled upon some online pics of 'naked' owls – and no, I certainly had *not* been Googling 'weird bird porn'! But from the photos, it seemed a sensible assumption to make that, since Karl's bulk is purely feathers, he'd be as light as one. Nope. Karl's bones must be extra dense or something because I could barely hold my arm steady as he perched inches from my face, and regarded me calmly with his mismatched eyes.

Mismatched because he's blind in one, easily noticeable by its cloudy colour. Apparently, he was attacked when he was younger by an angry swarm of bees; I don't know what he'd done to antagonise them but blinding him in response seemed a tad excessive. But that's nature for you – dangerous and wondrous in equal measure, so actually, exactly like Karl.

And his eyes merely added to his charismatic mystique; I was in love, and I didn't care what other birds Brian might subsequently bring out to meet us. I knew that (in more *Love Island* parlance), my 'head wasn't' gonna turn' for any of them. Unfortunately, Karl's frequently did, to around 270 degrees. He was clearly a flighty one.

After we'd spent a *lot* of quality time together, mainly doing a Vogue-worthy photo shoot, Karl decided he'd had enough, swooping off to a high perch and waiting for Brian to take him back to his owl house. Basically, I'd been 'mugged right off'.

After that, Brian brought out three more birds for us to meet, and it was rather like ornithological speed dating:

Caesar, aged twelve, a saker falcon, with sleek good looks and bright yellow feet. This avian George Clooney was a fanciable fellow, but he had some side-eye action going on which, frankly, made me a bit nervous, and not in a good way. Next.

Tilly, a twenty-three-year-old red-tailed buzzard, (aka chicken hawk, so named because . . . well, if you can't guess and you keep fowl, make sure your coop is well protected and has an exceptionally sturdy roof). The Beyoncé of the bird world, she was undeniably beautiful, but her beak curve looked lethal, and I wouldn't, ever, want to turn my back on her. Next.

Nickel, the youngster of the group at nine, slim and sinister – think Javier Bardem in *No Country for Old Men*. And that's an appropriate analogy since Nickel is actually the sole entrant in an avian identity parade to find . . . a killer!

See, I'd told Brian about a bird who, a few months ago, caused a pigeon to literally explode in my back garden. I'd only seen the culprit's tail as it took off, but from my vague description, Brian knew exactly what the baddie looked like. And, as soon as I met Nickel the harris hawk, so did I. Those white tail tips were unmistakable.

Brian said that I should ring him if I spotted it again as these birds aren't native to the U.K. and so was either 'being flown' by a handler – unlikely due to my suburban location – or was an 'escapee' and needed catching, hopefully before breeding with any indigenous species.

I realise I'm coming off as some avian racist but, apparently, it can pose a threat to local wildlife and might upset the ecological applecart too. Right then, the moment I get home, I'll be on to our Neighbourhood Watch team and start rustling up some 'Wanted' posters. We'll find this trespasser Brian, don't you worry.

It really was a terrific afternoon. We were wowed by these giants of the bird world and seeing them flying at such close quarters was hypnotic and glorious. But the location of *Perriswood* is pretty glorious too, offering bird's-eye views (*Obvs*) of Oxwich Bay, and beyond. And Brian was a great host who put up with our numerous, and often ridiculous, questions with good humour and great forbearance.

And even though I didn't get that peck on the cheek, and even though Cath and Karl *did* seem to have the 'better connection' (*Sigh*), I'll definitely be booking in to meet him again soon. Because that's owls for you – the feathery, flighty, and fabulous head-turners of the raptor world . . . and I bloody love 'em!

Perriswood Country Pursuits offer a variety of activities for the whole family, whatever the weather and whatever your ability (or disability). As well as archery and falconry, there's a rifle range, coffee shop, and an array of farm animals that you can meet. So, if you fancy a day out with a difference, give Brian a call on (01792) 371661 or visit perriswood.com for further details.

Parting the Veil, Episode 2

16th July 2022

I've mentioned before that, though I possess a healthy Scully-like scepticism for all things abstruse and esoteric, there is a tiny part of me that, like Mulder, truly *wants* to believe. And really, we're only here for a bit of a giggle, but who knows? Maybe Freddy Moon (not his real name, but close), is the real deal?

His website certainly says so, encouraging us to come on a 'fascinating, eerie and spiritual journey with heart-racing accuracy, hair-raising moments, and psychic mediumship second to none'. *Wow!* Sounds like we're in for an otherworldly odyssey, so buckle up because 'Psychic Night' at the Holiday Inn Express, Swansea (East), is about to go down!

So, Cath and I are on another paranormal adventure, excited and a little nervous to be meeting 'an acclaimed British Psychic Medium, like no other'. I think it's because we've both suffered quite a lot of loss lately, and I know Cath would love to get a message from her mum.

I'm hoping to get something too: maybe from my mum, who if she does make an appearance, would probably to tell me I need a haircut, or would express displeasure at my idea of selling up and moving to a park home in Scotland. Or from Dad, who came up with that top secret, cryptic phrase for an occasion such as this. Basically, if Freddy Moon utters those random words, it would prove to me, beyond any doubt, that there really is an afterlife. *Eek!*

The event was taking place in the Gower Room, which seated a max of thirty, was configured in their theatre layout – three semicircular rows of ten seats, facing a wall of whiteboards – and which, unbeknownst to us, nicely foreshadowed the fact that the evening's event was going to be pure (and rather poor), theatrics from start to end.

The chap on the door handed us a flyer which listed all of Freddy's past events in 2022, though strangely, no future ones, before ushering us in with a jolly, 'Sit anywhere, ladies'. We chose two seats at the front and a quick glance around showed that we were nowhere near capacity – twenty at most. It was a much more intimate scenario than we'd envisioned.

The fire-door was propped open with a rubbish bin, the blackout curtains were battling, in vain, against the blistering sunlight, and the tinny portable speakers were doing an outstanding job of distorting the melancholic muzak – though were no match for the riotous stags who were cheerily checking-in for 'a weekend on the lash like!' and who had, plainly, started early.

A purple disco ball luridly illuminated the room, and I was getting strong Kit Kat Club meets Speed Awareness Course vibes; add to that a carpet that wouldn't be out of place in The Overlook and you had the perfect venue for those boy-racers who, when not performing wheel-shredding doughnuts to a booming Ray Brown bass line, liked to kick back with a hefty Stephen King. It was all rather jarring.

It was also the bleakest, most soulless space I'd ever had the misfortune to visit, and my hopes for a good night out – which, in fairness, hadn't been that high anyway – plummeted. I certainly doubted it provided the necessary ambience to encourage drop-ins from any dear departeds, and I knew that Mum, literally, wouldn't be seen dead in a Holiday Inn after an ill-fated, and enormously rowdy, overnight in Liverpool for the 2003 Grand National.

To give it a bit of pizazz, two roller-banners had been placed either side of the 'stage', which displayed images of Freddy looking moodily intense, legs akimbo, white silk shirt unbuttoned to his navel. They also boldly proclaimed Freddy's talents, along with his websites and his '24-hr Psychic Phone hotline'. *Sigh*. The signs of chicanery were strong with this one.

The three chatty ladies behind us had brought a cool bag bursting with bottles of wine and *nibbles* and were noisily settling in for the duration. They'd been to several of these types of evenings before: 'Saw that famous Sally something, in Cardiff once, but we didn't get no message or nothing. Waste of good money she was. Pringle? Mind, dunno what this Freddy's like, never even 'eard of him before'.

Well, we were about to find out exactly what he was like because the music, thankfully, faded, to be replaced by an upbeat, showbizzy announcer: 'And here's the star of the show, celebrity psychic to the stars, from Sky TVs *Psychic Today,* give a warm welcome to . . . Freeeeeeeeddy Moon!' And then, to non-deafening applause, in trotted the man himself, and immediately I felt sorry for him.

Because as well as celebrity psychic, it transpired that Freddy was also the doorman – those pics of him must have been taken years back – and, unmistakably, the voiceover MC. It was clearly a one-man band kinda show.

He was a chirpy fellow and began showering us with compliments. Apparently, we were a 'lovely lot' and, though he'd done several 'very large' shows already this week (*doubtful*), this was his favourite because he knew that everyone would be getting a message, 'with validation', tonight (*Hmm?*).

He'd already meditated – the 'lovely staff' at this 'lovely venue' had given him a 'lovely room' where he could cogitate and prepare himself for the 'rigours of communing with those lovely, loved ones that are now in spirit'. And then we had to meditate too, since it helps 'open up the channels'. This caused raucous hooting from behind us as one woman muttered something about her channels always being open, and I heard the unmistakeable sound of another bottle of wine being unscrewed.

Freddy was unfazed. 'That's it, close your eyes and let the physical world drift . . . drift . . . driiiiiiift away'. And we tried, really, we did, but 'driiiiifting' is pretty difficult when you're a hundred yards from the incessant rumble of the M4 during Friday night's rush hour.

But soon we were ready to 'receive the validations', and the first spirit who came through was 'possibly a male, holding a blue teddy'. No response, so he asked, 'Has anyone here lost a child? Had a miscarriage?' *Oof!* Not the most sensitive approach to such a topic, but it had stated on the booking form that Freddy's 'performances are known to shock, amaze, intrigue and emotionally move even the toughest of sceptics' so I guess we had been warned. I was just hoping that the lady who tentatively raised her hand was mentally prepared for the coming interaction.

Thankfully, she was. And she was a good one to start with because there were messages for her, her sister, mother, auntie, and two cousins, who made up almost a third of the audience.

He started with generic clichés: her child is happy; he loves her etc. which caused some half-nods and half-smiles. But the best bit was when he mentioned the dead grandmother's clock: 'I think it needs to be fixed?' As one, the whole family gasped, before the mum explained it had stopped that morning. Then he mentioned a 'pram, or something similar?' and it transpired that one of the, visibly, heavily pregnant cousins had ordered a pushchair from Boots yesterday. He was definitely winning them round, but the rest of us needed more persuading.

And for Cath and I, the opportunity to be convinced came almost immediately as he homed in on us because Cath's mum, Margaret, had joined the party. At first came the standard guff: 'I'm seeing cancer, around here', and he motioned to pretty much every area of his body. 'And her lungs filled with water when she passed'. Correct. But cancer is the leading cause of death worldwide and when you die, your lungs often fill with water so . . .

Then he mentioned that Cath was having problems selling a house. Correct, though I'd wager it'd be true for the majority of people who had lost older relatives, inherited property, and were trying to sell during a cost-of-living crisis. I wasn't blown away.

But though I had no confidence in him, I've got to admit that at this point, I was feeling a tad envious. Where was my message? So far it was all Cath! Oh, but wait . . . now Margaret had her hand on *my* shoulder, and she told him I was having trouble with my 'knee or leg'. Um, this was accurate'ish and semi-impressive – or it would have been if he hadn't seen me limping out of the disabled toilet with my walking stick, minutes before the show started. *Sigh.*

Anyway, Margaret also said that everything would be fine, so that was nice, even if I was mentally rolling my eyes. Good as it was to be included in her visit, I would have preferred one of my parents to pop in, but such is life, or to be exact, death.

Hang on though, someone else was coming through, though Freddy couldn't say if they were male or female. But there was 'something to do with cremation, and water?' I threw him a bone. Might it be scattering Mum's ashes off Mumbles Pier? 'Yes, yes, that's what she's saying. She wants to remind you to do it soon'. *Yawn.*

Between you and me, I'd already taken a handful of Mum down in a Tupperware box and done a mini-sprinkling, but I didn't want to knock his confidence, so I nodded encouragingly and said I'd be sure to remember.

His style of mediumship leant towards constant repetition of 'Ooh, we're having a good time, aren't we?', to which we all dutifully replied, 'Yes', and which, I suppose, was meant to be a type of subliminal manipulation. But unfortunately, it didn't work. As the evening advanced, the audience gradually left his cries to action unanswered. Poor Freddy.

And also, out of a four-hour show, I'd estimate a good two were spent in total silence while he 'communed' wordlessly with whoever had entered the 'mystical arena'. These silences were *much* too long to be comfortable, and it didn't take a psychic to sense the increasing irritation in the room. If you've ever watched that episode of *The Office* where David Brent gives a talk to business leaders, you'll understand exactly how we felt. To say it was third-rate is a huge compliment, and it was becoming progressively more awkward to watch.

In fact, it was so cringey that people had started leaving. One or two initially, but after the first interval, a few more didn't reappear. And you could tell from the sheen of sweat on his brow that he was desperate for the remaining audience to stay – even the wine ladies, who were becoming more boisterous with every bottle, especially in the sphincter department. Loud farts kept interrupting proceedings, causing widespread guffaws, but Freddy pressed on regardless.

In terms of his 'spirit-imparted knowledge', if he wasn't garnering a positive response from an individual, he would dodge the negatives by suggesting it was yet to come. 'Watch out for that because you will do', became his catchphrase.

Examples: You've been on holiday? No. Well you will. You've split up with your partner? No. Well, watch out for that. You're selling your house? No. Well you will soon, so watch out for that. It was a ridiculous diversionary tactic, and unfortunately for Freddy, we all knew it.

But for Cath and I, the zenith of the evening, in terms of entertainment value, came during his conversation with a deceased chap called Samuel. Blank faces all round so Freddy dived into a description of the spirit that was trying to come through.

'Okay, so this man, I think he's called Samuel? He's saying . . . that he's wearing . . . shoes. Yes, they're very shiny . . . and black. Ring bells with anyone?' *Oh dear, Freddy. Slow headshake.*

The audience response – stunned silence followed by gales of laughter – made Freddy hastily announce another interval, saying he wanted to try something different, and that he'd 'rearrange the room' while we were gone. Intriguing. No, not really but, unlike many others, Cath and I were still up for prolonging the evening.

We returned to a circle of chairs, surrounding a small, square table which had a glass tumbler on it. Then he invited those of us who wanted to 'get involved', to place a finger on the base and 'try to catch a spirit. *Ah, c'mon Fred!* This was risible because:

1. If Freddy was to be believed, we'd already been visited by eleven spirits, so it made no sense that we needed to try 'catching' one now.

2. The glass didn't move. At all. For over nine minutes (I timed it).

3. Freddy realised it needed his special 'psychical energy to get things moving'. And he was right because once his finger touched the tumbler, it was off, jerking around the table in fits and starts. Unbelievable!

The wine ladies cottoned onto this *coincidence* because they tutted loudly, packed up the cool-bag and headed off, a strident, 'Well, he were crap!' left hanging in the air as the door swung shut behind them.

And that was it for Cath and I too. Sod waiting 'til the end, and good manners be damned. We said good luck to the, very few, remaining diehards and scuttled out, leaving as Freddy started shuffling his tarot cards and asking if anyone fancied a shot on his Ouija board.

We barely got to the car before collapsing in cackles, and I had to keep stopping on the way home as fresh waves of hysterics overtook us. I'd get myself under control and then Cath would murmur, 'A man . . . wearing shoes'. And so it continued. It really was a night to remember.

Poor old Freddy. Even though I think I can safely say he was a charlatan, he was such an abysmal one, Cath and I actually ended up rooting for him, willing him on to come up with 'validations' that were actually valid. But alas, it wasn't to be.

So, if you're looking for a competent display of psychic mediumship, I'd give Freddy a miss. But, if you don't mind paying £20 for an evening with the Alan Partridge of the clairvoyant world, then he's definitely the man for you. Just remember, take wine – you'll definitely need it!

Fear Factor 1

Getting Slammed

7th August 2022

My cadence has crumbled, my voice ricocheting through the panoply of pitch, bouncing from bass to soprano and back again, and I'm trembling so much, I'm in real danger of keeling over. I've heard of knees knocking from fright but, until now, I'd always assumed it was just a metaphor. I realise, with a shocking clarity, that this was a mistake of genuinely epic proportions – and it's all the fault of a stupid motivational post I once saw on Twitter.

Because it seems you can't go on any social media these days without stumbling across them – those inspirational quotes, presented in saccharine, swirly handwritten fonts, set against backgrounds of soft pastels, or scrawled over the silhouetted image of someone doing yoga on a beach at sunrise.

'Dance like nobody's watching', 'Live, Laugh, Love', and a personal favourite, 'You can, if you believe you can', which is basically bollocks; believing I *can* fly a plane is very different to actually doing it. And I've had over ten hours of lessons so well know the panicky pitfalls of overconfidence whilst in control of a light aircraft – as does my instructor, Phil, when, for no good reason, I once decided to pull back on the throttle immediately after wheels up. (And if you're reading this Phil, once again, I'm really, *really* sorry.)

Anyway, in amongst the mawkish phrases, which are often hackneyed and frequently ridiculous, you can occasionally chance upon one that resonates. A few weeks back, I noticed a tweet – 'Do one thing that scares you each day'. I'd heard it before, but it must have been a slow news day on Twitter because, instead of scrolling past, I got to thinking about what frightened me, what activities I'd find challenging, and thought, 'What the hell!'

I wasn't going to take it to extremes though – no swimming with Great Whites or jumping off mountains in a wingsuit. These had to be fears I could face daily, though I soon discovered that I wasn't scared of enough things to manage seven a week, so I changed it to a once-a-month kinda deal.

I started off big, with my bête noire, after reading a lovely poem by a friend of mine about spiders. It later transpired that it was actually a commentary on the judgement delivered by Lady Hale (wearing her, now infamous, spider brooch), when she found Boris Johnson guilty of the illegal proroguing of Parliament, but I clearly didn't get the subtext. Anyway, I began trying to exist alongside these leggy lodgers rather than throwing heavy books at them and leaving them in situ until Tim could hoover up their spiky remains.

I even befriended one that lived in my bedroom curtains – it was pretty tiny, but still . . . Every night, she(?) would drop from the tiebacks to sleep, legs akimbo, on one single, webby strand. It was *Charlotte's Web* meets *The Silence of the Lambs*, with our quid pro quo being I won't kill you if you don't crawl into my mouth when I'm asleep.

Then came Plantasia's 'Meet the Reptiles', which was actually more awkward than scary. I rocked up, only to realise it was an experience for kids, and out of around twenty of us, I was the only participant who could go a whole hour without either peeing my pants or screaming for mummy. On the plus side, I was easily able to use my superior height and strength to get to the front of the queue where I handled the snake, then exited asap, before the parents complained to management.

Next, the aforementioned flying lessons which were, and will always remain, terrifying – though the views of the Gower Peninsula were so staggering, I really couldn't be blamed for the occasional loss of concentration.

Despite severe Coulrophobia, I watched *IT* when I was home alone – and at night! I went to the *Gower Christmas Tree Farm* to confront the reindeer – yeah, I know they're cute, but those antlers and pink gum-teeth really freak me out.

And then, only the other day, I set off for my own graduation, which was several neuroses rolled into one horrendous bundle: Absurd academic robes (of the finest polyester) + sweltering heat + menopausal flushing + abhorrence of formality = Heavy Pass! Sorry to say but I bottled it. We took a few photos outside then I ditched the costume, and the ceremony, and we buggered off to the pub. Seems this particular event was a fear too far.

So, back to the here and now. In 2020, I'd entered the *Swansea Poetry Slam*. Because we were partially in 'Covid Times' it wasn't being held live and entrants had to video three poems, one for each round, and send them in. This was way out of my comfort zone. Not the poetry side of things, though I'd never entered a Slam before. No, it was because I was overweight and felt really self-conscious about appearing on camera. I'd have much preferred doing it in real life, but I bit the bullet, spent days trying to record myself without my chins dominating the shot, and eventually sent them in.

I was gobsmacked when I came third; I won £20 – the first money I'd ever *earned* from writing – and that inspired me to keep going with my lyrical ballads and upbeat verses. And so, when Slam '21 was announced, I was first in line to book my spot in the live event, being held at Cinema & Co on High Street.

Arriving, we were greeted by a cheery lady, who encouraged us to remove our Covid masks so she could see our 'lovely smiles'. That set Tim off on a, 'If I catch Covid from this lot' rant. *Sigh*. Pacifying him with a lager, we headed to the cinema/theatre space and got as comfortable as possible on the low, cushioned pallets that they use for seating. The room was artistically rustic, gave off strong boho vibes, and seemed like the ideal place for an evening of spoken word poetry.

It wasn't a large venue and there were probably only around sixty people milling about, waiting for the kick-off. I was, understandably, a little nervous, but that was hugely outweighed by my excitement at sharing something I'd written with the wider world.

I'd been working on my Round 1 poem for a few weeks and was chuffed with it. I thought it had enough rhythm, and gravitas, to see me into Round 2 when I intended to pull out the big guns and head down a more literary, free verse route. While I couldn't wait to get started, Tim couldn't wait to get home. He was the one facing fears that night because 'arty-farty stuff' wasn't his cup of tea. I got him another lager.

Eight o'clock and the organiser appeared on stage, the crowd fell silent, and *Slam* got underway. First came the news that only eight of us would be competing. Fab! Much better odds of being placed, and Tim, who'd been agitating to leave before we'd even arrived, perked up and murmured, 'We'll be home by nine'. *Eyeroll.*

Competitors had two minutes from the moment they began speaking, the judges ringing a bell once time was up – and when, finished or not, you had to stop. The running order had been picked at random and I was #2, which you might call prophetic if you're a fan of literal toilet humour, but more on that later.

So up went #1, an edgy, flat-capped fella in a blingy waistcoat and Doc Martens, and he set the bar pretty high. He was loud, animated, acting his poetry with every fibre of his being, and the audience loved him. It seemed that it wasn't so much about the quality of the verse but rather the energy of the performance. Two minutes later he jogged off the stage to enthusiastic applause. Then it was my turn.

And, given what would happen in the subsequent two minutes and three seconds, the weird thing was, as I approached the microphone and got settled in the spotlight, I didn't feel nervous . . . at all. I'd practiced, a lot and knew my poem was no more than eighty seconds long – and that was reading it reeaalllly slowwwwwly. And I've never been scared of public speaking – probably helped by being a teacher for twenty odd years – so talking in front of a hundred eyes felt easy and natural. And I'd written a deliberate crowd-pleaser, with a lively tempo, some cool internal rhymes, and a little bit of word play. Okay, it was about death, but I'd approached the topic in my usual, light-hearted way. I was 100% ready and raring to go.

Nope. Apparently, I wasn't. As soon as I opened my mouth, it started. My voice began quavering, like a pubescent boy who'd been on the helium, and a tremor coursed through me before settling into a pulsing, and very visible, shudder – and which, ironically, was way more rhythmical than my delivery.

Then my throat seemed to swell and close, sweat burst from every pore and I heard a deafening thrumming in my head. *WTAF?* As each physiological symptom worsened, I realised that for the first time in my life, I had zero control over myself (discounting my sixteenth birthday where I necked two bottles of wine and spent the evening in a flowerbed on the Kingsway), and it was terrifying.

But, despite my body's betrayal, I did what anyone would do under such circumstances, and ploughed on through; really, there was no other option since my mobility issues meant doing a runner was impossible. Plus, I was determined to finish within the two minutes, or at least before my voice became audible only to dogs.

And I almost managed it, squeezing out my final line a few seconds after the bell, in a small, squeaky act of rebellion. I vaguely remember wobbling off stage to sporadic pity-clapping, before downing a pint of cider that didn't touch the sides – though the relief of it all being over was infinitely more intoxicating. Obviously, I wasn't going through to Round 2.

But I had company in the bottom slot. Mind, she'd turned up with a butterfly emblazoned across her face, told the organiser he could f**k off if he expected her to stop after two minutes, and proceeded to wail for quarter of an hour whilst strumming erratically – and tunelessly – on her guitar. Guess I was worse than I'd thought. *Sigh.*

We stayed til the end though. Tim was all for legging it once I'd been dumped, but I didn't want to look like a sore loser, and most of the performers – because that's what they were, true performers, unlike me – put on a really great show. Clearly, I needed considerably more practice.

But, of all the phobias I'd faced thus far, weirdly, this was my proudest achievement. Because, as it turns out, it's the fears you don't even know you have, the ones that sneak up on you and catch you unawares, that are the real killers.

So yes, I was dreadful, yes, it was mortifying and yes, for the rest of the evening, when I glanced in anyone's direction, they quickly lowered their eyes or looked away. But sod 'em! I tried, I failed but as Einstein once said, 'Failure is success in progress'. And that's one inspirational quote I can actually get behind.

As for my fear programme, I do intend to carry on. Next week, I'm off to the hairdressers which I realise sounds ridiculous but I'm majorly phobic after I once requested a few highlights and a trim, ending up with a Keifer Sutherland in *The Lost Boys* mullet. Then there's nuns (those *Armchair Thrillers* of the late seventies were horrifying for a nine-year-old), and anyone clad in head-to-toe yellow oilskins (*Hammer House of Horror: The Two Faces of Evil*). Both'll be tricky to accomplish since traditional black habit sisters and crusty old seadogs are thin on the ground around my way. But they're deffo on my 'To Do' list.

And then I'll probably be penning, and practicing, my poetry because, mostly in the words of The Temptations: 'Get ready, Slam 2022, 'cause here I come'.

Sadly, Slam '22 was cancelled – either that or, more likely, the organisers deliberately kept the date and venue from me, unwilling to give me a platform so I could repeat the cringe fest – and I was away for Slam '23. So, my return to spoken word poetry will have to wait until later this year, and if you find yourself in the audience, apologies in advance. Lol.

Good Vibrations

Awakening My Inner Stag

20th August 2022

So far, during my *DIY life enhancement programme*, I've tried some new, and oftentimes strange, activities, and met many interesting people along the way. I've had highlights – with the #1 spot, by some margin, still being that sensory deprivation tank. But *this* experience will *never* be a favourite, and despite my promise to try everything with an open mind, I think I knew, even before setting foot inside the venue – a bleak architectural fusion of eighties student halls meets sheltered housing – that *this* probably wasn't going to be my cup of chamomile.

The class had been recommended to me by Si, a long-standing devotee, who I'd actually met at the float centre. He'd raved about it, advised me to book well in advance because, 'It's *very* popular and spaces for newbies are limited'. And he assured me I was, 'Gonna love it!' *Hmm?* I confess I was intrigued, so when the next available date popped up on Facebook, I messaged Grace, the instructor, and prepared for my first ever Gong Bath.

Gong Baths are a type of meditation where you 'bathe' in sound vibrations. This 'healing practice' has many beneficial effects according to Si, including, 'a deep trance-like tranquility, pain relief and emotional release'. It was definitely worth a shot.

But, given that I was there on a quest for serenity and relaxation, I wouldn't say I got off to the greatest start. Initially there was quite a bit of queuing, which I find difficult at the best of times. The line was barely moving and after ten minutes of propping against a table whilst juggling two orthopaedic pillows and a walking stick, my back began spasming in sympathy with a manifesting migraine, wholly caused by the heavy scent of incense that was smouldering in reception. Surely it shouldn't take this long for forty of us to file in.

Oh yeah, it does! Eventually reaching the threshold of the 'sacred space', all became alarmingly clear. Grace wasn't just there to welcome us in with a wide, friendly smile. Nope. Before we could take even one step into the large hall, whose parquet floor was carpeted with neatly arranged rows of yoga mats and blankets, there was a three-phase 'cleansing ritual' to be endured. *Sigh.*

First came the 'Venus Spray, in honour of the Goddess', which Grace liberally squirted around my head and shoulders. It smelt of lavender and jasmine, was a blessed relief from the pungent patchouli, and would help with the removal of impurities from my, apparently, 'muddy' aura.

Next Grace whipped out, what I can only describe as a sort of wafting stick. Two foot long and topped with a clutch of feathers, it rattled loudly as she fanned away whatever pollutants had been squatting in my 'energy field'. And to be fair, I did feel the impact of it – but only insomuch as I needed to curb the chuckles of discomfort that were threatening. Maybe that was the 'emotional release' Si had been talking about?

Then Grace unveiled the pièce de resistance, theatrically whipping a red silk cloth off a low table to reveal a deck of 'Goddess Oracle Cards'; I needed to 'pick the one that calls to you'. Now, I'm always up for card tricks and sleight of hand, but this was a bit much. Still, I listened hard, but none whispered to me, so I grabbed the nearest and turned it over. Grace exhaled sharply. 'Ooh, now that's an interesting one. *Elen of the Ways.*

And? C'mon Grace, I might not be fully into this oracle stuff, but it'd be nice to know if Goddess Elen is good or bad? Of course, I had to ask, and after a pregnant pause, she said, 'Well, we all have damaging patterns and habits that we need to break'. *Lol!* I could feel the gurgle of more giggles growing so I moved off to bagsy a spot in the rear of the room, where I could do my 'bathing' in relative privacy.

It was rather like being at a grown-up sleepover – but a nightmarish one where you don't know anybody, and there's no alcohol; everyone was stretched out on yoga mats (which did little to soften the unforgiving flooring), some with blankets pulled up to their chins, others wrapped in duvets. As Grace worked her cleansing magic on the stragglers, I assumed the foetal position, arranged my pillows until I was semi-comfortable, before swathing myself in the provided fleece blankie. I was snug, settled, and ready for ninety minutes of idyllic inaction.

Unfortunately, the gong bath, like admittance, also had a three-phase plan, *Phase One* being a lecture on the purpose and origins of Goddess Cards. Long, *long,* story short: Women have been forced to hide their true 'divine' natures for centuries. Men are to blame. Celebrations of 'the Goddess' used to be held on Friday 13th but wouldn't you know it, bloody men ruined this too, by choosing to burn witches (aka 'true women'), on this same date. Men are basically knobheads. The end.

I wasn't 100% convinced of the accuracy of Grace's homily, and I wasn't sure how well her anti-patriarchal starter was received – mainly because I could only see the back of most people's heads. But the young man, laying two feet from me, widened his eyes before rolling over and pulling his duvet a little tighter around his shoulders.

Phase Two, and we're into a torment of titanic proportions – this isn't only mantra chanting, this is ancient Sanskrit mantra chanting! Now, personally, I think it's a bit unfair to expect first timers to remember all the 'words' without advance warning, or more helpfully, a phonetic crib sheet, but I gave it a good go since it was meant to loosen our throats and 'unmuzzle' us.

After a few minutes of ragged chanting – which proved I wasn't the only one who was struggling and sounded as soothing as a dentist's drill – I managed a few reps of 'Ohm granny pooh knee bum ohm bam ham pooh' before I retired behind my blanket and waited for signs that it had worked. Grace said there might be coughing (*meh*), rumbling stomachs (*meh*) or, if we were *lucky,* 'you'll feel something building deep within, that will eventually free itself through your unbound throat'.

What now? *No! Oh no! NO!*

You can guess the reason for my panic. Remember those float tank 'mini purges', where my body, apparently, expelled toxins? Well, since they manifested as the deafening, uncontrollable roaring of rutting stags, and was embarrassing enough in isolation, what if it was to happen here, tonight, in front of all these people? *Good Goddess*, it didn't bear thinking about! So then, obviously, I couldn't *stop* thinking about it, and my stress levels started surging. I needed out of there, pronto.

But, as I was about to sneak off – as unobtrusively as an overweight woman with a walking cane can – Grace instigated *Phase Three* (*dammit!*), and we got down to some booming, big gong action.

Initially, the sound was muted, almost like the noise you get when you run a wet finger round the rim of a glass. Not unpleasant, but not calming either. I could feel the slightest of tremors through the floor, which was actually quite pleasant but, after ten minutes, it wasn't floating my boat.

The people I *could* see seemed truly out of it, breathing deeply, eyes closed, totally at one with the gong, but the impact of those good vibrations were passing me by. The guy next to me started snoring.

Then Grace branched out, adding in an occasional jangle of seashells, or plinky-plonky wind chimes which I found quite grating. In fact, it seemed that, whenever I felt my eyelids droop and I was, *maybe*, on the brink of blissing out, there'd be a series of shrill *chings*, or a sharp *clank,* and I'd be wide awake and back in the room.

As Grace threw herself into even wilder, percussive multi-tasking, playing instruments with the energy and abandon of Animal in *The Muppet Show*, I gave up. Frankly, it seemed ridiculous that I was having to *force* myself to relax. Plus, it's pretty difficult when your arse is numb, your legs won't stop twitching, and you're suddenly desperate for a pee (the fault of that sodding *waterfall shaker*, I'll wager!). It was ridiculous, and the absurdity of the situation hit me, hard.

We've all been there. Something tickles you and no matter how much you try, there's no way of suppressing the hilarity. I buried my face in the blanket, but my whole body was trembling with conspicuous mirth, and my snorting garnered irritable shushes from supine neighbours. Grace shot me an assessing glance but continued with her singing-ringing bowls.

As the last vibration gave way to absolute silence, people began yawning, stretching, and rubbing their eyes, as if waking from a really restful sleep. Grace said to take our time getting up and, if we wanted, she'd come around with a book that explained the meanings of our cards. According to Goddess Elen, the three aspects I should focus on are:

1. The need to embrace new things. Well, I've already started but it's always nice to be ahead of the game.

2. Breaking my 'destructive' habits. Okay Elen, but honestly, who hasn't got a bad habit or two?

3. Jettisoning those things which are holding me back from attaining my full potential. *Hmm?* I think another moon ceremony could be on the cards.

As I was leaving, Grace stopped me to say how pleased she was that I'd exhibited such a 'deep connection to the gongs' because, 'I could see you vibrating from here'. *LOL!* I managed to keep it together, but the second I got to the car, I crumbled, and it took several minutes before I could explain, to a bemused Tim, exactly why I was creased with laughter.

So, did I achieve tranquility? No, but in all fairness that was down to me. I was so genuinely fearful of having a 'stag' outburst in public, I know that I deliberately refrained from fully letting myself go. Basically, I kept my 'muzzle' firmly in place throughout. And that's why I think I've been a bit hard on Goddess Elen because self-sabotage is one of the habits I could certainly do with breaking.

Did it help my pain? Nope. But again, that was my bad. Grace had asked if I'd be more comfortable sitting in a chair, but I'd insisted I wanted the full experience, yoga mats and all, so them's the breaks.

But though I found it a bit underwhelming, don't let me put you off trying gong therapy for yourself. No, it didn't do much for me, but the majority of people there *did* experience positive results. As animated post-bath chatter filled the room, I heard reports of mental lightness, dreamy visions, and perfect peacefulness, and it seemed that most attendees left feeling refreshed, re-energised and wonderfully rejuvenated.

And, weirdly, it did feel surprisingly sociable, this gathering of strangers, cocooned and quiet, sharing an unorthodox hour. It was a bit like being back in infant school when, every afternoon, we would troop to the hall for 'sleepy time'.

So, all things considered, though gong therapy didn't deliver in my search for serenity, it was certainly valuable in other ways, and I met some smashing individuals, which is another key aim of my life-enhancement plan.

We've already been for coffee and, next month, we're off to a local Pagan Moot – yeah, I know, but I could really do with some expert help on that ritual I'm planning. But, best of all, the lovely Grace has promised to give me lessons on controlling my inner stag and, if I can master that, I might possibly give sound bathing another try. But first, I'd better brush up on my Sanskrit.

Good Grief! Part 2

Back in the Doghouse

3rd September 2022

So far, we've lost two bath towels, a Laura Ashley cushion, three pairs of my best *going out* knickers, a pillowcase, five slippers, one sandal, and a golf umbrella. Add in irreparable damage to Tim's glasses, a vase of tulips, a jar of faux peonies, a lamp, two charging cables, and an inflatable kayak, and you might understand why we're beginning to think we've bitten off *much* more than we can chew.

The lawn is pitted with holes of varying depths and Tim's veggie patch has been annihilated, the perimeter now securely fenced with rolls of green steel mesh. Basically, it's an arcadian Alcatraz out there but, as Lynda (next door down), wearily calls over the wall for the third time today, it's obviously not secure enough. Turns out that confining two puppies in one compact garden is *way* harder than we'd imagined. And yes, I did say two!

I guess you might be surprised that, within months of losing our lovely lurcher, Barney, we've already welcomed new canines into the family. After he'd gone, I'd been inconsolable, bursting into noisy sobs with no warning, and mourning my furry pal with more intensity and tears than any deceased human relative.

When friends, tentatively, suggested that a new dog might help the grieving process, I was vehement in my refusal to even contemplate a replacement – I vowed that I would, 'never have another dog again, *ever!*' End of!

But, as my grief lost its fire, settling into a softer sorrow, I found I could scroll through the photos of Barney (and Tommy Zoom), and remember the good times with a gentle nostalgia, and an occasional sniffle. But still, I stood firm – no more dogs.

So, why do we currently have a pair of fourteen-week-old lurcher pups gnawing on our dining chairs and tearing our rugs to pieces with teeth that, though tiny, are huge in terms of destruction? I blame social media, Stepdad, Tim, and Lizzie – in that order.

I'd been idly scrolling through various dog sites when Puppy 1 popped up on screen. He was a ball of yellow fur with giant feet, an angelic expression, and just like that, I was in love. No, it wasn't the thunderbolt I'd experienced with Barney, but I felt a smile on my face and a stirring in my heart, along with the faint fizz of panic – what if he'd already been reserved, or rehomed? Puppy 1 was meant to be ours and my 'No Dog Ever' pledge was all but forgotten. And all it took was one stupidly, fluffy face.

See, during the Barney-free months, life instantly became *'too'* everything – *too* quiet, *too* lonely, *too* aimless, *too* empty. I missed the *clack* of his claws on the laminate floors, I missed his fat head resting on my legs when I ate toast, I missed the daily ambles in our favourite woods, and I missed the routines we'd kept for nearly fifteen years. I even missed the regular *pffts,* and the accompanying noxious odours, as Barney slept the sleep of the just, snoring deep and dreaming of rabbits. Yep, everything felt *off*, and it didn't pass.

I was so struck by Pup 1, I showed his pics (which included some of his siblings), to my stepdad to canvas opinions, and this was my first mistake. Stepdad commented, 'Yeah, I like him, but look at that black one. Maybe you should get him as well?' *Lol!* As if. One was more than enough for us to handle.

So, after a Zoom call, where I virtually escorted the rescue centre's owner, Sandra, around every inch of our house and garden, babbling as I desperately tried to demonstrate our eminent suitability as 'dog parents', we got the green light, and I went shopping.

I purchased everything the new arrival could possibly need: food, collar, lead, harness, bed, travel cage, treats, toys, bath robe, shampoo, more toys etc. Yeah, it was *OTT*, but I couldn't help myself – some women love shoe shopping, but I've always preferred a sank around Pets at Home, and one person's Jimmy Choos is another's puppy chews so . . .

When collection day arrived, I tanked up Geoff and we headed north, staying overnight with the family to break up the journey, and then the next day, my stepdaughter, Lizzie, drove me to puppy central.

It was all wonderfully chaotic – nine pups in total, plus their mum, the uniquely named, Askit. While I spent time with Pup 1, Liz attempted to restrain the rest of the pack, but her efforts met with little success. Askit, a beautiful dog of exceptionally large proportions, flung her front paws over Liz's diminutive 5 ft. frame and slow-danced her around the yard.

My coaxing of Pup 1 also seemed doomed to failure because he simply wasn't having it, preferring to stay curled up on the path as the others swarmed around me. He was the most reticent of all the pups, only perking up when his brother, Pup 2 (dark, dishevelled with spiky hair), bounded over.

I was a trifle worried. How would Pup 1 cope when removed, not only from his mum, but from his favourite bro too? When Sandra, a no-nonsense northern lass, with a wicked twinkle in her eye and an encyclopaedic knowledge of everything 'Dog', brought us a cuppa, I voiced my concerns.

'Oh, he'll cry a bit at first but'll settle in a few days, don't you worry'. I knew she was probably right but still . . . I rang Tim.

After explaining the situ, I was gobsmacked when he said, 'Well, get them both then?'

'What? *Two*! We *can't* have two!'

'Why not? We've always had two. And they'll be company for each other'.

Of course, I discounted it as ridiculous, but watching Pups 1 and 2 play . . . *Hmm?* Maybe two wasn't such a bad idea? I mentioned it to Lizzie as she foxtrotted past with Askit.

'We can't get two, can we? That'd be mad, wouldn't it?'

'Well, you've always had two, haven't you. And you know you want them both, so do it!'

Reader, I did it.

Sandra waved us off with a lengthy list of feeding instructions, plus lots of 'top secret' advice to ensure our boys stayed fit, healthy, and in tip-top condition. (I'd love to share some, but she made me swear I'd keep them to myself – 'Lurchers Honour!') We headed home.

In the two days I'd been away, Tim had puppy-proofed the garden, and letting the boys out for the first time was a joy to watch. They sniffed, squeaked, gambolled, and frisked, thoroughly exploring, and christening, every grassy corner before leaping into Tim's potatoes, digging ferociously, and then collapsing in a rapid-onset puppy coma under the broad beans. *Aww!* They seemed so happy with their new surroundings, though Tim was already muttering about getting more fencing sorted if he was to save his onions.

Puppy High Jinks

Names next. I'd already decided I wanted Puppy 1 to be named after either Tim's dad (Donald), or mine (John). But these days, Donald's a no go; I couldn't run the risk that other dog-walkers might think I'm a secret MAGA, so John it was. Tim wasn't happy because John 'isn't a *proper* dog name, and there'll be blokes'll turning round if I shout that in the park'. *LOL!* But what about Puppy 2? We canvassed opinions from family, but nothing suited – not until Grandson #4, a long-standing werewolf obsessive, suggested Wolfie. John and Wolfie? Yep, perfect!

Their behaviour, however, was far from it. The first issue is that they move at pace – mainly trotting, eight massive paws thumping across the floors, which only ceases when they reach turbo speed. Then it becomes the rolling thunder of galloping horses, followed by violent thuds as they use the sofa cushions to slow their charge, before ricocheting off to begin their breakneck laps of garden, kitchen, and lounge once again. And again. Ad infinitum.

They eat/chew/ravage everything they can get their teeth around – stones, pegs, cabinets, sofas, sticks, shoes, fishing nets, garden furniture, the paddling pool, and on one memorable day, even their own vomit. *Heave!*

They also thoroughly enjoy antagonising each other, sneakily biting a passing tail, leg, head, or neck, and their wrestling is high energy, only stopping when I fire a water pistol to shock them into letting go of the other's throat.

Since their arrival, our days have been spent trailing them around the house and removing things from their mouths before they can destroy it/swallow it/both. We've had to toddler-proof the whole of downstairs because they are *very* long (tall?), already, and can reach the kitchen worktops with ease.

Tim is still in the midst of his ongoing struggle to keep the garden, and his veggies, safely enclosed and protected. The mesh he first used is now easily jumpable, so he's redoing it with the 6 ft. version. Basically, it's the fencing equivalent of painting the Forth Road Bridge

They might be adorably entertaining but we've both discovered that puppies are very, *very* hard work. And though they're already well-versed in the art of innocent-puppy-dog eyes, their capacity for mischief, like their size, seems to double daily.

We needed to get a grip before:

a) They demolished any more home furnishings.

b) They morphed into the big, speedy dogs they'll become – and which, judging by their current growth spurt, won't be too long.

Professional assistance was required asap, and luckily, we found it! (play *A-Team* intro)

'If you have a problem (dog related), if no one else can help (there are others, but these are the best), and if you can find them (they're on Facebook), maybe you can hire . . . the *J & K Dog Training* Team'.

We signed up for the five-week starter course and set off for our first class, eager to learn how to gain a modicum of control over our dynamic duo. But I'd be lying if I said we weren't slightly apprehensive; and when J & K, (Jim & Karen), saw our boys, they seemed apprehensive too. According to Jim, getting two puppies at the same time 'really isn't recommended'. Yeah, thanks Jim, but I think we've already established that. And so it began.

As well as training dogs, and more importantly, owners, the session included three short 'socialisation playtimes', where all the pups were let off-lead, to charge around with gay abandon and varying degrees of good manners.

At first it was bedlam, a canine version of WWE, with our two tag-teaming to spring heavily onto their unsuspecting classmates. Sooki, a sausage dog, retreated under the chairs, growling, and showing her teeth, and ours quickly got the message that they were too rough and backed off.

But, by playtime three, John and Wolfie were exploring and cavorting independently of each other, and even Sooki had come out of her shell, galloping after John with a definite come-hither look in her eye.

We learned recall, along with *Sit, Down* and *Off,* and it was an exhausting, but informative, ninety minutes for humans and canines alike. Though, as a gruff Yorkshireman, Tim's attempts at the 'high-pitched and happy, *come'* definitely needs work. But as we were leaving, Karen came over to say that our two had done 'remarkably well' so I was one very proud mum.

As well as training, we've had several vet visits already –

inoculations, sickness, diarrhoea, anal glands (most unpleasant for *all* concerned), and suspected kennel cough. Turns out, that when one pup is off-colour, *both* need the treatment, so it's been an expensive few weeks – but thank God for multi-pet insurance!

All our neighbours are now used to the falsetto festivities when wees and poohs are done outside – 'Clever boy, doing your biz!' – and Haydn, the lovely old chap who lives next door up, shouts encouragement through the trellis and applauds every toilet triumph.

Rapid-Onset Puppy Coma

They're also used to the low-pitched, 'No, bad boy!' when either pup is too lazy to walk the three steps to outdoors. But we've discovered that these 'accidents' always occur on drizzly days so I'm guessing our boys, like TZ and Barney before them, are rather rain averse. Maybe it's a lurcher thing, but it's certainly not great when you live in the 11th wettest city in the UK.

But we're getting there. It's been – checks calendar – eight days since we last had to disinfect the kitchen floor, and they've started crying to be let out, which is a massive step forward. They, mostly, will *'Come'* if there's a frankfurter on offer, though any distraction – dog, person, bird, leaf, blade of grass etc. – and we've got no chance.

We took them to Clyne Gardens on Monday, which is a lovely park that overlooks Swansea Bay, and it's fair to say there were a few minor kerfuffles – leisurely picnics were flattened, sandwiches snaffled, and we had to send the grandkids to collect our wayward pups as we were too shamefaced to retrieve them ourselves!

Since they've arrived, life's been hectic, eventful, tiring, frustrating and much, *much*, busier than it ever was when living with two grown-up dogs. Ironically, it seems that puppies are a very different animal.

But the *clacking* of claws on the laminate is back, along with soft heads resting on our legs when we eat, and those daily, dog-driven, routines. We're even okay'ish with the malodorous *pffts* that they emit with alarming regularity, because, though we miss Barney and TZ terribly, life suddenly seems a bit brighter. And being dog-parents again? Well, that's just absolutely, bloody magic!

J & K Dog Training can be found on Facebook.

When Life Gives You Melons

The Ups and Downs of *The Change!*

17th September 2022

In my family, it was never called the menopause. I recall Mum, my aunts, and grandmothers, all referring to it as 'The Change' – spoken of in hushed tones, and definitely capitalised. And as a child, I would frequently wonder what that actually meant. What were my female relatives going to *change* into? I had visions of the Incredible Hulk, maybe werewolves, or any of the variety of metamorphosis characters I'd seen on *Dr Who*. And I was *really* excited to see it happen.

Now, having gone through the worst of it myself, I can confirm that what I became, for a time, was a fretful, forgetful woman, filled with a simmering rage that could turn to tears in an instant, with an insatiable hunger for carbs, and zero for sex. Actually, apart from the colour mutation, the Hulk wasn't that far off the mark.

And though I've never really warmed to Davina McCall (whose presenting style is a tad too frenetic for me), that the menopause is finally out of the shadows and has become a hot topic is due, in large part, to her. And, for that, us women should be grateful because it's been overlooked, mocked, and downright ignored for far too many years.

I'm fifty-two, so you'd probably expect me to be starting with the whole 'hot flush, brain fog, low libido' issues about now. But mine actually began twenty years ago, six months after meeting Tim.

Back then, I was working as a teacher in a rural school in Gloucestershire, and I loved my job. In fact, it consumed me, pushing thoughts of boyfriends and kids to the very bottom of my imaginary priorities list. See, I'd never been a woman who craved ankle-biters. Of course, I knew that, *someday*, I'd have children, but the timeframe for becoming a mother was nebulous. And I knew that I couldn't consider starting a family until I'd met my *Mr Right* – who, it turned out, was a rather irascible Yorkshireman, with quick wits and kind eyes.

And meeting Tim when I did was serendipitous because *he* was actually the one who first diagnosed that there might be something amiss 'down there'. *Hmm?* So, off I went to the GP where, red-faced, and mortified, I explained that I might need an internal examination because, 'my boyfriend said it feels like I've got a fruit basket up my foof'.

Long story short, it wasn't a basket, just a couple of melon-sized tumours – one Honeydew, one Galia. Cue familial panic, *many* maternal meltdowns, and me, in the eye of the storm, calmly trying to lay everyone's fears to rest. It didn't work, so I was actually quite glad to get to hospital seven days later and away from all the emotional drama that frequently accompanies occurrences like this.

The surgical team paid me numerous visits, all promising to be 'conservative' since I was young and childless, assuring me that they would save what they could. But waking up afterwards, it transpired that, like a closing down sale, everything had to go.

I'd had a 'total abdominal hysterectomy with bilateral salpingo-oophorectomy' (aka 'radical hysterectomy' which is *much* easier to say, and I still find it rather thrilling that, at least, something about me can be classed as radical.)

Truthfully though, it was a bit of a blow and I definitely struggled to wrap my head around the long-term implications of such a procedure, as well as coping with the immediate after-effects. On the bright side, I was alive, cancer-free, and could wave farewell to tampons, pads, PMT, and stomach cramps. But the downside was, obviously, no kids. And that's life I suppose – the universe gives, and it takes.

However, despite the conversation I'd had with the hormone nurse prior to going under the knife, I clearly hadn't fully grasped that, within hours of coming around from anaesthesia, the joy that is the menopause would immediately, and aggressively, kick straight in.

Describing my very first symptom as a 'hot flush' severely understates the blazing fire that was pulsing through me, and the resultant sweat which saturated my bedding within minutes. They put me on an oestrogen oral HRT, which helped a little, but still, I was burning up, miserable and mentally exhausted.

I should have stayed in longer, but the worst place to recover from illness or operation is, oddly enough, a hospital, where the routines keep you awake, and you yearn for a dark room, your own bed, and blissful silence. After five long days (and even longer nights), I begged the surgeon to allow me to leave and, with a little persuasion, he finally agreed.

For six weeks, I sat at home, giving mind and body a chance to heal. Of course, there was the pain and discomfort that came from a wound which ran from belly button to bikini line – and which had me back in hospital for a few nights when it became infected. But it was the menopause that hit me hardest. I guess I'd never thought hormones could play such a massive part in my mental (and physical), health but, by God, they did!

I struggled on with my existing HRT for three months, but when I next saw my specialist, the floodgates opened and I sobbed for a good half hour as I tried to explain how even the easiest tasks were now insurmountable, how my thoughts were no longer my own, and how I had completely 'lost myself'. He recommended implants, and these were, to put it bluntly, the dog's bollocks!

Because of my age, I had oestrogen *and* testosterone. *What?* Yep, apparently women produce small amounts of testosterone physiologically which 'drives their libido', and which, I confess, was news to me – but then I did get a D for Biology 'O' Level so . . .

Anyway, twice a year I'd have a local injection in my belly, a nurse would make a small cut and then shove in (none to gently, it has to be said), a couple of slow-release balls of hormones. And that was it. I'd skip happily away, knowing that my debilitating symptoms would be under control for the next six months or so, brimming with zest and bursting with vigour.

However, one fateful day, I trotted along for my implants only to be told that, 'due to supply issues', the NHS couldn't continue offering that treatment! *Alert, alert, panic mode activated! Shit!* It takes time to adapt to different medication, alongside the attendant 'tweaking' of doses, so the thought of it being possibly months before I felt human again was pretty damned depressing.

Back on the pills, with a testosterone gel which didn't have much effect – *Sorry Tim* – I battled on, but within weeks, I hit rock bottom. I was at work and remember leaving my classroom, only to have a sudden, and total, mental absence – I didn't know what I was meant to be doing or where I was going. I didn't even have the energy to carry on walking, so I sat on the stairs and cried my heart out, supremely unconcerned that the pupils might see me.

Luckily, I was rescued by the aptly titled caretaker, who took me to his shed, gave me a mug of sweet tea, and patted my back until I'd stopped blubbing. Next day, I saw my doctor again and the whole HRT routine began anew.

With hindsight though, I think that I was actually lucky to have a 'surgical menopause'; at least I knew the *exact* reason for my lack of reason, for my tears, my plummeting libido, and my total character change. For those women who slide naturally into the menopause, well, you have it much tougher than I ever did.

But time marches on, and now I'm *mainly* on an even keel though it seems I can't, fully, say goodbye to the brain fog, flushes, or night sweats. But these days, I have learned ways to mitigate them.

I always carry a hand fan, and I'm talking about those old-fashioned, folding ones. They not only shift a ton of air, but

Fan Flirtations.	
Carrying in right hand in front of face	*Follow me.*
Carrying in left hand	*Desirous of an acquaintance.*
Placing it on the right ear	*You have changed.*
Twirling it in left hand	*I wish to get rid of you.*
Drawing across forehead	*We are watched.*
Carrying in right hand	*You are too willing.*
Drawing through the hand	*I hate you.*
Twirling in right hand	*I love another.*
Drawing across the cheek	*I love you*
Closing it	*I wish to speak to you*
Drawing across the eye	*I am sorry*
Letting it rest on right cheek	*Yes.*
Letting it rest on left cheek	*No.*
Open and shut	*You are cruel.*
Dropping	*We will be friends.*
Fanning slow	*I am married.*
Fanning fast	*I am engaged.*
With handle to lips	*Kiss me.*
Shut	*You have changed.*
Open wide	*Wait for me.*

you can also pretend you're in *Bridgerton*. (And, on a side topic, we really are missing a trick if 'Fan Flirtations of the Victorian Era' doesn't become mainstream again.)

I used to slap on foundation but found it exacerbated the 'face sweats', so I binned that in favour of powder, now a mainstay of my make-up bag. It's ideal if I need to tone down pink cheeks or, more likely, repair the after-effects of sweat rivulets and mascara runs.

Deodorant, and I mean spray and roll-on. Yeah, I know that's a given, but now I put it *everywhere*, paying particular attention to under boob, under stomach, inner thighs, and arse cheeks. Anything to guard against buttock-shaped sweat stains on leather chairs or car seats.

Because I can't rely on my memory, long or short, the most used app on my mobile is the calendar which I fill in *as soon as* I make any arrangements. Not only that, but I also set alarms because it's no good using an aide-memoire if you keep forgetting to check the bloody thing.

Diamonds? Nope, it's layers that are a hormonal girl's best friend. Top tip: Ensure your base garment is made from a natural fabric such as cotton or cheesecloth. Both are cool and also great for absorbing excessive sweat. However, avoid polyester like the plague!

I used to take my HRT each morning – one 2mg pill. But a few years back, a hormone nurse mentioned that, throughout the day (and night), the effects of the HRT begin to wear off. *What?* I mean, it's obvious now that I think about it, but I never really had! *Hmm?* So maybe that's why my symptoms were more apparent during the evening and overnight?

I rang the practice, asked if I could have 1mg tablets prescribed instead, and now I take them morning and evening. And touch wood, I'm sleeping better than I have for years, and the night sweats, which still episodically occur, seem milder too.

Some women, me included, find that alcohol and spicy foods often kick off the sweats and flashes, so I kept a food diary for a while which helped me work out my triggers. Cider and curries were the enemy, but there was no way I could abstain from a pint of Brothers' Toffee Apple or a Madras. So, now I just indulge earlier in the evening, and find it keeps the menopausal symptoms to a minimum.

And when Tim and I pop out for a Sunday roast, we avoid a carvery, where queuing next to boiling hot food is guaranteed to set me off – plus it's sodding awkward when you use a walking stick. Instead, we go to a local pub where I always reserve the table furthest from the kitchens, and which also happens to have windows that actually open. Heaven!

Lately, as friends of a similar age have begun entering this particular stage of life, I've heard, too many times to count, how they feel down and depressed, fatigued, lacking in confidence, and how they are 'losing' themselves. And that's really the crux of the matter. Because the menopause *is* about loss. But there are gains too which we certainly shouldn't ignore – and no, I don't mean those sneaky extra pounds which are an absolute bugger to shift.

Now, I feel surprisingly free; free to try new things, make new friends, explore new places. I'm more comfortable in my skin than I've ever been – despite sagging tits, greying hair, and a pudgy menopausal midriff. (Not to mention a budding beard! *Sigh.*)

I've discovered that I'm more self-assured and can say what's on my mind without the fear of being judged holding me back. I've got a better understanding of what's really important to me, and because I know that I can't please everyone, I no longer feel obligated to try.

I'm in the midst of what traditional Chinese medicine calls, 'The Second Spring' – a phase in a woman's life that marks new beginnings, wisdom, and flowering feminine potential. *Wow!* Isn't it great to take a positive approach that speaks of rebirth, renewal, and growth? And they're absolutely, bloody spot on!

So, grit your teeth ladies, we'll get through this! And once we do? Well, spring is just around the corner, and it's going to be blooming fabulous!

If you're struggling or need advice, speak to your GP, or ask to see the doctor/ nurse in your practice who specialises in dealing with menopausal matters. There are many treatments available that can help you get through it as painlessly as possible, whether HRT or natural therapies. Or you can visit any of these Twitter (X) accounts for lots of useful information:

@menomatters
@BrMenopauseSoc
@Menopause_Cafe
@BLKMenopause
@Pausitivity2

Fear Factor 2

Where the Wild Things Are

15th October 2022

We're surrounded by hordes of excited children, Tim is rolling his eyes and muttering darkly that he 'knew it was only for kids', and I'm guessing I missed *that* crucial detail when I chanced upon this event on Facebook.

But I don't let it put me off because I've been gearing up for it all week and I'm not backing out now. Plus, the seductive smells of *proper* coffee and homemade cakes are enough to keep him happy whilst the wonderful Gemma tries to organise my one-to-one with Dylan.

We're at Dewkes of Sketty, a pet shop and café combo, which offer tempting treats for humans and pooches alike. It's basically a Costa for canines, but with a cosier vibe and, after seeing one four-legged cutie demolishing a 'doggy-chino' (topped stylishly with a swirl of cream and gravy bone), I'll definitely be bringing our two for a visit – once their psycho-puppyhood is behind them and they can abide by the Dewkes 'House Rules'.

Tim has just got started on his flat white when Gemma reappears, says it's all sorted, and if we can wait ten minutes for the kids' group to finish, she'll take us up to meet him.

Fabulous! I'm delighted and terrified in equal measure . . . Nope, scrap that. Now that it's happening, if I'm honest, it's more like 1% delight, 99% terror.

My palms are suddenly clammy, there's a tremor in my hands, and I have to put down my coffee cup for fear of spilling it – think *Keeping Up Appearances*, when Elizabeth has tea with Hyacinth.

Sod the coffee! What I really need now is a calming cider, but in the absence of human alcohol, I might have to give their 'dog wine' a whirl – and pop a diazepam, or two.

Some time ago I wrote an article about facing fears and phobias, triggered by that oft-quoted phrase, 'Do something that scares you each day'. Attempting this on a daily basis was somewhat ambitious – I'm not frightened of enough things to manage three hundred plus per annum. So, I changed it to a one-a-month kinda deal and have managed to stick with the program thus far.

And now that autumn is upon us, it seems fitting that today I'm going to come face to face with, literally, my biggest bête noire. You see, much as I love this 'season of mists and mellow fruitfulness', it's also the season of sneaky incursions, with homes invaded by eight-legged devils who scuttle, spikily across floors, walls, and ceilings, and fill me with constant dread.

For as long as I can remember, I've had a horror of spiders, and can even pinpoint the exact moment it began. I was six, it was autumn (*obvs*) and Dad had scooped up an exceptionally large specimen that was hunkered down behind Mum's hostess trolley.

We had our 'Donkey' routine (that's what we called the big ones) down to a fine art; I'd open the back door, Dad would put the leggy intruder outside, then we'd both wag a finger at it while singing 'Mr Spider go away, and don't come back another day'. (*I dunno, so don't even ask.*)

But, that night, Dad didn't reach the back door. Instead, with a sudden 'Ow', he dropped the spider (which hot-footed it into the curtains) and said the four words that fuelled my phobia into being – 'The bastard bit me!' *What!? They have teeth!?* Remember, I was only six.

Anyway, since starting my dangerous living project, I *have* managed to stick to my resolution of co-existing with arachnids, rather than crushing them under heavy books before getting Tim to hoover up the remains.

And it's not *all* spiders that freak me out. I'm not bothered by those flimsy, brownish ones that hang out in corners doing not very much at all, small ones – £2 coin-sized or less – are acceptable too, and Daddy-Long-Legs don't even count.

But those giant donkeys, which appear with such frightful frequency this time of year? Well, they're another matter entirely. So, if I was to continue with my 'live and let live' commitment, I needed urgent help.

Enter Animal Cwtch, a mobile animal encounters company, with a menagerie of fluffy, feathery, and scaly pets, which you are very welcome to meet. And that was why I was there – to meet, and maybe hold (*Eek!*), Dylan, a *Tliltocatl albopilosus,* aka curly-haired tarantula. As immersion therapy goes, this was hardcore.

But Dylan actually sounded perfect for the job because, in my mind, anything furry, or 'curly-haired', couldn't be that scary. Could it?

I should also add that my thinking was heavily influenced by the 1970s kids' programmes I grew up with, in particular *Paperplay*, which featured two high-vis spiders called Itsy and Bitsy, who happily helped a smiley lady with her arts and crafts. And it was these squeaky sweethearts that informed the mental image I had of Dylan.

I was in for quite a shock.

Gemma led us upstairs to the activity room and introduced us to Animal Cwtch's Jo and Kevin, who were terrifically supportive of what I was aiming to do and brimming with knowledge about their much-loved pets.

They started explaining a little about the various animals but, sorry to say, I wasn't listening; my full attention was on the glass boxes which I incessantly, and anxiously, scanned for signs of Dylan.

Kevin, immediately realising I was a woman on the edge, decided to ease me in gently, so he sat me down and handed me a guinea pig called Dusty. *Lush.*

She was a tricolour fluff-ball with the softest fur and sweetest nature, and after a few minutes of cuddling, I did feel slightly less stressed and a tad more in control of myself. Unfortunately, it wasn't to last.

As Jo returned Dusty to her cage, Kevin reached into a glass case

85

that I'd thought was empty of everything except leaves, and I got my first look at Dylan and . . . *No. Oh no! Mission aborted!*

Dylan was *nothing* like Itsy or Bitsy – in fact, he was their polar opposite. He was squat and monstrous, with menace emanating from him with each languid leg movement, and I could barely watch as Kevin eased him out of his den.

I started sweating and, for once, this it was no menopausal flush. Nope, this was pure, unadulterated terror. My whole body was trembling, and if I hadn't already been sitting down, I know my legs would have gone from under me. I was truly petrified.

Kevin clocked that I was entering full-on fight/flight mode, so quickly began imparting information about Dylan which he thought might help allay my, very evident, fears.

Curly-haired tarantulas are, apparently, the best 'starter spiders' for arachnophobes due to their docile nature and a bite less painful than a bee sting. They are also only interested in attacking things that are much smaller than themselves.

Thanks Kev, but words like 'bite' and 'attack' were causing spikes of adrenaline to course through me, and I felt my eyes fill with tears. This was clearly a terrible idea, and I couldn't go through with it!

But, by now, I had a small audience; Kevin and Jo, Gemma, James (the owner), and several other staff members – not to mention Tim, who seemed to be enjoying my discomfort a little *too* much.

It was apparent to everyone that I was on the verge of chickening out. But then Kevin suggested I should watch him handling Dylan first

– so I could get more accustomed to his movements, and average velocity.

This was a surprisingly good idea because *that's* the biggest problem I have with spiders – the startling speed of the scurry, combined with the ability to move in any direction at pace.

I remember Dad telling me a spidery-fact years back, and it's stuck with me ever since; how, in a 100m sprint, if you scaled a spider up to the size of a man (*Shudder!*), you could give the bloke an 80m head start and still the spider would win. With hindsight, it's no wonder I evolved into an arachnophobe . . . Thanks Dad! *Eyeroll.*

So, back to Dylan. I peeped through splayed fingers as he slowly ambled across Kevin's palms before grinding to a halt. In fairness, as spiders go, he did seem pretty chilled – though, for me, he was still absolutely chilling.

And then it was my turn. Was I going to do this? Apparently yes, I was!

Another phobia of mine, one I *have* managed to overcome, was the fear of injections, or any procedure that involved needles. I used to be completely incapable of looking when one pierced my skin. But that primordial reaction kicked in as soon as Kevin began his approach to place Dylan carefully on my bare arm. I turned my head away and squeezed my eyes shut, powerless to even glance in *that* direction, despite sympathetic encouragement from the onlookers, and calls of, 'Aw, look at him, he's gorgeous'.

At first, I couldn't feel anything at all – no huge, hairy feet thumping across my skin, no sinister weight upon my arm. In fact, I had to ask if Dylan was actually on me because, 'No, I'm sorry, I can't look. Not yet!'

And I'm sure that Tim, who was videoing the experience, thought he was being helpful (*Bollocks, did he!*), by interjecting with, 'You will do – he's getting up to your face', a statement which caused some laughter amongst my audience, and a sharp, tearful 'Sod off!' from me.

It took time, quite . . . a . . . lot . . . of . . . time . . . (so belated apologies to those parents and kids who were patiently waiting downstairs for their own animal encounters), but eventually I managed to, not only look at Dylan's fat, black body, but also to move him closer to my face so I could see his eight beady eyes.

But when he began moving his pedipalps – the two mini leg-like appendages spiders have on their heads which they use to locate food – I decided I'd had enough desensitisation for one day. With a relieved exhale, I passed him back to Kevin, and got a round of applause from the spectators. *And breathe, Del! Phew!*

Giddy with achievement, I happily posed for photos with Leia, the Royal Python, who was a piece of cake in comparison to Dylan – though Jo said that when it comes to fears, snakes top the list by some margin. Frankly, I envy them *that* phobia – I mean, how often does one of those slither out from under your sofa?

Hyperventilating!!! (Me, not Dylan)

So, am I glad I did it? Yes, deffo. In fact, looking back at the photos and videos, I still can't believe it's me with that solid lump of spider resting on my arm.

Has doing it helped me master my fear of 'normal' spiders? Yes, to some extent, though I remain hyper-vigilant. I still shake out the duvet and pillows each night, ever since a friend mentioned how a donkey had once run across her face as she was falling asleep. *Screeeeeam!* Now *that* is the stuff of nightmares.

And, speaking of nightmares, I'm fifty-three next month (*sigh*) and instead of the usual pub get-together, I'm seriously considering booking in at Dewkes for an Animal Cwtch birthday party.

They're advertised as 'for children', but I'm sure being a big-kid-at-heart counts too? (Plus, I think I'd really, *really* enjoy seeing how well Tim would cope when *he's* the one up close and personal with the delightful Dylan. *LOL!*)

Dewkes of Sketty, (and Mumbles) stock a wide range of pet products as well as coffee and treats for you and your pooch. They also host a range of events throughout the year and can organise children's parties in conjunction with their Animal Cwtch partner. Find out more at www.dewkes.co.uk or via their Facebook page – Dewkes Boutique Pet Shop & Dog Spa.

Animal Cwtch is a family run animal encounter business. They can take their menagerie of animals to visit care homes, groups such as scouts, brownies, and youth clubs, and to schools and nurseries. They also do parties and private events. Find out more at www.animalcwtch.co.uk or via their Animal Cwtch Facebook page.

Licensed to Kiln

29th October 2022

Right, so being upfront from the get-go, I'm not remotely arty, crafty, or creative. The highlight of my aesthetic abilities thus far in life is the donkey head I first drew in Junior school, and which I have spent the intervening forty-six years refining – I've added a neck bow.

In secondary school, art continued to be a subject I couldn't master, along with a new circle of hell known as Home Economics, which added to my misery and garnered similarly abysmal results. My highest mark during three years of cooking (and my only edible outcome), was a '4 out of 10' festive chocolate log; and when we did sewing, the baby doll pyjamas I made – and was *forced* to model in the third-year fashion show – were consigned to Mum's duster pile as soon as we got home.

I've often wondered if my lack of prowess in the crafty arts might be partially genetic because Mum wasn't particularly artsy, though she did have a way with counted cross-stitch, which she encouraged me to try. I didn't take to it – simply sorting skeins into various colour shades almost defeated me. And when I did try my hand at a Christmas robin, the final result looked as if he'd had a run-in a with a cat. Apparently, my 'tension was all wrong, and dreadfully messy' – an accurate and succinct commentary on, not only my stitching, but also my life. *Sigh*.

Over the years, I've tried many, *many* creative classes, but my artisanal accomplishments have generally been met with familial incredulity, tears of hilarity, and gentle encouragement from tutors to 'Maybe try a different type of craft, eh?'

No longer do I hold any desire to learn how to arrange flowers, make rag rugs, or dabble with decoupage. Now I stick to Conversational French (*C'est bien amusant*), and seated Tai Chi, where my 'parting the wild horse's tail' is truly a sight to behold. Yep, these days, I know my limits.

But, despite this lifelong hopelessness with handicrafts, there is one branch that I'm still tempted to explore – pottery. Only once have I ever worked with proper clay and that was also in Junior school when my teacher gave us each a lump and said, 'Make whatever you'd like'. *Hmm?*

At the time, Mum was in hospital, Dad still enjoyed the occasional cheroot, so I decided to make a present both parents would enjoy, so allow me to present the practical, if paradoxical, nurse-ashtray!

Through youthful, rose-tinted glasses, my finished piece was a triumph. And when I showed my parents what, in essence, was a squashed clod of earthenware, they were fulsome in their praise.

But with hindsight, I realise that Mum and Dad's brimming eyes were not unshed tears of pride, but rather heroic attempts at stifling incipient hysterics. I can also understand why it rapidly disappeared, never to be seen again.

But tonight, I'm about to dive back into clay in a big way, and I'm actually feeling quite enthusiastic about it.

See, some weeks back, Cath and I went to Craftsea in Mumbles to try pottery painting. Obviously, this was Cath's idea since she can turn her hand to anything – painting, sewing, making, doing etc. She's hugely skilled in *all* the crafty arts.

I wasn't looking forward to it at all, but walking into the bright interior, I was pleasantly surprised. We were the only two there so I was relieved no one would be looking over my shoulder and critiquing my creation. And the range of items we could buy, to then paint, was huge.

Eventually, I stumbled across an exemplar egg-tray (painted in a faux Kidston palette), which I loved and decided to emulate. Unfortunately, Cath also decided to paint an egg-tray (*Bugger!*), so the pressure was on. I was determined I'd win this battle!

And, after a pleasant two hours, I honestly thought that I had. Okay, mine was a bit darker than the original and my brushstrokes weren't as fine, but it was eye-catching and vibrant. And I have to say that, in comparison, Cath's seemed a smidge underwhelming. *Tee hee!*

We left them there for firing, assured by the obliging assistant that we could pick them up in around a week, and I took some photos before we headed off to Verdi's for a celebratory milkshake and sundae.

Later, when I showed the pics to Tim, and forced him to choose between the two *anonymous* pieces – I certainly didn't say which was which – the one he thought was best was . . . *drumroll please* . . . mine! *Huzzah!* I was made up.

Made up, until it was time to collect them. Where Cath's had been a touch insipid, now it looked stylish – the sort of egg-holder you'd see on a sleek countertop in *Country Living*.

And I certainly didn't need Tim's surprised interjection of, 'Oh, yeah, Cath's does look better than yours now', to realise that the firing had done me no favours. In comparison, mine could, at best, be termed rustic, with a large side of garish. And yes, it also appeared to have nipples. *Humph!*

Anyway, despite the disappointing outcome, those few hours had got me thinking. Maybe I should be a bit more adventurous and have a shot at making my own ceramic creation?

I dithered for a time, but after catching the nineties classic *Ghost* on Film4, I gave Emma, owner of Cwtch Pottery and queen of clay, a call.

Fast forward two weeks and I'm in the, slightly damp, vestry of a local church, with a ball of clay squatting ominously in front of me and a mind devoid of ideas. I hadn't considered what I might like to make in advance, but in my defence, I wasn't fully *au fait* with the properties, or possibilities, of clay.

As other potters arrived and began collecting their, very impressive, fired pieces ready for glazing, Emma sat beside me and gave me a 1-2-1 lesson on the process of creating exquisite things from earthenware.

She was absolutely brilliant, a fount of pottery knowledge and expertise, and she put me at ease immediately. Within ten minutes I'd learned four methods of 'building', was ready for action and just needed to hit upon something to make, or more importantly, something *I'd* be capable of making.

I panicked for a time before recollecting the witchy-ritual I've got pencilled in for next month. So, my nebulous notion was to create a ceramic jack-o'-lantern tea light holder which would be a cool addition to my makeshift 'altar' (aka coffee table).

Plus, something hollow was, apparently, more straightforward to make, involving basic 'hand-moulding', so simples. Turns out, it wasn't.

All the class were really friendly and more than happy to respond to my numerous calls for help. My neighbour even let me borrow her 'special tools' but, despite such expert assistance, I found it nigh on impossible to get an even thickness throughout.

And then, attempting to form it into a rounded, pumpkiny shape meant teasing in the top edges. It was hopeless and I basically ended up with a clay version of a crumpled paper bag.

I kept fiddling, making it somewhat worse but when I began carving the eyes and mouth, I realised I'd forgotten a nose hole, and I didn't have any space left to put one in. *Grrr!*

So, I threw in the towel – and a horrified gasp rippled around the table when I rolled my clay back into a ball and prepared to start afresh.

But it's not quite that easy. If you've been working the clay for any length of time, and I'd been at it for around forty-five minutes, it automatically develops air bubbles which can make the finished piece explode when it's being fired. *Uh oh!*

So, how to remove them? This was, without question, the most pleasurable part of the evening. You simply throw your lump onto the floor, where it lands like a cow pat with a satisfying splat. I admit, I kept going for far longer than the five times Emma had advised.

(On her website Emma mentions the health benefits, physical and mental, that come from moulding clay, including regulated breathing, mindfulness, improved dexterity, and lower blood pressure. And frankly, after my splatting stress reliever, when I got going again, my mind emptied, I was wholly 'in the moment', and I did feel myself relax.)

Once I had a smooth and airless ball, Emma gave me a few more pointers, obviously realising that when I'd emphasised my complete inexperience, I wasn't being modest. She demonstrated the best way of moulding, how to hollow out the shape with your thumb, and then use the other fingers to smooth the outside.

And it worked *way* better than my original method of punching the clay into submission. I began to feel a slight buzz of belief – maybe I was capable of constructing something rather splendid after all?

When I got home, I was bubbling with enthusiasm, couldn't wait to tell Tim all about it, and, as always, he was delighted to listen to my excited chatter (*Eyerolls – from both of us*). But then, it was a nervy seven day wait, keeping everything crossed, that when my pumpkin emerged from the kiln, it would be in one wonderful piece. And reader, it was! *Phew*!

My second lesson was all about the glaze, and I didn't make it easy for myself. See, I was aiming for a degree of realism, trying to avoid an all-orange, and obviously fake, pumpkin. And achieving *that* meant several colours and layers.

Emma said to apply three layers for a professional finish, and I took this to heart. I began with black, aiming to add, and emphasise, shading. But then the orange caused my black to run in places where it hadn't dried sufficiently so I waited before adding a little more. And then a bit more. And thus, I ended up with *many* layers in some areas, with only one or two in others.

When I finally put down my brushes . . . no, it didn't look great. But the memory of the egg-tray transformations (for better, or worse), made me hopeful that my finished piece would magically transform during the second firing, morphing into something damned impressive.

Nope. I'd been on tenterhooks all week, giddy for the next class when I'd finally see my pumpkin revealed in all its spooky glory. I got there early, and, despite Emma's congratulations, it wasn't – at all – what I'd been hoping for.

Maybe it would look better with a candle inside? And yes, it did – mainly because viewing it with the lights off hid the multitude of scumble-sins and fat fingerprints that had been baked into it.

Look, anyone with eyes would think it the work of a talentless toddler, and clearly, I was no Clarice Cliff. I felt blue. *Sob.* I mucked about with my new ball of clay, but my heart wasn't in it. So instead, I set about dreaming up believable excuses for why I wouldn't be coming again.

The finished article – Sigh!

One hour, and a full pack of wet wipes later, my hands, face, hair, and shirt were free of earthenware residue – I've always been *gung-ho* when launching into any endeavour – and Emma came to ask if she'd see me next week. And I was genuinely dumbfounded when I heard myself say yes.

Surprisingly, despite numerous problems with my moulding, despite inglorious glazing, and despite having to park my perfectionist persona at the door, messing about with clay is actually bloody good fun. And at the end of the sessions, I came away feeling mentally refreshed.

I think I enjoyed it because, for those hours, I was a kid again, messing about with Plasticine, or the more fragrant Play-Doh, with no real-world worries weighing me down. Fears about the cost of living, the febrile political landscape, and spiralling mortgage rates didn't wholly disappear, but they definitely eased as I focused on the job in hand – literally.

So, I'm going to keep on potting. And since money is tight, this Christmas I'll be crafting ceramic gifts for all the family – and can't you envision the joy on their faces as they read this?

Obviously, I'm not going to let slip exactly what I'll be making since I don't want to spoil the surprise. But what I will say is that, if they're lucky, there might be a modern iteration of the legendary nurse-ashtray under the tree. And, if they're even luckier, they could even discover a donkey head ornament hanging on it. *Ho, ho, ho!*

Craftsea Pottery Studio is a lovely venue for a few hours of gentle painting. Check them out at www.craftsea.co.uk. Or, if you're interested in making your own, you can find details about all services and classes offered by Cwtch Pottery on Facebook, Instagram or by visiting Emma's website at www.cwtchpottery.co.uk.

Under a Mourning Moon

Dining with the Dead

12th November 2022

It's Tuesday, 8th November 2022, and there's an unusually auspicious moon overhead. Firstly, it's full and, according to *The Old Farmer's Almanac*, is commonly called a 'Beaver Moon', though that's mainly in the USA where, at this time of year, those buck-toothed rodents begin to get busy dam-building – and where *that* moniker doesn't induce the juvenile sniggers you'd probably hear in the UK. *Snigger!*

However, over this side of the pond, the Celtic term of 'Mourning Moon' is much more fitting for the cabbalistic ceremony I've got planned.

Tonight is also the last *total* lunar eclipse until 2025, though unfortunately this cosmic event won't be visible in the UK. But, as it happens, neither is the moon, which is currently shrouded by thick banks of rolling rain clouds. *Sigh.*

On the advice of my online Wiccan mentor, Lady Nightshade (aka Audrey), I'm attempting to try a little 'moon-bathing' in advance of the ritual. Apparently, absorbing the rays of the final full moon before the winter solstice will help energise me.

But all this darting in and out, dodging the downpours, is leaving me feeling less vitalised than when I began – though I'm guessing that catching the occasional, erratic moonbeam is better than nothing.

After consulting her about my plans, Audrey also mentioned that 'tonight marks the true astrological observance of Samhain', and that I should, 'ward well during this blood moon eclipse'. *Uh oh!* Sounds a tad ominous.

This is only the second time I've consulted Audrey, and I do have doubts regarding the accuracy of her instructions. I asked for advice some months ago, when preparing for my first ever rite, and she had omitted to pass on a key piece of information – that my crawling should have been deasil (clockwise) rather than widdershins (anti). *Humpf!*

To be fair though, it probably didn't make that much difference since the whole thing became a bit of a fiasco, due to thousands of toadlets, a raft of rats, and weather so wild, burning manifestations at the 'sacred space' was impossible; eventually we gave up, and had a mini-bonfire in the back of Geoff.

Since that night, I've detoured from the pagan path, instead devoting myself to less esoteric endeavours, such as pottery, painting, and attempting to stop John and Wolfie eating the kitchen table, with limited success.

But tonight's the night when I will, once more, dip my toe into the Wiccan ways, as I prepare to honour my ancestors, and past pets! The table (and teeth marks) are covered in natural calico and I'm almost ready to host my very first 'Dumb Supper'. But with Audrey's words of warning (and warding), in mind, I initially needed to do a little bit of 'smudging'.

Yeah, I didn't know what that meant either. But, as it turns out, it simply entails wandering around the house, wafting smouldering sage into every corner of every room, while chanting positive affirmations. Okay. That sounds eminently doable, even for a total novice like me.

But first I needed to get hold of a 'smudging stick', plus some other pagan paraphernalia, and luckily for me, I knew exactly where to go – the Gypsy Wishes Magical Market at Swansea's Brangwyn Hall. *Epic!*

There were numerous stalls selling everything the modern witch, Wiccan, pagan, Viking, druid etc. could possibly desire. Plus, it offered the 'full psychic, holistic craft experience'. *Wowzers!* I made a list, picked up Cath, and off we went.

Our expectations were *maybe* a little too high. We'd anticipated a chamber, alight with flickering candles, the heavy scents of mystical herbs and spices in the air, with stall owners, robed in black, conical hats set at jaunty angles as they hawked their arcane charms and spells. We were very excited! *Eek!*

So, of course, it wasn't like that at all. The only candles we saw ran off batteries, the hall smelled rather fusty, with very occasional whiffs of sandalwood, vanilla, and 'Dragons Blood' (Yep really! I asked). But most disappointingly, not even one vendor wore either liturgical apparel or a pointy hat. *Bummer*!

However, there was an enormous array of stuff for sale, and some stalls looked quite enticing, so we swallowed our disappointment and started shopping. Top of my list was the 'smudger', and almost every stall had them. Clearly this, allegedly, purifying bundle was a best seller in occult circles.

Cath was off like a rocket, accumulating items at a rate of knots; jewellery, a Christmas wreath, two display cases, and some delicious fudge – After Eight and White Chocolate. *Yum!* She also bought me a cute little illuminated ghost which would make an ideal table decoration for my planned silent supper.

I browsed, sniffed, and discovered that unburned sage smells bloody awful! So, instead of a pure sheaf of the herb, I got a combo, and could only hope that the lavender would be powerful enough to stifle the other.

Then we moved onto crystals, of which there were many, *many, MANY* types available. But I knew exactly what I was looking for.

So, you can keep your Topaz, Amethyst, Lapis Lazuli, Carnelian, Hematite, Black Obsidian, Selenite, Pyrite, Black Tourmaline, Citrine, or the numerous colours of Quartz, because all I wanted was a simple Moonstone. (It was Mum's favourite, and I thought it would be a nice addition to my 'altar'.)

Turns out, everyone else must have wanted one too, because after trawling the whole hall, there was only one stall which had one for sale – and it wasn't the perfect milky colour I'd wanted. But for £3, I got it anyway. And it did look quite lovely in natural light.

Finally, I needed that witchy cliché that is a cauldron. And though Audrey had said 'large, metal and suitable for a stove top', I couldn't afford anything like that. Instead, I stumbled upon a dinky, ceramic version, with a lid and china spoon, and at £6.50, it was a bargain. (When I unwrapped it at home, I discovered it was a novelty soup bowl but, what the hell? It'd do the job).

My cauldron for the evening

Now I had all my necessary bits and bobs, it was time to prepare the house, altar, and table. I would have liked a hand, but none was forthcoming, with Tim, as usual, refusing to have anything to do with my 'weird shit'. *Sigh.*

However, fate was on my side in the form of my friend, Dawn. She needed someone to look after her daughters for a couple of hours and was happy for them to help me prep for my pagan ritual – once I'd assured her it didn't involve child sacrifice. *Epic!* Right, let's get cracking little witches.

And we did. Obviously, being the responsible adult that I am, I was somehow talked into relinquishing this role when faced with the sort of unanswerable logic that only an eight and ten-year-old can sell.

Thus – and please stop reading now, Dawn – Olivia carried the lit candle, Leia was the smudger, and I was 'allowed' to carry a saucer, which they thought would be 'useful for catching potential sparks'. I couldn't help but feel they were humouring me.

We began in the lounge where Tim (grudgingly), and the pups (unconcernedly), were banished of their negative energies through excessive clouds of smoke, hugely enthusiastic wafting, and a cheery banishing chant. Then we tackled everywhere else.

And I have to say, the kids were fantastic. As well as infusing the whole house with joyous positivity, they also provided, unasked for, feedback on my décor (occasionally blunt, mainly valid), along with suggestions for the installation and locations of further smoke alarms because 'just one isn't really enough, Del'.

Yep, where fire was concerned, they were *very* well versed in preventative measures, but they also had a keen eye for potential colour palettes for the bedrooms. Thanks girls, much appreciated.

(Oh, and I can confirm that burnt sage smells a *lot* more pleasant than its dried form. And that's fortunate because I couldn't detect even a hint of lavender.)

Then it was time for the main event – dressing the table. We started with flowers. Mum died just over a year ago, so to cheer me up on the first anniversary, Tim had bought me a lovely, autumnal bouquet (*he has his moments*), so it seemed fitting to use these.

Then came candles, tea-lights, my handmade clay pumpkin, a real pumpkin, ghost and skull ornaments, the moonstone, place settings, and our fancy Christmas crockery. Frankly, the reindeer struck a slightly bum note but it's the only matching set I have. And Leia and Olivia thought they looked 'SHAMAZING' so who was I to argue.

I put out posh glasses, a bottle of Prosecco to liven up proceedings, and then it was time to add the 'guests'. Since all four invitees were dead, Audrey advised using photographs – *Well, duh!* – so pride of place was an old wedding pic of Mum and Dad which I had on my iPad, top dog TZ was next, and then our beautiful Barney completed the set.

Leia and Olivia did the ceremonial lighting of the candles, we turned off the big light and . . . *Wow!* It looked gorgeous. I was ready, set, and good to go, and so were the girls. Dawn turned up in the nick of time because, though the kids had been a wonderful help, the supper itself was a dinner for five.

Audrey had said that, food wise, I should serve homemade bread, seasonal soups, and vegetables but I'm not a talented cook, and am certainly no baker. Instead, I bought Co-op's 'irresistible sourdough' to accompany the Bœuf Bourguignon I'd knocked up in the slow cooker.

(Side note: I've discovered that, even with my severely limited culinary skills, a slow cooker makes anything taste good. Plus, in these straightened times, they're an energy efficient way of cooking, costing around 5p per hour to use. So, I'd recommend one to anybody who's counting the pennies or isn't gifted in the kitchen department. It's genuinely changed my life and I've become quite boringly evangelical about it! Though, Stepdad has just started lobbying for air fryers, so either/or.)

Right, no more talking. Let the silent supper begin.

It's strange to say that the 'dumb' aspect of the ritual had, sort of, passed me by. Despite Audrey's wise advice to 'fully embrace the silence and focus on staying in the moment' – *Eh?* – I hadn't really considered how *that* would actually feel.

But, once I'd piled each plate with a hearty ladleful of posh stew – yes, your incorporeal guests 'eat' too – and filled each flute with a hefty slug of Prosecco, the atmosphere shifted and, instead of the bit of fun I'd imagined, I suddenly felt the solemnity of it all.

My dinner guests – Mum & Dad, TZ and Barney. (Can you spot my tealight holder?)

The kitchen seemed to shrink around me, and all that existed for (most of) the meal were the memories I had of my four guests. Very occasionally, my mind would stray to the everyday – especially when I heard Tim bollocking the pups for eating the rug. *Sigh.* But, as Audrey had advised, I forced myself to stay in the moment and kept on, silently, celebrating (and mentally talking to), my dear departeds. And it might sound fanciful but, at times, it actually felt as if they were sitting at that table with me.

Twenty minutes later, my plate was empty, and the next step was to burn the short messages I'd prepared for each guest. Mini-cauldron, your time has come.

If you don't mind, I won't share what I wrote with you because it was heartfelt and hugely personal. But, as each note flamed then turned to ash, and I blew out that guest's corresponding candle, I admit that *Regina XXL* was recruited to mop tears and a runny nose.

Now all that remained was to wish each visitant a final, soundless goodbye, before leaving the table and exiting the room. Done.

There's no question that it was an uncanny, unsettling experience, but it's one I'm seriously considering making an annual event.

Of course, I think of my late parents and pets frequently, but this ceremony provided a reflective focal point for my mourning, and suddenly the weight of grief seemed a little lighter. I felt surprisingly refreshed and it was a truly cathartic experience.

Back in the real world, and with the big light switched on, there was a table to clear and washing up to do.

Apparently, the uneaten food and drink should be buried outside, to 'return it from whence it came'. *Bugger that, Audrey!!* There was no way I was going to squander a tasty casserole that would feed Tim and I for another two days. And pouring Prosecco over the lawn would have been just criminal.

So, I put the stew back in the slow cooker, and prepared to polish off five glasses of Prosecco – acid reflux be damned!

And I know for a fact that all my loved ones – Mum in particular – would definitely applaud such a truly selfless display of thrift. *So, waste not, want not. Cheers!*

Hello From the Other Side

So, it's 9:30pm on a foggy Friday evening, and Cath and I are idling in the Aldi car park, Crosshands. I've been flashing my lights at the few cars that have driven in but the only person who's shown any interest, thus far, is a middle-aged lady who stopped to ask if we were 'signalling for help'. Of the men who, we hope, are going to give us a night to remember, there is, as yet no sign.

I know what you're thinking but, much as I'm up for anything, I doubt I'll ever pen an article entitled, 'Del Goes Dogging'. Mind you, I think I might have, accidentally, dogged once when, parking in a quiet country lane at midnight, an ex and I launched into an impassioned snogging session only to be suddenly torchlit on all sides.

Cue screaming (us), rapping on the windows (them), and me driving away in a spray of gravel and shower of expletives.

With hindsight, I guess it's possible they weren't actually doggers; after all, this happened in Burford, an idyllic, thatched Oxfordshire village with a doddery demographic and an overly zealous Neighbourhood Watch. But, whether sexual voyeurs or elderly vigilantes, that's one experience I don't fancy repeating.

Anyway, back to tonight's activity which will be, I'll wager, *much* more thrilling than any 'Peeping Tom' pastimes, because Cath and I are . . . *drumroll* . . . going on a ghost hunt! And I can't wait. *Eek!*

I've got mood music blasting through the car stereo ('Bad Moon Rising', 'Thriller', 'Don't Fear the Reaper' etc.), the heated seats are set to a bum-baking 25°, and we're ready, willing, and waiting to meet the guys from *Ghost Watch Wales*, Wales' foremost paranormal explorers.

And we soon spot them, as a spectral hand appears from the depths of a parked car and beckons us over. Closer, and we see they're not in anything resembling the iconic *Ecto-1*, instead driving a rather more prosaic Fiat 500. *Oh well, a girl can dream.*

Introductions are made; Geraint is the owner of GWW (and lead investigator), and this evening he's being ably assisted by two further team members, Gethin and Mark. They tell us to follow them, and we proceed, in solemn two-car convoy, the 10.6 miles to the secret location, known in the GWW arena as 'Area 51'.

[Tip #1: Some locations must remain undisclosed, for fear of potential paranormal poachers. The world of psychic exploration is, apparently, a cut-throat business! So, if you find an 'active' spot, keep it to yourself.]

And I've got to say that the journey definitely enhanced our anticipation. We threaded through twisting lanes, verges shrouded by thick ribbons of mist, and didn't encounter another *living* soul.

Eventually we reached a wide driveway, blocked by wrought-iron gates – we had arrived at Ground Zero. *Gulp.* It was a single-storey, half-timbered house comprising two dumpy towers, with a front facing gable and a steeply pitched roof.

Though a fair way removed from the sizable country house we'd been imagining, it certainly looked eerie enough, ominously squat and illuminated only by headlights . . . and just as my playlist switched to 'Tubular Bells, Pt 1'. *Yikes!*

Gethin unlocked the gates and we drove in, parked up and donned coats, scarves, hats, and gloves – we'd been warned in advance to wrap up warm since it was a cold night and we'd be there til around 3am. Then we, trepidatiously, followed the ghost gang inside.

[Tip #2: Even on the mildest night, you might still feel a ghostly chill so layers are a must. I also went with tights, leggings, two pairs of thermal socks and a knock off Oodie from Dunelm, and remained happily toasty for the full five hours.]

As the team trooped back and forth, armed with a variety of intriguing silver suitcases, Geraint got Cath and I settled with a fan heater and a mug of tea in the building's tiny kitchen, and outlined how the investigation would proceed.

[Tip #3: Set up a temperate base camp, ideally with access to a kettle. Otherwise, take a large flask. And plenty of food too, because you don't want your blood sugars dropping when you're a world away from the bright lights of a Co-op, and in a place where no delivery drivers would ever venture.]

There were two zones we were focusing on – the Main Hall (MH), a massive space with high vaulted ceilings and well-preserved parquet flooring, and the Back Room (BR), a more intimate chamber, currently being used by the property's owner for storage.

Geraint also filled us in on the 'ghosts' that he'd seen/sensed/smelled on their last visit. The main man was Reg, a

Ghost Hunting Kit

Victorian labourer with a dry sense of humour and whose appearance was presaged by an 'overpowering smell of pig shit'.

Apparently, Reg also possessed a fair knowledge of modern mechanics as he'd been known to restart the cars of those unfortunates who'd broken down outside. Reg sounded like a stand-up guy.

106

Though, that he'd also been known to appear in the back seats of visitors' cars changed my opinion somewhat. (Note to self: Check car *thoroughly* before heading home.)

Then there were three young women, assumed to be maids from a local manor house. Their passing was due to cleaning arsenic-soaked wallpaper while omitting to keep a window open. Despite such an awful passing, their spirits retained a keen sense of fun and they'd been heard giggling occasionally and whispering between themselves. *Uh oh!*

And then there was the tragic tale of two children who had been murdered by their mother. It was a heartbreaking story, but I really hoped *they* wouldn't make an appearance – child ghosts freak me out.

By now, Gethin and Mark had finished lugging in the equipment cases, and we were given a quick briefing on some of the paranormal paraphernalia that the team, and we, would be using. Here comes the science bit:

The EVP-R (Electronic Voice Phenomenon Recorder) is designed to pick up sounds and voices that might not otherwise be audible. Gethin told us it's the most frequently used piece of kit during GWW investigations and gets excellent results. *Ooh!* Fingers crossed for disembodied voices tonight.

EMF (Electromagnetic Field) Meter is probably the most recognisable device in any ghost hunter's arsenal. If you've watched *Ghostbusters,* you'd easily identify this small, handheld apparatus. It has coloured lights – green, amber, red – with the whole spectrum sparking to life when a 'spirit force' turns up.

I'd bought my own, having spotted one on Amazon for £6.99, and I had great fun wandering around our house, testing for the presence of phantoms. Based on my limited research, I can confirm that we're spectre-free – unless you count the kettle which is clearly haunted as it caused the meter to hit red whenever it boiled. *Lol!*

The Aeroflux II, a bland-looking white box, with a powerful purpose, was making its debut tonight. The guys were extremely excited because 'It measures temperature deviations and logs air pressure 23 times a second'. It also indicates any changes via a colour coded LED:

Green = the device is actively monitoring.

Amber = fluctuations occurring, so we might notice 'minor' events such as small noises, EMF spikes, and slight temperature changes.

Red = it's all kicking off, big time! Expect loud noises, strong EMF spikes and visual anomalies.

I caught Cath's eye and we silently agreed that if that box flashed red, we'd hightail it out of there and burn rubber down the M4. Call us chickens, but red sounded *far too* intense for fledgling phantom hunters.

By now, we'd finished our cuppas and were eager to get started. But not before Gethin had given us our own 'monitoring devices'. He handed us each a mobile phone which contained some incredibly special apps.

I got the 'SLS Camera with Night Vision' which detects 'humanoid bodies in your environment', displaying them as stick figures. It was simple to use so I tested it out and it make stickmen of us all. Great, but I wasn't sure how I'd react if a stray angular figure popped up on screen. *Shudder!*

However, Cath's app was more interesting for she had the 'Paratek Ovulus'. No, it's nothing to do with *Harry Potter.* It's an app that holds a databank of words which a passing spirit can dip into and use, if they'd like to communicate. *Epic!* We were good to go.

[Tip #4: You can never have *too much* kit. But check out the range of apps available before you start seriously splashing the cash.]

En route to the BR zone, I asked if the team had ever captured a ghost on camera and there were nods all round. Gethin handed me his phone, displaying a photo he'd taken at our current location, during a previous visit. 'Take a look at this and tell me what you see'.

It was blurry, with a yellowish cast and had clearly been snapped with a lower resolution camera than was common these days. But you could make out what *appeared* to be, the shadowy figure of a man, with something resembling a noose around his neck. *Oo-er! I've got chills and they're definitely multiplying!*

Now, suitably scared, Cath and I made sure we chose seats between the guys, based on the irrational assumption that nothing could 'get' us if we were in the middle of the herd. Then Gethin pressed record and began the EVP sessions by 'calling' the spirits.

It was totally chilling, and I don't mean that pleasurable thrill of fear you get when you're watching a scary film. The air felt damp, it was pitch black, and all we could hear was question after question being asked of the ether, with pauses for potential answers.

At the same time, Cath began nudging me because her Ovilus was flashing (*Oo-er, missus!*), with words were slightly disturbing: *Satan, Death, Malevolent, Hate*, and what really freaked us out, *Stay. Uh oh.*

But, in the spirit of scientific honesty, we also got *Nose, Smell, Sandwich,* and *Sausage*, which caused some silent shoulder shaking and left us feeling a bit more relaxed, though *that* didn't last long.

After some time, Gethin decided to play back the recordings for us to hear because he'd noticed 'spikes' occurring throughout the session and, in almost every one, he'd captured some kind of sound anomaly.

And this was the most petrifying part of the night, listening to those breathy voices(?) – which had *not* been audible at the time – whisper, whistle, and chuckle beside us. We also heard several muffled bangs,

Gethin's reaction to the EVPs!
(Our reactions were similar tbh.)

and what sounded like the scrape of furniture being moved, maybe across a well-preserved parquet floor? *Double Yikes!*

At that point I quietly suggested to Cath that we might make an early exit, but her blood was up, the MH zone was next, and she really wanted a shot at 'communing'. So, of course, we stayed. *Bloody Cath and her puppy-dog eyes!*

During another 'tea and get toasty' break, Mark arranged five chairs around a small table in the centre of the MH zone and, nervously taking my place, I admit that I felt intensely vulnerable.

Just like the best spies in the business, I generally prefer sitting with my back against a wall so that any threat comes at me head on – and certainly can't creep up behind me and place icy hands around

109

my throat. Yep, my imagination was running wild.

Gethin asked if I'd like to have a go at 'calling', and I tried, but after a stilted and clichéd start – 'Hello, I'm Del . . . Is anybody there?' – which earned a definite corporeal tut from someone – Cath took over and was, surprisingly, excellent. She kept going for ages, was applauded by the experts on her 'good rhythm' and was even rewarded with a few spikey anomalies. *Sigh.*

[Tip #5 – When 'calling', find your flow. Yes, leave pauses for inaudible replies, but keep your questions coming.]

It was around 2:30am, and nearly time take our leave of Area 51, when Geraint, who'd been doing more EVP questioning, gave a wide and welcoming smile.

He then imparted the *happy* news that, 'There's a young boy standing there', and pointed to an empty space behind my left shoulder. *Gulp.* Then he continued: 'Can you try to touch one of us? Or come and play under the table? You like to play, don't you?'

Klaxon alert! Shit got real! I did *not* want any little boy ghost 'playing' anywhere near me. I had visions of a pale, wild-eyed face peeping up from between my thighs and so, on the pretence of a loo stop, I made a swift exit, dragging Cath along to stand guard outside. I'd had enough excitement for one night.

And yes, I realise I'm a big fat scaredy-cat, but it was a *very* unnerving place, and I was glad when the boy disappeared, and the guys began packing away.

They escorted us back to the car, which I checked thoroughly for any visual, or olfactory, evidence of Reg, and we headed home. It had certainly been a night to remember.

And it might be fanciful (and most likely due to low blood sugars) but, as we drove away, I swear I caught a malodourous whiff of pig shit, and heard a muffled voice call out, 'Duh, I could murder a sausage sandwich!' *EEK!*

If you fancy experiencing a serious paranormal investigation for yourself, you can find the Ghost Watch Wales group on Facebook.

Untamed Melody

Experiencing the Rhythm Method

11th December 2022

I can't feel my arse, my extremities are numb and, clearly, I'm not dressed for the occasion. I should have guessed that my Rudolph poncho wouldn't vibe with the bohemian 'atmos'. *Sigh.*

I'm currently sitting in a *very* rustic wooden structure which has a grassy roof, no walls, and a smouldering fire pit at its centre. It's located in the middle of an ancient woodland and, despite the stunning surroundings, I'm regretting deciding to come. The fact that it's also daylight, December, and sodding freezing doesn't help.

I'm here because, as you know, over the past nine months, I've pushed myself to try out new activities, to explore the esoteric, and to inject a little fun and adventure into my life.

But I've also tried my hand at more conventional hobbies such as painting and potting, which I strangely found *almost* as dreadful as allowing a large tarantula to amble across my arm. (Mind, I still can't look at the photos of *that* encounter with Dylan, except through splayed fingers!)

But it's, indirectly, because of my pottery class that I've come. A few weeks back, some of the girls were ribbing Rosemary (advanced potter, excellent coiling skills), about her 'naked romping', and my ears pricked up. I was, understandably, intrigued.

After the bawdy asides and laughter had finally died down, I asked her what they were talking about and she told me all about 'free-dancing, which instils a feeling of liberty and well-being. And no, we don't do it naked'. *Hmm?* Interesting. But then she added, 'And there's a cocoa ceremony too', and *that* sealed the deal.

So, I've come along to the 'Winter Dream Ecstatic Dance & Cacao Activation' event, DJ'ed by Osara, facilitated by Seagypsee (aka Marie) and aided by Gordon – accomplished keeper of the sacred flame, and official photographer.

Myself and thirty-odd 'like-minded individuals will be going on an ecstatic dance journey, to express our wildness, to release emotions and to revel in community magic'. We'll also be creating 'a powerful portal for creative freedom and untamed expression as we celebrate life together'. *Um, okay?*

Frankly, it sounded *much* too advanced for someone like me who has never tried anything this 'out there'. Plus, I can't remember the last time I felt *truly* ecstatic. And, in case you were wondering, you should know that I'm no dancer, and that's not only because of my stupid back.

Even in my pomp, when I'd occasionally venture to a nightclub, I was never a great mover. In fact, you'd often find me sitting in a quiet corner, guarding coats, and handbags, rather than attempting to 'pump up the jam' on the dance floor. So, you can imagine how *way out* of my comfort zone this was taking me.

But, putting the oddness of the occasion aside for a moment, another concern was how I'd get from Caswell Bay car park up to the venue itself. Luckily, it was a level third of a mile, and the footpath was, mainly kind underfoot, and under wheel. I'd taken my trusty rollator (Roy) because a walking stick doesn't cut it over distance, and as well as helping my balance, Roy provides a handy seat when my spine starts screaming at me to stop.

After a leisurely twenty-minute roll, I arrived punctually for the 3pm kick-off but was actually one of the first there. I guess the free spirits who normally attend this kind of thing aren't quite as anal as me when it comes to timekeeping.

If I'm honest, I was really nervous. I'd have liked to have taken a pal along for moral support, but all my friends were busy – apparently *(Hard eyeroll)*. Only Cath was blunt enough to say she didn't fancy 'capering about in a freezing forest for four hours'. And fair play to her for that.

So, approaching the primitive structure, it was more than the sub-zero temperatures that were causing my legs to shake. But I needn't have worried because Marie (ethereally beautiful, green handkerchief skirt, luxuriant hair) and Gordon (outdoorsy, cool tunic, also luxuriant hair), couldn't have been more welcoming, not even raising an eyebrow at a total newbie who'd rocked up to a wild dance event pushing a mobility aid and wearing a reindeer hoodie with ears, and antlers!

As Gordon worked on getting the fire cracking, Marie explained what I should expect, handed me a pair of wireless headphones – 'to be respectful to the preserved wildlife whilst immersing you in the sound' – then introduced me to a few other early birds. And it happily seemed that I wasn't the only dance-virgin in attendance.

Lorinda, a bubbly blonde, had driven from Ammanford to be here, explaining that today marked the start of a new life phase, after several very tough years. 'I thought, what the hell! I'm going to be a hippy for the weekend'. And George agreed. 'I've never tried anything like this but, you only live once, right?'

It was a phrase echoed by others, and there was a palpable sense of anticipation; I think we were all hoping we'd experience some sort of release from the stresses and mundanity of the everyday. Fingers crossed.

Thirty minutes later, we had the full complement of participants, DJ Osara was setting up his decks and Marie announced it was time to begin. *Eek.*

We started with 'grounding', closing our eyes, and imagining 'roots growing out of our spines and coiling down to the earth below'. I did my best but I'm not good at visualisation and, despite Marie's hypnotic chanting, I couldn't seem to picture it. But the breathing exercises were effective and, for a few minutes I, almost, forgot about my frosty fingers and toes.

And then, it was time for the 'ceremonial' cocoa (or cacao, which I'd assumed was pretty much the same thing). *Nope.* Cacao is a *vastly different* animal – or rather, vegetable. According to Marie, as well as being delicious, cacao can help 'enhance the dance experience and gently guide us to connect with hidden dimensions within ourselves'. *Wow!* This cacao had some *serious* heavy lifting to do.

As Gordon circulated with steaming cups of the 'natural medicine', Marie gently intoned the steps she had taken to prepare the cacao, reassuring us that 'it has been meditated over, been sung to and been honoured'. *Phew! I'm so glad about that.*

First, we were instructed to smell it, ensuring we were 'present' as we did. *Sigh.* I inhaled deeply and tried to keep my wandering mind focused on the contents of the paper cup. Yes, the rich chocolatey notes were as expected, but when they blended with the damp, peaty odours of the woodland, a heady mix of earthy aromas hit my olfactory nerve and . . . *Wow!* It was truly lush.

I couldn't wait to get stuck in, so I eagerly took my first sip, and— *Ugh!* It was absolutely, bloody dreadful! I struggled to swallow, others began to cough, and it seemed clear that this particular cacao needed *a lot* more prayers and song to make it palatable. (On the upside, I was very glad to wrap my frozen hands around a heat source.)

I took a second, tentative, taste and forced myself to explore the texture and flavour. It was thick and extremely bitter, but since I'd lowered my expectations – I'd originally thought it would be like a Starbucks' hot chocolate, only better – it didn't seem *quite* as unpleasant. I continued sipping.

Now we were all nicely 'grounded', it was time for the main event. As Gordon's fire began flaming warmly enough to bring some feeling back to my feet, DJ Osara stepped up, told us to don the headphones and suddenly, we were cocooned in our own individual dance bubbles.

And then the roundhouse really started to swing – big time! At first, the music (much like me) was chilled and slow. Osara had talked us through the process, explaining how to 'reach out into nature and embrace anything that your bodies, voices, and souls are drawn to do'. Okay, sounded a bit bizarre but, to echo Lorinda, 'What the hell!' *Let's do this, Del.*

As my fellow dancers drifted out into the woods, I sat on Roy and began to sway, albeit somewhat self-consciously, as I allowed the waves of sound to overtake me. But I couldn't ignore the dog-walkers or the groups of ramblers.

One Ecstatic Dancer

They scuttled past, casting bemused glances in our direction, and weaving warily between the oblivious dancers who were rhumba'ing around the roundhouse. And when two spaniels and a Weimaraner, literally, crashed the party – leaving their human handlers aghast and calling in vain – the absurdity of it all hit me, hard. *LOL!* (Though I was, thankfully, able to swallow my hysterics more easily than Marie's cacao.)

But then Osara's set began to swell into a global fusion of basslines and rhythms, and it filled my body with what, for me, was a wholly unnatural and irrepressible desire to dance. And once those toe-tapping Indian oboes kicked in – I'm a bugger for a *shehnai* – I finally felt myself begin to let loose as my shoulders embraced the tempo, and the experience.

(Between you and me, I admit that I was a tad envious at first, watching my dance-mates leap around the fire, shake their tail feathers, and get well into the groove with every inch of their bodies. But it passed – I'm not big on navel-gazing, and it didn't take long to get Roy rocking and rolling.)

And, suddenly, I didn't care. I didn't care if I looked ridiculous (which I did), arms windmilling madly and feet propelling Roy on a mystery tour through undergrowth, shrubbery, and mud. Because that was the beauty of this event – nobody gave a damn what anyone might think of them, or their dancing, no matter how unconventional, idiosyncratic, or downright ludicrous it was.

We weren't bopping to look good or impress others. We were

letting our bodies do exactly what felt right – and it was liberating, and truly marvellous.

For the next three hours I was, basically, away with fairies, throwing some full-on-far-out sedentary shapes, and dancing my elbows off in the best upper body workout I've had for years. And when, as I should have expected, I felt one of my shocking *stag moments* begin to build, I didn't even attempt to stifle it.

Instead, I roared my heart out, loud, and proud, antlers aquiver, because it felt totally natural to be bellowing in a forested glade on a Saturday night in Swansea. *Hmm?* (Note to self: Ask Marie if there's something other than cacao in that 'medicine'.)

As the music reached the 'wild abandon' stage of proceedings, it seemed to have been perfectly timed to coincide with the appearance of a cold moon, which caused zealous howling from those atop the limestone slopes. The energy was raw and feral, and when a bare-chested chap in harem pants pulled out his fire stick and started twirling, things hotted up even more.

All fired up and loving it – big time!

I was even moved to take an *extremely* rare selfie (after a certain age, no amount of filtering helps), because I had a massive, cheesy grin plastered across my face. And it wasn't for the camera, but simply due to the pure joy of the moment. I knew I needed to capture it, as a reminder of how wonderful life can feel, if I only let myself go enough to fully enjoy it.

As the pace slowed, people began emerging from the black depths, blinking as if waking from a harmonic hibernation. Their headphones winked a path through the oaks and beech, as they shuffled towards the fire. It was time to 'cool down'.

Once more in a circle, we waited for the final chords to fade before removing our headphones and, grudgingly, returning to the here and now. Marie asked if anyone felt like sharing their experience and I was one of many who were buoyed up enough to do so.

I wanted everyone to know that, despite an inability to do standing shimmies, I was proof that even us 'sitting-downers' can reach ecstatic, dizzying heights, and I actually felt a tiny bit tearful.

I could have stayed longer, for the 'community dinner', or the planned evening swim (*Brr!*) but time was ticking, and I had another ghost hunt starting at ten. So, I thanked the guys, said goodbye to the group and rolled back to the car, Lorinda lighting the way for me with her torch.

We were in complete agreement. Yep, we'd had the weirdest four hours of our lives, but we were buzzing and fizzing with energy. We'd both experienced a, very real, sense of release, and for a time, were completely freed from the conventional, and it had been absolutely fabulous!

We'll definitely be going again because, as it turns out, Gloria Estefan was right. Someday, 'the rhythm *is* gonna get'cha', and it'll be freaking fantastic!

If you fancy having a go at ecstatic dance – and I'd really recommend that you try it at least once – you can find Marie (Mystic Cocoon) and Osara (founder of Ecstatic Dance Bristol) on Facebook, where their upcoming events are posted. They're also on instagram as @seagypsee and @osarasound. And if you'd like to hear some of the music before committing to a session, search for Osara on Mixcloud.

Blue Christmas

The Gasman Commeth

25th December 2022

Look, I love Christmas as much as the next woman, and despite being, at fifty-three, old enough to know better, I still get childishly excited about the annual visit from the *Big Man*. Of course, I don't *believe*, but sometimes, even if just for one night a year, it feels right to suspend the cynicism and simply embrace the magic.

When the neighbour's fairy lights first flash into life in early November, or when I pass a house festooned with sparkling stalactites, garden filled with swaying snowmen, surrounding a radiant Santa in his Rudolph-drawn sleigh, I still feel that fizz of excitement and delicious anticipation of the festive delights to come.

And, despite the *many* stresses of the season, I still love loading the tree with old, and new, decorations, draping loose coils of sparkly ribbon and strategically placing strands of lametta, to give it that frosty look.

I love deciding what presents to buy, so I see smiles of genuine pleasure on the grandkids' faces, and on Tim's, though with him it's nigh on impossible to gauge his true feelings, masked as they are, by (stereo)typical Yorkshire stolidity, and brevity. *Eyeroll.*

The shops are rammed, everyone's rushing, but there's a good-humoured joy about it. People are nicer, more inclined to engage, to chat, to share a smile and resigned shoulder shrug with strangers who are queuing, mostly patiently, at the next till.

I love wrapping presents, though I'm pretty inexpert, a bit slapdash and can never manage those razor-sharp corners my stepdad does with ease. But I love sitting at the kitchen table with my 3-for-2 festive rolls of puddings, robins and polar bears, scissors, and Sellotape at the ready.

I put on my fave Christmas film, 'Die Hard', (and yes, it *is* a Christmas film), and begin cutting, sticking, and labelling before filling the sacks, ready for transportation – by SUV, not sleigh – to the, frequently, snowy wilds of Yorkshire.

I love Christmas Eve, donning new pyjamas ('cause I've got to look nice for Santa) and curling up on the sofa with a bag of posh crisps and tray of dips, cosy, and content because we're as ready as we can be, and all that's left is to crack open the Quality Street and relax with a pint of Snowball. (We don't do things by halves in this household.)

But this year, I'm not feeling it and, in Elvis' immortal lyrics, it's shaping up to be 'a blue, blue, blue Christmas'. *Sigh.*

See, 2022 has seen a fair number of relatives pop their clogs, including our beloved dog, Barney, so I suppose it's understandable I've been feeling pretty low. But really, it's because of Mum.

She died in early November '21, so last year's celebrations, coming mere weeks after, were a low-key affair. There was no *proper* tree – my stepdad wanted to use the faux silver birch we'd bought for Mum's death party – so I bought one too, threw a few baubles on both, didn't do presents, and a quiet time was had by all.

But, for some reason, this year feels *way* worse. I'm melancholic, got no *hwyl* and just can't be bothered to bother.

I looked up the 'Seven Stages of Grief' on Google and I think that last Christmas, I was probably in a combination of Stages 1, 2 & 3: Shock, Denial and Anger. We knew she had Covid, knew that due to existing heart issues there was a high chance of her dying, but still, when it *actually* happened, it rocked my world.

I've been in a daze for months, desperately seeking someone to blame, a simmering rage bubbling up on occasion, causing tears and mood swings, with poor Tim having to pick up the pieces.

But it did lead to Stage 4: Bargaining/Questioning. What if we'd tested her for Covid sooner? What if her booster jab had come a couple of weeks earlier? What if I'd been more careful when I delivered the shopping? What if? What if? Ad infinitum.

I was consumed by these thoughts, whilst also remaining steadfastly in Stage 2 – She wasn't gone, she was on holiday, in hospital, staying with friends. And she'd be back soon.

Then, during the Autumn, Stage 5 descended, casting a black, depressive cloud over my every day. And that's where I am now, or rather, where I was until yesterday morning, because I think that I've finally moved on to Stage 6: Acceptance, and Hope.

Sounds encouraging, doesn't it? As if I've finally reached the end of the heartache highway. But, by default, with acceptance comes the realisation that she's *really* dead. And that's why this Christmas is the worst ever, because, as it turns out, it was Mum who made it magical.

In Christmases past, like most, we had our traditions. First was the tree, a bushy, fake six-footer that we'd decorate excessively, with copious strands of tinsel and migraine-inducing flashing lights.

The 'How many sleeps?' countdown, the secret present wrapping, Christmas Eve's 7am shopping trip to M&S, followed by toast and hot chocolate in The Kardomah. Then home, to spend the morning helping/hindering Mum as she prepped the veg, and Dad sorted bird, beef, and gravy.

The afternoon would see me in new pyjamas, waiting to start my yawning routine once the daylight began to wane, logic being the sooner I was in bed, the sooner *He* would come.

But it was the one night each year when my parents would deliberately keep me up late – anything to ensure that they'd manage to get a couple of hours kip before being woken by a shrieking, hefty child, with a pillowcase full of presents and giddy as a kipper.

Once, as I was drinking Mum's 'Special Christmas Eve Cocoa', I found a green jellybean(?) in the bottom of the mug. Yep, they'd thought it a good idea to try spiking it with one of Dad's Temazepam (Street name = Green Eggs.) *WTF?* But the 1970s were a vastly different time, and these days, I've heard that harried parents often resort to Calpol so . . .

After the sack came 'tree presents'. Dad would always make us a cuppa and bacon sarnie before we could begin the unwrapping, so I'd have to sit on my hands to stop myself ripping in. Waiting was an exquisite torture, but worth it to curl up with a new book and new favourite toy, while Mum did a quick once over with the hoover and Dad began filling the first of many bin bags with shredded paper.

Then the day unfolded in, what is probably, the usual way for most. Visit family/friends, home for turkey and flaming pudding, Queen's speech, board games, dozing, picky bits, TV specials, and then bed. And it was always wonderful.

Mum & Dad, Christmas 1976, 2:47am – LOL!

As time forced some of our traditions to change, Mum was still the one constant that remained. Mum, and her profligate approach to present buying. Because, when it came to Christmas, she pulled out all the stops. *Big time!*

Her gifts were always thoughtful, invariably extravagant, and frequently useless – she subscribed to the school of thought that presents should be something you wanted but could never justify buying for yourself. And I bloody loved them.

So, at age twenty-four, I didn't *need* a sound-activated robot cat, or at twenty-six, a video player and the complete BBC series of 'Pride and Prejudice', or a dancing Shaun the Sheep at thirty, or a quarter-life-sized electronic pony at thirty-two, a Nile cruise at forty, or iPads for both Tim and I at forty-five, or the innumerable other silly toys and splendid presents that she'd shower us with.

And no matter my age, I was always Mum's little girl, and her gifts were guaranteed to bring out my inner child – and definitely not mark my middle-age slide into the *Bayliss & Harding* era, an epoch of bath salts, smellies and slippers. (Of course, I'm always grateful for any gift but, even in Covid times, a girl can have too much Grapefruit & Mandarin Hand Wash. *Sigh.)*

But back to yesterday when everything changed, and bizarrely, it was Hugh the Gas who was the catalyst. He'd dropped in to assess our boiler leak and as he prodded the 'right manifold', he happened to mention that he was on his way to watch his daughter's nativity play. And that's what did it.

I literally felt something fracture inside me as it suddenly dawned that I was nobody's child anymore. In fact, I was an orphan, and a childless, sibling-less one at that.

And yes, I realise I'm being hugely dramatic, and I know it's not *technically* true, but it does give you some sense of where my head was at right then. Plus, who'd come and watch me if I was in a nativity?

I felt alone and adrift, with the full weight of adulting squatting heavily on my shoulders, and I saw a fleeting vision of a future filled with endless responsibility, boiler breakdowns, and a bathroom rendered unusable from the sheer weight of Royal Jelly hand cream and soaps in the shape of flowers. *Sob!*

Thankfully, this maudlin phase didn't last longer than a couple of minutes because, after the thunderbolt of acceptance, came an almost instantaneous lifting of my mood, a strange sensation of release, and my mother's voice, echoing through the ether, with a heartening, 'I might be dead but you're not, so stop moping, Del, and get some bloody decorations up . . . and don't forget the Stork!'

(Top Tip: Mum's Stork-infused roast potatoes were legends of fluffy, crispy scrumptiousness and honestly knocked Nigella's out of the park – one year we did a blindfold taste test. So, forget goose fat and go with marge.)

Wow! In the space of fifteen minutes, I'd experienced a maelstrom of emotions, moving from despondency to acceptance, pessimism to hope. And Mum was right – I needed to pick up her Christmas baton and run with it.

I suddenly buzzed with an energy I'd lacked all year and was more than ready to get the party started. *Yippee-ki-yay mother–* (If you know, you know.)

Within hours, the wreath was on the front door, our silver birch was twinkling in the lounge, the garland was draped over the fireplace, (stockings of past pets hanging jauntily from its branches), and the presents for the grandkids were wrapped and sacked.

When Tim got home from work, I informed him that 'Tonight's the night', seeing his face fall when I added the words, '. . . for the Big Shop!', though much, *much* less big than previous years. (Don't get me started on the cost-of-living crisis or we'll be here til next Christmas!)

At 9pm we braved M&S, for a small beef and ham, then popped across the road to Tesco Extra for the rest. We were home, unpacked and on our second Snowball by 11.30pm.

(Side note: Going late is definitely the way forward – especially if you have a decent sized freezer and don't relish the cut and thrust of battle for the last tray of Brie & Cranberry parcels.)

Our tree, with some special decorations

And now that everything's done, I'm starting to wonder what lay at the root of my mourning breakthrough. Maybe it had something to do with the ecstatic dancing I tried a few weeks ago which was *very* freeing, and certainly released some pent-up emotions?

Or, if I'm being *very* fanciful, I might wonder if Hugh was an angel, sent by my mother, to jolt me out of my brain-fogged fugue? (And at £285 inc. VAT, for *several* hours labour, a couple of expensive parts *and* a service, I certainly wouldn't be surprised if he's got a pair of feathery wings folded neatly beneath his hoodie.)

Maybe it's a good, old-fashioned Christmas miracle? Or maybe it's that time truly *is* a great healer? Who knows? But I'm finally feeling festive and intend to enjoy this Yule as much as possible.

And, with traditions in mind, I've decided to instigate a new one this year, in honour of Mum. So, let's hear it for Del's Cracking Christmas Eggnog! It's very rich, very sweet, a tad eggy (but in a good way) and is seriously worth trying if you've got a dusty bottle of Captain Morgan knocking about in a cupboard.

So, for now, I'm *mostly* at peace with the world. Tim said he'd pay good money to see me in a nativity (as did friends, Lizzie, stepdad, and Cath). Hugh's fixed the boiler so, when we can afford to turn it on, it'll be more energy efficient and will actually work. And I'm snug in my pyjamas, raising an eggnog to Mum, but also to those of us who, for whatever reason, might find this festive season a bit of a struggle.

I can't promise things will get easier but, as tonight happens to be the Winter Solstice, I can definitely promise that the dark will stop rising and there'll be brighter times ahead! And here's hoping that 2023 brings happiness, cheaper bills, and is kinder to us all.

So *Iechyd da* to the return of the light!

If I've given you a hankering for Eggnog, my secret recipe can be found at www.allrecipes.com/recipe/57028/amazingly-good-eggnog. Okay, so I lied – it's not mine – but whoever wrote the recipe and called it 'amazingly good' absolutely didn't.

For a nostalgic Christmas Snowball, take a 1/2-pint tumbler, add 2 measures of Advocaat, and fill to the top with full fat lemonade. Stir well. Add a tiny splash of lime juice (optional). Add at least three maraschino cherries and allow them to sink to the bottom. Finish with a long straw. This is a very moreish drink, not too alcoholic, and the cherries add a slight almondy flavour which is extra yummy.

If you have gas issues (that aren't due to Christmas over-indulgence), Hugh the Gas of Hendre Gas Services is your man. Call him on 07306 310267. He's a marvel.

And finally, if you're struggling this festive season, for whatever reason, mind.org.uk is an excellent website, giving tips and advice and it also contains contact details for numerous charities and agencies who will be able to help you.

Cultural Highlights of 2022

31st December 2022

When real life becomes too unsettled, too sad, or simply too alarming, and the continual lurch from one crisis to another threatens to overwhelm me, I often retreat from the world with a blanket, a large mug of tea, and a good book. But not just *any* book.

Over the years, I've found that I can recapture the carefree, contented days of my youth by diving back into the books I discovered as a child – and when the only worries I had were whether Jamie Davies fancied me (he did), and if he'd ask me to the Christmas disco (he didn't! Damn your eyes, Jeanette Grove!)

Agatha Christie, Dick Francis, and Alistair MacLean have all been dusted off again recently, and I've enjoyed the cosy, nostalgic contentment of reconnecting with characters and stories I've loved for over forty years. These authors might not be classed as giants in the true *literary* sense, but they could certainly tell a bloody good story.

So, if you haven't dipped a toe into the arctic waters of *Ice Station Zebra* (and met the dreamy Commander Swanson – *swoon*), or encountered the ingenious *Murder of Roger Ackroyd*, or followed Sid Halley, plucky ex-jockey, taking on racecourse corruption in *Odds Against*, I think it's odds-on that you've got a real treat in store.

Next, as a Tolkien fan, I've got give a shout out to Amazon's *Rings of Power*. The series was released in September, with an episode dropping each week. So now, if you want to learn more about the First

Age, there's a full season waiting to be binged. Okay, so it's had mixed responses, and there's *a lot* of haters out there (mainly the JRR purists), but personally, I adored being *visually* back in Middle Earth for the first time since Peter Jackson's *Lord of the Rings* graced cinemas in 2003, and *The Hobbit* trilogy in 2013.

I loved the storytelling, the expansive settings, the old (and new) characters, and thought the acting was on point. The only downside is that Season Two probably won't be released until 2024 so there's a bit of a wait. But I'll be filling the time re-reading *Lord of the Rings*, and attempting to, finally, finish *The Silmarillion*. (Wish me luck with that one - it's complex, weighty, and rather dry!)

The final delight I stumbled upon in 2022 was a podcast on BBC Sounds called *Uncanny*, hosted by award-winning writer, Danny Robins. This little gem sees him investigating first-hand accounts of paranormal encounters, before throwing open each case to us, the audience, and asking for our theories and questions. Like me, Danny is a 'sceptic who wants to believe', and this will appeal to ghost lovers and cynics alike. From spectral phantoms to sinister folklore, poltergeists to UFOs, it's a veritable supernatural smorgasbord – as well as being a *very* chilling listen. So, if you fancy uncovering some blood-curdling stories, or want to find out why the phrase, 'Bloody hell Ken!', keeps trending on Twitter, tune in for some truly terrifying tales.

Beating the New Year Blues

Tuning Up for a Toe-tapping 2023

7th January 2023

Every Boxing Day morning, without fail, Dad would greet us with the cheery, tongue-in-cheek, 'Well, it's as far away as ever', and Mum and I would groan at him for casting a dampener over the remainder of the festive season.

But now that the Christmas sparkle has been boxed up and stuffed back in a cupboard for another year, in the words of Soul II Soul, we're definitely, 'Back to life, back to reality', with a bleakly depressing bump.

The bridge between those festive frolics and the dark and dismal blanket of January is, obviously, New Year's Eve, a time when we often reflect on the achievements (or failures), of the last twelve months and set goals for the coming ones.

'New Year, New You!' is a phrase I've seen plastered across social media ever since Facebook became a thing, and I admit, I've bought into it; in the past I've enthusiastically thrown myself into resolutions – stop smoking, lose weight, give up chocolate, blah, blah, blah . . .

But that I oft repeat these same promises on the 31st of (most) Decembers, tells you all you need to know about me – I try, but never quite manage to stick with them for the long-haul. In fact, being totally honest, they rarely last past January, and sometimes even less.

One year I gave up meat, but caved six days later when, after a particularly boozy night out, I found myself in a local curry house, halfway through a Chicken Korma and a Keema Naan before I, guiltily, remembered my heartfelt pledge to all animals. (I tried restarting the next day, but Tim makes a mean bacon butty, and the temptation was just too great.)

So basically, December 31st sees me setting myself up for yet another year that showcases my total lack of resolution and self-control. *Sigh.*

But this year, I'm approaching it differently – I'm giving up, 'giving up'. Instead of intentions littered with transitive verbs that are heavy on the prohibition, I've decided that 2023 is going to be a wholly positive and upbeat twelve months.

Yep, I'm diving into this shiny new year with an optimistic mindset and focusing on more favourable verbs such as 'to start', 'to gain' and 'to persevere'. (The one rider I'll add is that, when I say 'gain', I don't mean weight – at least, I sincerely hope not.)

So that's why, on 3rd January 2023, Geoff is idling in the deluged car park of Dunvant Rugby Football Club (DRFC), while I give myself a mental pep talk on why I ever thought *this* was a good idea. Right now, I'm seriously debating whether I should head home.

See, I'm not here for the rugby, either as a spectator, or player (though with my bulk, I'd make a great prop forward – but only if I could use my mobility scooter for the scrums.)

Nope, I'm here because of a stupendous Christmas gift that I got from Tim – and which, given his normal custom of panic-buying *Bayliss & Harding* on Christmas Eve, was hugely surprising.

So, unwrapping an irregular-shaped oblong box, I was staggered to discover that it contained a mahogany, concert ukulele. *Crikey.*

Okay, bit of background. Firstly, I'm not of a musical bent . . . at all. I can't read music, I've never, properly, learned an instrument, and have only ever tried three, all of which met with scant success.

My inaugural attempt was with everyone's favourite – the recorder. Those of you of a *certain* age will recall learning to play this frightful fipple flute in primary school – and kudos to Mum and Dad who, I now realise, were tortured for many months by my breathy, grating, and barbarous attempts at 'Baa, baa, Black Sheep'.

Then, in the late seventies, when marching bands became big

business, I joined the newly created, 'Tycoch Silver Spurs'. I was hoping for drum major but since I wasn't able to twirl the mace without injuring myself (and others – I'm still *really* sorry about your eye, Tracey Woodman), I was instead handed an instrument that required no expertise and could cause little damage, other than to eardrums . . . the kazoo.

This version had a large trumpet-like flared end, which functioned as a megaphone for tuneful (and tuneless), humming and was a remarkably simple way for any child to make loud and excruciating sounds, guaranteed to induce migraines in long-suffering parents.

Every summer Saturday, we'd don our uniforms and stomp around local carnivals, fairs, and competitions, giving our all to 'When the Saints Go Marching In' and butchering the less traditional, 'Six Million Dollar Man' theme tune.

Resplendent in black cowboy boots, mint green mini dresses with silver chording and tassels, and topped off with a jauntily angled Stetson, we were a sight to behold. *Yee-haw!*

(I stopped going when my kazoo – somehow – got furniture polish in the blow hole and, no matter how hard I hummed, I couldn't rid myself, or it, of the taste of Pledge. Plus, my arch-enemy, Sharon Peters, was promoted to drum major, and watching her flinging the mace around with consummate ease was too much for my youthful heart to bear. *Grr.*)

Finally, there was the piano. Both Grandpa and Mum were accomplished pianists and I used to enjoy playing easy, one-handed duets with them when I was little. But then I hit my teens, discovered the joys of boys and, as my hormones waxed, any interest I had in learning that instrument waned. And this remains a lifelong regret.

Whenever I watch Jools Holland's Hootenanny, I always mourn my inability to sit at any *old Joanna*, tinkle the ivories, and get a pub, or party, rocking, as everyone marvels at my skill.

I guess I'm secretly a frustrated entertainer. And so, since I don't have a piano, or the funds for lessons . . . the ukulele it is.

In recent years it's become a popular choice, with clubs popping up all over, but the initial craze passed me by. I think it was because, whenever I heard the word 'ukulele', George Formby's nasal, 'Leaning on a Lamp Post', would leap, unbidden, to mind and, though my older relatives loved him, I was definitely not a fan.

But, after spotting some videos on YouTube, it seemed that this little strummer might be the perfect instrument to try and master. *Fingers crossed, literally!* I mean, have you seen some of those chord charts?

So, over the twixtmas period, I spent an inordinate number of hours tuning, plucking, and thrumming my new toy, whilst splashing a fair chunk of my Amazon Gift Card (also from Tim – this year the boy did good, on books to help me get to grips with Duke (my uke).

Duke the Uke

Within an hour, I was playing 'You are my Sunshine', and delighting Tim with both the music, and vocals. No, it wasn't great, and the chord changes were hugely challenging, taking me too many seconds to move from C to G (or even F), but still, I was making music, after a fashion, and I was hooked.

Over the following days, I added 'House of the Rising Sun' and, a personal favourite, 'Leaving on a Jet Plane', to my repertoire – again, nowhere near perfect, but I think I made a fair fist of them. Then I began practising chord transitions.

By Dec 29th, Tim kindly suggested that I might be able to concentrate better if I was in a different room and away from the TV – he's so considerate – but then ruined it by adding, '. . . because all this twanging bollocks is doing my head in'. *Humph!*

(Actually, he had a point. Some of my practice sessions were a *tad* discordant, which I'm putting down to water-retentive hands, a pathetic span, and a distinct lack of dexterity in my digits.)

But I kept at it, doing a little more each day, and that brings me back to the rugby club. Frankly, if I hadn't spotted a couple of smiley ladies carrying ukulele cases, I might still be dithering in the car park, but . . . *Oh, bugger it! I'm going in.*

I was nervous for two reasons. #1 It's always disconcerting meeting a large group of new people for the first time. #2 These people were part of a ukulele band. Yep. A band. A *real* band. For *proper* ukulele players. What the hell was I thinking? This was clearly a massive mistake.

Turns out, it 100% wasn't. Within minutes of anxiously crossing the threshold, I'd been warmly welcomed by the genial John, Richard, Debra, Josie, Jean, Maggie, Lynsey, several Chrises and Ian (plus others), and was cosily established beside Dawn, a beaming beauty – think rockabilly Julie Andrews with a wicked twinkle – who, metaphorically, held my hand all night.

She helped me tune up, she shared her music, showed me the chords – *numerous* times – and taught me more in a couple of hours than I'd learned during a whole week of solo sessions.

And, as well as ukes, there were other instruments in attendance – double bass, drums, keyboards, guitars, harmonicas, and a tambourine. I was surrounded by a myriad of musical talent but, despite my extreme amateur status, I strangely didn't feel out of place.

Me, who'd only been *sort of* playing for seven days, was shamelessly strumming along with a roomful of real musicians, and it felt bloody brilliant.

We did a whole gamut of crowd pleasers – 'Great Balls of Fire', 'You Never Can Tell', 'Brown Eyed Girl', 'Three Little Birds' – and, when it came to request time, as the newbie, I was asked to choose. Well, there could be only one:

'Leaving on a Jet Plane?'

'Yep, we've got that'.

And away we flew.

Of course, I made mistakes. I got completely lost during most of the songs, ground to a sudden halt during 'Crying in the Rain', repeatedly had to put down Duke and watch how others changed chords, and was easily defeated by F7, E major and the finger-squishing D, but none of that mattered. All that mattered was that I was there, I was trying, and I was having a ball.

It was the most joyous evening I've had in a very long time. The music, the singing, the laughter, the supportive atmosphere, the sense of achievement, the cider (DRFC has a *very* competitively priced bar. *Woohoo!*) Everything was simply marvellous.

And even as we began packing away, someone launched into 'Piano Man', and we belted it out in true rugby club fashion. It was the perfect end to a perfect evening.

So, you can probably guess that, yes, I'll be going again. In fact, every Tuesday evening until my fingers finally seize up with old age, I'll be there at DRFC, strumming, thrumming, and singing my heart out.

And I know, beyond doubt, that this is one resolution I'll have no difficulty keeping. (Though I'm betting that F7, and E major, will forever remain my bête noires. *Sigh.*)

Whether you're an absolute beginner like me, novice, intermediate or expert, Swansea Ukulele Club is a great place to learn, socialise or come for a gentle strum and a good old singalong. Visit their Facebook page for more details.

Cider, Skulls, and Saucepans

When you rock up to a pagan festival and the very first random stranger you speak to has one of the most awesome names you've ever heard, you just know that the heavens have aligned and, surely, some sort of adventure lies ahead.

And that's exactly what happened last Saturday, when I braved the inclement weather to attend Gower Heritage Centre's Wassail and Mari Lwyd Festival. Frankly, given that I'm well into folklore *and* cider, it seemed strange that I'd never, in all my fifty-three years, been before. Plus, I love horses, though I usually prefer the breathing variety.

Anyway, Tim didn't fancy it after I mentioned horse skulls and Morris dancing, but was delighted to drop me off so that:

1. I wouldn't have far to walk,

2. I could have a few drinks, but mainly

3. Because it meant he could enjoy an uninterrupted evening playing golf on his iPad and take ownership of the TV remote. *Men.*

But it was lucky I didn't drive myself because when we got there, the car park and surrounding roads were gridlocked. Wassailing was clearly more popular than I'd realised.

So, with Tim muttering darkly about 'amateur drivers' – *yawn* – as he reversed along the main road, I was unceremoniously deposited outside Shepherds, from where I strolled the short distance to the Heritage Centre, before joining the queue of people waiting for both admittance, and alcohol.

Though the Mari Lwyd has its skeletal hooves rooted firmly in Welsh folklore, wassailing (from the Old Norse *Ves Heill*, meaning good health) is a more geographically widespread tradition. It's celebrated in the cider-producing areas of the West of England, and Wales, around Twelfth Night (5th/6th Jan) or, if you happen to be a Julian calendar purist, on 'Old Twelvey Night' (17th Jan).

There are two types of Wassail – House and Orchard. The House Wassail was where people went door-to-door, singing and offering a drink from the wassail bowl in exchange for gifts. On Gower, this practice came with its own regional song, the imaginatively titled 'Gower Wassail' and which, for some unknown reason, was recorded and released by Steeleye Span in 1971. (It's on YouTube if you fancy a listen.)

But tonight is an Orchard Wassail, and its purpose is twofold – first, we need to 'wake up' the apple trees, and second, we need to 'scare away evil spirits', thus ensuring a rich and bountiful autumn harvest.

And that explained why my carrier bag contained a whistle, saucepan, and wooden spatula – I was tooled up and more than ready to make some noise. And, judging by the weight of cookware on display, so was everyone else, though I'm sure the couple who'd brought a *La Creuset* crock pot were simply showing off.

Anyway, after no little wait, I finally found myself at the Shed Head cider counter. Their cider is made on site, using handpicked Dabinett apples from the very orchard we were there to wassail, and I was encouraged to sample the full range of their traditionally made tipples, finally settling on a pint of Shed of Heaven. *Lol*. Compared to the fizzy varieties, this was flat, strong, and definitely an acquired taste, though happily, I acquired *that* taste very quickly.

Then, since the *Sweyn's Ey Morris & Sword Dancers* weren't on for an hour – and were themselves currently milling about and drinking deeply from tankards – I wandered outside to find a table where I could people-watch. And *that's* where I met the shaggy-haired young man who gloried in the name of Satchel Baggins. This was kismet – my favourite bag *and* hobbit combined.

Over the next thirty minutes I learned that:

He was a bit of a cider connoisseur.

He was aiming to set up his own orchard in Llanelli.

He shared my love of folklore.

He had a wide knowledge of ancient Welsh literature.

He lamented his inability to speak Welsh. (*Yep, me too, Satchel.*)

And he was waiting for his mate who'd apparently gone for a shower somewhere in the car park (?), which seemed a bit odd but then, that's youngsters for you. (With hindsight, it's possible I *might* have misheard. Did I mention the cider was *very* strong?)

The Mari Lwyds are coming!

Anyway, Satchel was great company, we chatted like old friends, and when we decided to head inside to see the festivities kick off, we exchanged phone numbers so I could keep in touch regarding the progress of his orchard, and no, that's not a euphemism.

And really, he set the tone for the rest of my evening because, over the course of some hours, I met a plethora of fascinating folk, two lovely dogs, and had an absolute ball.

Dog #1 was Maxwell, a chunky yellow lab (and therapy dog), who was sublimely unconcerned by the noise and crowds around him. He rested against his owner's legs, lazily accepting the numerous pats and ear scratches from all and sundry. And it was while I was fussing him that I noticed Lesley.

I'd spotted her because she was wearing the most amazing headdress, fashioned from antlers, holly, and crystals, and which I later discovered she'd made herself. So, I gave Maxwell a final tummy rub, and headed over to ask if I could take her photo.

And that was fortuitous because, as it turned out, Lesley was a witch (and a *chaos* witch at that), who'd been brought up in a poison garden and grew her own healing plants and herbal remedies. *Epic!*

We chatted as we queued and she explained a little about plant lore, invited me to visit her garden, 'when it's in bloom', and mentioned some witchy rituals, saying she'd be happy for me to tag along. *Extra epic!* (Well, it's been a while since my last attempt at anything esoteric so I'm well up for trying again.)

Inside, the Morris group were preparing to start the revels, so I squeezed through and found myself sitting next to a festively garbed bloke called John, who was accompanied by his 'Day of the Dead' inspired Mari Lwyd. He'd driven down from Brecon and explained that he was always in demand around this time of year.

He told me about his forthcoming events, one of which was taking place in the Forest of Dean. Apparently, the Foresters were wassailing fanatics, but chose to relinquish the standard pots and pans in favour of shotguns. *Wow!*

That's some hardcore carousing, but I wasn't hugely surprised. See, I lived and worked in Gloucestershire for over twenty years and there are some areas in that ancient forest that have a strong *Land that Time Forgot* kinda vibe. And side note: If you ever visit – and you should because it's glorious – don't mention the bear! (If you know, you know.)

I'd have liked to chat more, but the sound of a fiddle cut us off, the

136

Morrisers were good to go and, with a quick shake of their bells, off they jolly well went. I've only ever seen Morris dancing on telly, and I've always considered it a rather gentle, bucolic activity – some simple country folk skipping about, with an occasional waft of a handkerchief, or inflated pigs' bladder.

But in reality, it's filled with a fierce physicality, and the stamina required to complete the numerous routines was evident in their flushed faces and laboured breathing. They were seriously brilliant, and though I was a tad disappointed there was no swordplay, the use of hefty sticks more than made up for it.

As they bounded about with choreographed extravagance, a shiny collie woofed in frustration as it tried to catch their dangling bells, and the many Mari Lwyds present ground their giant teeth and snapped their jaws in time with the music. It was totally surreal and bloody brilliant.

Rosie & Bronwen, Lesley, and 'Morris'

After twenty minutes, the fiddle stilled, the dancers took a well-earned break, and it was time for the next stage of the proceedings – the grand Mari Lwyd pageant. *Eek!*

By now it was twilight, and as the horse skulls (and 'handlers') gathered outside for the torchlit parade around the local environs, I got definite *Wicker Man* vibes; I honestly wouldn't have been surprised if Christopher Lee, complete with bad wig, yellow turtleneck, and sickle, had appeared to lead the procession.

But no. Instead, we had a genial Green Man, dapper in an ivy-covered bowler, waistcoat, and red cravat, and not a sickle in sight. *Phew.* He was accompanied by a range of atypically attired stewards, some distinctly steampunk (shoutout to Chris and Donna). There was also a jolly man on an accordion, a menagerie of kiddies dressed as animals, and the local musical legend that is Andy Tamlyn Jones, had been persuaded to put down his guitar – he was playing a set later in the evening – and pick up a drum.

After some minutes of semi-organised chaos, (That down to you, Lesley?), we were suddenly silenced by a smart drumroll signifying that the horses were under starter's orders. Then, with a thunderous cheer, they were off, swaying drunkenly along the narrow road, an eager crowd at their heels.

I'd set myself up on a picnic bench halfway along the route so was perfectly placed for taking photos, and for nipping through the hedge behind me which provided a sneaky shortcut into the orchard.

I happily snapped away as the merrymakers trooped past, singing, shouting, and jigging the hundred yards to the village shop, before circling back and into the orchard, in readiness for the evening's finale.

That the orchard had been under flood water a few hours earlier was evident from the ankle-deep mud, and I was glad I'd decided to wear wellies. While I waited for the procession to return, I noticed that some branches were bedecked with ribbons and, more strangely, slices of toast, so I asked the bohemian lady standing beside me if she knew what that was all about. And boy oh boy, she certainly did.

Rosie, who happened to be a true, ex-travelling Roma, now unwillingly domiciled in Burry Port, was the owner of, not only a heritage vardo (round-topped decorative carts), but also Bronwen, the shiny collie who'd taken exception to the Morrisers' bells.

Rosie told me all about wassailing and the toast tradition – you soak stale toast in apple cider and then hang it on the spurs of the dormant trees as a way of attracting friendly, helpful spirits who are thought to encourage the trees to thrive.

She also mentioned that we should pour our cider on the base of the trees as an 'offering', but that was a tradition too far for me – and for Rosie. Instead, we loudly raised a glass and toasted the orchard, then Rosie went to get us another pint and I played with Bronwen until all the stragglers turned up.

Satchel trotted past, friend in tow, and gave me a wide grin and a double thumbs up. Despite being liberally splattered with mud, he was clearly enjoying himself, but his pal was clearly regretting getting a shower beforehand.

Suddenly the drum, and crowd, fell silent and the Green Man took centre stage as master of this final, most important, ceremony. There was a lot of staff-waving, and several songs which I couldn't really hear, but I caught a few time-honoured *fol-de-rols* and a couple of *da-di-das*.

Day of the dead Mari, with handler

Then, with a wild flourish of his bowler, the drumming started anew, we readied our pots, pans, whistles, bells, tambourines, pan pipes and the like – though no shotguns, unfortunately – and began beating, bashing, yelling, and shaking the bejesus out of them.

It was discordant and deafening, but if that cacophony didn't drive any lurking evil spirits out of that orchard, it wasn't for lack of trying. It had been one hell of a night.

As the crowd dispersed, some wandering back to the warmth and live music of the Heritage Centre, Rosie and Bronwen headed to the bus stop, and I texted Tim, who arrived ten minutes later with the pups who were delighted to see their *mum*, though more delighted to have their evening walk a few hundred yards up the road in Park Wood.

While they galloped and chased, Tim and I ambled and the night was so still, we could hear the echoes of continued carousing. I found it rather affecting, though Tim said he was glad he hadn't gone because he 'couldn't be doing with that sodding racket for more than a minute'. *Sigh.*

But I'd loved it – the mayhem, the rituals, the noise, the cider (*obvs*) and all those wonderful characters I'd met. And I found it heartening that the old ways, and accompanying traditions, are still remembered, and celebrated, today. Long may it continue. So, Ves Heill, and a happy 'Old Twelvey Night' new year to you all!

The Gower Heritage Centre is a great place to visit. Find out more at gowerheritagecentre.co.uk.

If you're interested in getting into the Morris dancing business, Sweyn's Ey Morris & Sword Dancers can be found on Facebook (Sweyns Ey Morris).

If you've never heard Andy Tamlyn Jones play, you've missed a real treat. Check out his Facebook page where you'll find details of upcoming gigs.

And if my reference to The Wicker Man has piqued your interest, it's definitely worth a watch, if only for the music and Britt Ekland's naked door-dancing. But that's the 1973 classic starring Edward Woodward and not the Nicholas Cage remake (which is a total shocker for all the wrong reasons).

Wow, Voyager

5th February 2023

Last weekend was a doozy. I spent Friday night in Edinburgh, did some 'guided breathwork' in Rhode Island, had a brisk walk through the mountains of Banff, Canada, hopped over to Kobe, Japan, for Lunar New Year, and finished up in London with a creepy, candlelit bedtime story, read by the treacle-toned Gerard.

I also stopped off in Oz for surf boat racing, visited a pagan temple in Armenia and, despite some moral reservations, popped into the Ice & Snow Festival in Moscow. Clearly, that's some serious globetrotting, so it's no wonder I'm absolutely knackered – jet lag is a bitch.

Ah, you got me! I haven't actually moved off the sofa, but it's true that I've been travelling, with no passport, plane tickets or luggage required. I've also met hundreds of fellow travellers from across the globe and been shown around by expert guides who brought the locations to vivid and vibrant life. It's been fantastic.

It all started last week in Park Woods. Most nights, Tim and I take the pups there because it's generally very quiet and that means our giant boys can be, mainly, off lead, and while they're exploring, I have plenty of options for sitting and lurking.

So, I was squatting in the burial mound, trying to spot C/2022 E3 (ZTF) (aka that green comet that hasn't been seen since the Stone Age) and I suddenly started getting itchy feet – and no, it wasn't *only* my chilblains.

See, as the evenings sluggishly lighten and the shoots of spring slowly begin to unfurl, I frequently experience an overwhelming sense of wanderlust. Basically, I yearn to break away from the, mostly boring, confines of my everyday life and experience what the world has to offer.

After waiting twenty minutes for Wolfie and John to sniff me out, we ambled back to the car and I suggested that instead of heading home we should, 'Drive, see where the road takes us, have an adventure!'

Of course, we didn't, and for very sensible (if prosaic), reasons:

1. Tim had work the next day.

2. He didn't want to waste a quarter tank of petrol, '. . . driving aimlessly around, God knows where, on a whim'.

3. The dogs needed their supper, and more urgently, a shower because they were liberally slathered in that most prized canine treasure – fox pooh – and which, if you've never smelled it, is eye-wateringly pungent and revoltingly musky.

4. I had a Chicken Chasseur in the slow cooker.

5. 'We can't waste money on hotels when we've got a perfectly good bed at home'. Yada, yada, yada. *Humph!*

We got back, shampooed the dogs, shampooed the car, ate dinner, and settled down for 'Winterwatch'. *Yawn.* (I normally love these programmes, but I was craving excitement and the starling murmurations just weren't cutting it.)

Tim, sensing my mood – 'What's up? You've got a face like a slapped arse' – suggested London. 'Not tonight, obvs, but maybe at Easter?' *Yeah, maybe?* Until it dawned on us that I can't manage the walking required to fully explore the capital.

We debated the use of mobility scooter, but the pros – 16 miles per charge, ease of use, explorability – were outweighed by one massive con which is that London is bloody busy, and driving through crowds is unpleasant and claustrophobic.

Your eyeline (depending on an individual's height), falls anywhere between breast to crotch, and despite pootling along on a luminous orange mobility scooter, you're still invisible to many, and an annoyance to most.

Sigh. It's hard to be impulsive when reality takes a bloody big bite from your pie-in-the-sky. It seemed that tangible travel was off the table. But, as I sulkily doom-scrolled through Twitter, I happened upon a photograph of London with a link to a site called *Heygo*. Reader, I clicked it.

If you haven't come across it, *Heygo* is a mobile platform whose mission is to 'Give anyone who wants to explore the world the power to do so'. *Coolio!* But there had to be a catch, and I fully expected it to be in the form of a yearly subscription or one-off fees for each trip booked.

Turns out, it's 100% free. Yep, you sign up, browse, book whatever you fancy and that's it. The world on *Heygo* is available for all, no matter how deep (or in my case, shallow), your pockets. *Woohoo!*

I settled in with tea, biscuits, blanket, and iPad, and prepared to travel the globe. And as I browsed the hundreds of destinations available, it became clear that the big bonus of this site is that the tours are, mainly, live. And that's what sold it to me.

Because I didn't want to watch films of far-off, exotic places and meander around the world in a solitary bubble. I wanted to share the experience, meet my fellow 'voyagers', and pretend I was *actually* there.

My inaugural tour was relatively local – 'Haunted Edinburgh' – with a very experienced guide named Sam. I arrived ten minutes early which gave me time to 'chat' with the other 100+ tourists who had already joined from around the world, and for Sam to explain to us newbies how her tours work.

She was starting at the castle, impressively lit up behind her, and while we waited until the 9pm kick off, she explained the functions of the different buttons we were seeing on our screens. One was for snapping 'postcards', another was an interactive map showing our route and finally, there was a 'tip' button.

If you'd like to, you can reward your guide with a donation, but there's absolutely no pressure to do so. In fact, every guide I've met so far has taken pains to point out that 'following' their channels is a great way of supporting them too.

As the clock struck nine, the tour began, somewhat unexpectedly, with the arrival of a clearly inebriated young lady who had decided that 'Somebody needs a hug!' Once Sam had kindly, but firmly, disentangled herself, explaining she was 'broadcasting live to several hundred people', drunk woman was thrilled, swaying close to the camera, and informing us that she was having a 'night out with the boyfriend, but he's no mine!' Cue maniacal laughter, and then, 'But shhhhhhh . . . it's a secret'. And, on that bombshell, she staggered off down Castlehill, awkwardly supported by her beau. *Lol!*

Sam walked us around the streets for an hour, stopping at various points along the way to chirpily explain ancient torture methods or thrill us with ghost stories and dastardly tales of 'muurdah'. (Her Scottish lilt was a joy to spend time with.)

At Parliament Hall, we learned about 'The Maiden', which decapitated over one hundred and fifty noblemen, and women, and came handily flat-packed for portability (IKEA 'GILJOTIN' – Stylish beheading device with clean lines, and in neutral tones).

Then there were the thumbscrews which, as Sam pointed out, were 'brilliant, because they were easily transportable'. And 'The Boot' – a nifty leg sheath into which wood was hammered, resulting in broken bones, rotting flesh and, ultimately, amputation. *Ouch.*

We visited the 'Pubic triangle', an area where antique bookshops uneasily rub shoulders with strip clubs and sex workers, before viewing the premises where Burke and Hare 'found' the first of their sixteen bodies – and by 'found', Sam meant 'muurdahed'; Burke would sit on the unfortunate's chest while Hare placed his hand over nose and mouth and helped them on their way.

Finally, we learned something of the, somewhat ironically named, 'Age of Enlightenment', and its manifestation in Scotland. Spoiler alert: It wasn't particularly enlightening if you were a woman, graphically illustrated by the tragic tale of Maggie Dickson who ultimately became famous as 'Half-Hangit Maggie'. (Google her, because when Sam called her a 'poor wee lassie', she wasn't being flippant.)

When the tour ended, I left a tip because Sam had been engaging, interesting and very, very funny. And that opened the floodgates as I booked in for three more of her tours and started exploring further afield.

As well as excursions, there are also activities to try, so I attempted a breathwork class with Sophie in Rhode Island. It actually felt a little counterintuitive, booking a tutorial entitled, '*Learning the Bliss of Breathing*', as I reckon most of us have already managed to grasp the blessed importance of respiration.

However, according to Sophie, there is more 'ecstasy to be gathered from breathing, with only twenty minutes reducing brain strain, improving sleep, easing inflammation and strengthening the immune system'. *Wow!* Bold claims but worth a shot, and it seemed like a suitably relaxing activity to try before bed.

Nope. Within minutes I realised that this wasn't for me, especially when it became clear that breathing is far harder than I'd ever imagined. Frankly, it's a wonder that I've managed to reach fifty-three without expiring.

Sophie explained the process for 'full immersion and healing'. But come on, would you know how to 'use your breath like a progressional wave, moving it to the pelvic girdle, before allowing it to flow slowly up to the solar plexus, spine and skull'?

My short staccato huffs took me to the verge of hyperventilation, I couldn't force oxygen anywhere close to my own personal pubic triangle, and nothing good was happening to my brain – other than an increasing urge to launch the iPad across the room and silence Sophie's soporific instructions. Instead, I left Rhode Island mid-class (and *sans* tip) and headed across the pond to Moscow's Ice and Snow Festival.

Moscow Snow & Ice Festival

Okay, so I, and several other voyagers who posted comments in the chat, clearly felt a little uncomfortable booking this tour, with the situation in Ukraine being what it is. However, Tanya our guide, welcomed us whilst standing in front of an ice sculpture of Tolstoy, and immediately confided that her two favourite quotations of his were:

'In all history, there is no war which was not hatched by the governments, and governments alone, independent of the interests of the people, to whom war is always pernicious', and 'War is so unjust and ugly that all who wage it must try to stifle the voice of conscience within themselves'.

We did the tour. And though Tanya said it was a much smaller affair than previous years, 'because, for obvious reasons, we have no international groups exhibiting', it was still pretty magical, with my favourites being the icy Matryoshka dolls and a giant snow kitten, complete with ball of wool.

Saturday saw me head east to Kobe (the beef capital of Japan), to watch the lunar new year celebrations. Our guide, Kendal, was live in the Chinatown district for the whole *twelve hours* of festivities! Now *that's* commitment, and she well-deserved all the tips she received.

I wasn't dedicated enough to stay *that* course, so I popped in and out, catching various musicians, dancers, choirs, and a wealth of, incomprehensible, cooking displays.

But I was really there for the lion dance. This consists of two acrobats acting as one lion. According to Kendal, there are numerous types of dance but today we would be seeing the 'Southern Chinese style', where the lion imitates the movements of a cat.

Apparently, local kung fu clubs train hard to master the acrobatic skills required, before the top students are chosen to don the fluffy costumes and perform feats of unbelievable gymnastics. And all while eager crowds are trying to shove their heads between the lion's snapping jaws – being bitten is a sign of good fortune for the coming year.

They were breath-taking. As the accompanying drumbeats grew in both volume and intensity, the movements of the lion became vigorously balletic as it leapt over obstacles, jumped atop tall poles and, rather sweetly, played with a large ball of silky twine. *Aww.*

I was up at 3am the following morning for an 'Evening Walk Around Banff, Canada', accompanied by the charming Patrick; I spent the afternoon getting a much-needed dose of vitamin D, watching the surf boat racing Down Under; and was home in time for 'The Witching Hour', where actor and guide, Gerard, reads classic scary tales in flickering candlelight. It was Jackanory for grown-ups and he was totally awesome.

Phew! I'd sampled a whirlwind of cultures, countries, and curiosities, and you can probably tell I'm already a *Heygo* addict. With the tours being (95%) live, because you can't pause, rewind or fast forward, you have to genuinely invest in the experience, let go of your actual surroundings and embrace the journey. And it's certainly satisfying my current wanderlust – at

One of the Kobe lions

least until I can afford to go on a proper holiday which, by today's reckoning, should be sometime around 2035. *Sigh.*

But now you'll have to excuse me because it's almost time for my Italian adventure (with the dreamy Giacomo). Tonight, we'll be sharing a gondola on the Grand Canal and jumping straight into Venice's world famous, 'Carnevale'.

But first, I'm off to experience Viareggio's celebrations and spectacular carnival floats. With this year's theme being 'Dreams and Desires for a Better World', it seems like an excellent place to start the weekend. So, happy travels voyagers, or as we say in Italy, *buon viaggio!*

Since writing this, the Heygo website has shut down. But there are others out there which offer the same sightseeing opportunities. So, if you yearn to travel from your own sofa, search for 'virtual travel' and you'll find the world is your oyster.

Fear Factor 3

Getting Stung by the Sewing Bee

19th February 2023

From the off, I freely admit that I'm no domestic Goddess. Raised by a mum who was the first female in her family to actually go *out* to work, and whose 'bibles' were, somewhat paradoxically, 'Superwoman' by Shirley Conran, and the 'St Michael All Colour Freezer Cookery Book', I guess it's hardly surprising.

In the mid-seventies, a heady time when wallpaper was psychedelic and dinner parties were all the rage, I'd often sit at the top of the stairs, listening to the grown-ups become increasingly 'merry' with each course, and frequently heard Mum uttering her favourite phrase, 'Life's too short to stuff a mushroom'.

And, on the whole, she lived by that tenet, with her gastronomic offerings being mainly shop bought, though some were, occasionally, passed off as homemade. I vividly remember the night when, whilst tucking into her farmhouse pâté, someone asked for the recipe, and her ensuing, stuttered explanation fooled no-one, not even seven-year-old me.

Yes, she would, sporadically, come home on a Friday evening and spend the weekend cooking up a storm. But whatever tasty treats resulted from these culinary forays were labelled 'Chest Freezer Only', and there they stayed. Dad and I didn't get a look in, and woe betide us if we so much as sneaked a peek.

She tried flower arranging once, returning with a health and safety nightmare called a 'Christmas candle holder'. It sat squat and sparse on our festive table for over two weeks, the flame gradually causing the single, faux, Christmas rose to shed its plastic petals into a cold collation – leading to Gran's priceless comment: 'These crisps taste very stale. They *can't* be M&S!'

She tried knitting, spending more than five months on a jumper for me. Throughout, she insisted that the telly remained off, and Dad and I had to converse in whispers because, any sound, 'breaks my concentration'. And when it came to casting on and off . . . suffice it to say, there were tears.

But she did eventually finish it, a moment of pride which lasted the two hours it took for her new washing machine to shrink it to the perfect size for my favourite bear. Poor Mum. She wasn't cut out for domesticity, no matter how hard she tried. And I've clearly followed in her footsteps.

But what's surprising is that, despite having little interest in attempting such homely activities myself, I do enjoy watching those telly programmes where others create mouth-watering bakes, charming ceramics, items of clothing, or beautifully crafted chairs. It's awe-inspiring, seeing such expertise in action, but I get frequent flutters of anxiety too.

Anxiety, because I can't help imagining how I'd fare if I was transported to the Bake-Off tent or a scenically sited workshop and asked to blind bake, hand build, jigsaw, or bind a bodice. (Spoiler: *Dreadfully, obvs!*)

My culinary speciality is jacket potato with cheese and beans, a jigsaw is my standard go-to gift for elderly relatives, and I still haven't got the hang of our washing machine – as evidenced by Tim's new white t-shirts being a vivid shade of pink, with a funky tie-dye effect.

But it's the 'Sewing Bee', with its machines, pedals, patterns, and pins that always gets my heart racing and fills my chest with a palpable sense of panic. If I was plonked in *that* haberdashery, I'd be hightailing it out of there, snatching at scraps of Terrycloth to wipe away my fear-tears because, when it comes to needlecrafts, I'm 98% clueless and

100% cowardly.

(The 2% is because I *can* make a fair stab at reattaching shirt buttons, and I've taken up a few pairs of Tim's trousers. He used to do it himself, using those tiny sewing kits you get from Christmas crackers, but his eyesight isn't what it was, and that suits me fine because, one year on, he still hasn't noticed that I hemmed his work slacks with staples – genius because they're not only a quick fix but also add a smidge of sparkle to his understated wardrobe.)

Anyway, it's this fear whi ch I'm tackling today, and though I'm infused with trepidation rather than full-blown terror, I still needed to give myself a pep talk and take a few deep breaths before entering Killay Recreation Centre at half nine on Saturday morning for the 'Make a Cushion' masterclass.

No, I don't know why I booked it either. I can only think that my new zealous attitude to life has become so entrenched, it's automatically starting to smother my less intrepid character traits. Whatever the reason, I was just hoping that I'd make it through the full three hours and come away with both cushion, and dignity, intact. Fingers cross(stitch)ed!

I'd already messaged Helen, our teacher, to double check that this was going to be suitable for 'a complete and utter beginner who hasn't touched a sewing machine since secondary school', and she'd replied with a reassuring, 'You're definitely in the perfect group, so don't worry'. Okay, I'm going in.

I followed the buzz of conversation to the sewing room which was decked out with an array of machines and a central table swathed with fabrics, threads, ribbons, and any accessories we would need to complete our project.

My fellow needleworkers were already armed with Hobnobs and beverages, so I grabbed a coffee, tried to settle my nerves, and prepared myself for what was to come. As I chatted to some of my classmates, I was heartened to discover that, though there were some experts among us, several hadn't used sewing machines before and considered themselves as amateur as me. *Phew.*

Katie wanted to learn so she could make dresses for her granddaughter, which explained the Peppa Pig fabric she'd brought for

150

her cushion. Ann was a beginner too but had a secret weapon in the form of her teenage daughter, Tasha, who was doing sewing at school and was 'quite good'. *Envious much?* However, Ann was happy to share said daughter, and over the ensuing three hours, I benefited from Ann's moral, and Tasha's practical, support.

But first came the important job of textile selection. Our cushions would be square, and we'd be using two fabrics on the display side, with a plain but hardwearing, denim back. This perked me up because I do have a good eye for colour and pattern, even if Tim has hinted that he feels my design choices can be a tad restrained – 'Not more bollocking neutrals. Paint it red or summat!' *Sigh.*

Anyway, since hitting my fifties, I've developed a penchant for florid florals, so my first choice was a blousy cream rose on a green background, and I opted to pair it with a plain cerise. They didn't seem natural bedfellows, but I hoped the teal ribbon would tie them together and I'd have a finished article which would complement the other cushions on our sofa. (Obviously, that's assuming I actually ended up with a finished article, and not unsewn squares of mismatched materials.)

Once we'd chosen, Helen launched into the first of her demonstrations and I began taking notes. She pitched her teaching at exactly the right level for most of us, took time to speak to us all individually and dealt with my very basic, oftentimes stupid, questions with good humour and clearly explained answers.

She covered the various stitches we'd be using – mostly straight, which seemed doable – though the zigzag we'd be using to attach our ribbon seemed ominously advanced. And then it was time to fire up the Brother Innov-is 10A Anniversary and start sewing. *Eek.*

I certainly didn't feel ready but that didn't matter because I'm not sure it can *truly* be termed 'sewing' if you're not using thread, and you're merely peppering a piece of paper with needle holes? But that's how we started.

The A4 was printed with lines – several straight, a few angular and a couple of curvy. We placed it in position, hand wound the needle down and used the plastic foot to secure it in place. Helen said not to push, instead 'gently guide it with your fingertips and the dog teeth will pull it through'. Then I turned my speed to 1 (tortoise), pressed the pedal, and I was away.

Okay, so keeping lines straight is harder than you'd imagine. I kept veering away, mainly because my eyesight (which the optician says is very good) was definitely not good enough to see where the needle was punching through the paper. The only way to combat this was to keep my nose a few millimetres from the needle plate, resulting in a hunched position that did absolutely nothing for my spinal issues and, more upsettingly, absolutely nothing for the quality of my sewing. *Humph.*

And 'sew' it continued. I finally managed a straightish line, had a good go at the angular and curved, and was beginning to feel rather pleased with my progress. Though I was a long way from perfect, Helen said I'd done great and 'those errors won't show once you start on your fabric'. *Lol!* But I'll take any praise, no matter how faint!

My confidence was building, only for it to seep away when we undertook the task of transferring our cotton to a bobbin and threading the machine. This was what I'd been dreading, still haunted by memories of attempting the same during a Home Economics test which I failed miserably. *Gulp.* Well, here goes nothing.

The complexities of feeding thread through various levers, nooks, and crannies to finally emerge triumphant in the eye of a needle, were beyond my capabilities. We were reminded to 'use the handy numbers shown on the machine' which were helpful in theory, but in practise, *WTF?*

Helen said it was all about the 'tension' and, given that I was getting increasingly stressed with each failed attempt, I could well believe her. And don't even mention the bobbin slot, its 'P' positioning or what to do when your thread snarls. I was fraying around the edges but remained resolute – I'd figure it out.

Turns out, that's sodding impossible unless you're a qualified engineer with a side-hustle in mechanics and logistics . . . or you're a teenager called Tasha, who shyly confided that she'd got an A* for her textile project and was happy to help (and where 'help' = did it for me while I got another coffee).

So yes, I cheated. But come on, I was wasting valuable cushion-making time faffing around. And so, with teal thread expertly in place,

I started on the main event. And I swear that the rest of it was all my own work. *Honest, Miss.*

Once I got going, it wasn't that bad. My side seams were a little skew-whiff, but not massively so, and I even remembered to backstitch at the beginning and end of each line. Zigzagging the ribbon into place was nerve wracking, but it ended up, mostly, straight. In fact, I was going great guns until I hit the corners.

Corners with their stupid 90° angles. The technique was to 'stitch along the seam until you are 1cm away from the end, wind the needle into the fabric, lift the foot and then pivot the fabric into position ready to sew the next edge'. Sounds simple, but I struggled – and if you've seen the 'Friends' episode where Ross gets a new sofa, you should be able to imagine the sound of my inner voice as it repeatedly yelled, 'pivot, Pivot, PIVOT!' to my uncomplying fingers. But finally, it was done.

The Finished Article – not too shabby!

Helen handed out cushion pads to stuff inside our covers and when I turned mine over, it revealed . . . a cushion that wouldn't be out of place in a Laura Ashley catalogue. *Un-bloody-believable!* Despite the numerous snags along the way, I was chuffed to mint balls, and still can't quite believe what I managed to create.

Of course, those few hours haven't cured my sew-a-phobia, and I certainly won't be hot-footing it down to Cliffords to purchase a machine anytime soon. But whenever I catch sight of *my* cushion, sitting puffed up and pretty on the sofa, I can't help but feel pretty puffed up too, with a genuine sense of pride in a sewing job well done. So, while life is still too short to stuff a mushroom, I reckon there's time enough for me to tackle Tim's staples. Now where did I last see that sewing kit?

Find Helen's classes and events on Facebook at All Sewn Up Wales.

Just a Perfect Day

Sunshine, Snowdrops and Songs of Praise

5th March 2023

Road trip. I bet that when you read those two words, you immediately thought of Route 66, maybe the Big Sur, Australia's Great Ocean Road or, a corker that's a little closer to home, Scotland's North Coast 500.

(That is, unless you're an avid antiquer, in which case, those words will have you dreaming of hopping in a vintage Triumph, with Catherine or Phil, and visiting a couple of National Trust properties.)

For me, I hear *Road Trip* and it sparks vague memories of the romance and excitement of youthful galivants that my fifty-three-year-old, somewhat stolid, soul still hankers for. As snowdrops surge through grassy verges and daffodils tentatively trumpet beneath a cool sun, that wanderlust I often experience at this time of year, eagerly asserts itself.

Some weeks ago, I wrote of the joys of virtual globetrotting and how, to some extent, it satisfied my travel bug. But, as the skies lighten and we welcome sporadic spring-like days, I confess that I yearn to throw a few essentials in the car, take to the open road, and leave financial responsibilities and adult drudgery far, far behind. *Sigh*.

So, I got the maps out – and by maps, I don't mean Tim's road atlas – and began planning an adventure, or maybe it's more accurate to call it a pilgrimage? Whatever, Tim was on half term, the BBC weather app showed Thursday as a fat yellow sun, and I'd plotted a long, weird, and

155

winding route that hit upon places I'd visited, and loved, when I was young. All that was left was to load up the car and head off on a voyage of discovery – destination, Ystradffin.

Okay, so when I say road trip, I guess it could *technically* be called 'a little run out', but that lessens the allure of our undertaking, and it is around a hundred miles so, 'Epic (1 day) Road Trip' it is.

And it wasn't only Tim and I who were going. We decided to take John & Wolfie, our pups, because leaving them home alone for more than an hour meant returning to chewed kitchen cabinets and a scene worthy of *White Christmas*, with drifts of sofa stuffing blanketing the laminate.

Road Trip Provisions

We were also taking my mother, or around one fifth of her, and our two old dogs. All three died over the past couple of years and they've been sitting, patiently in their urns – two small wooden caskets for Tommy Zoom and Barney, and a Moët Jeroboam for Mum (*don't ask*) – ever since.

Before she died, we were lucky to have time enough to make detailed notes of her last wishes. And there were many. In amongst direct cremation, buffet food choices, music, and even the clothing that my stepdad, Tim, and I were ordered to wear for her 'Death Party', she

156

made sure to tell us exactly where she wanted to be scattered.

And Mum being Mum, and a woman with her own unique brand of wanderlust, she didn't make things easy. Not for her the local garden of remembrance. Nope. As she said, 'I haven't done enough in life to stay in one place for an eternity, so add these to the list'.

There are some far-flung places on *Steph's Farewell Tour*, but unless we land a lottery win, they'll have to wait 'til either the cost-of-living drops, or Tim cultivates enough fresh veg to make a killing. (Have you seen supermarket shelves lately?)

And, even then, when it comes to taking her abroad, I'm still, mildly, haunted by a French coach trip where several implacable customs officials wanted to know exactly what I'd stashed in my five *I Can't Believe it's not Butter* tubs. Apparently, Dad's ashes resembled something a little more Class A.

(Fair play though. After I'd clarified, in halting French, that *'Mon père veut être dispersé dans l'eau de France'*, I was warmly hugged, given twenty Gauloises – *Eh?* – and our coach was waved through without further ado.)

Anyway, Mum's top three are:

Pembroke – where Mum's brother, Uncle Clive, lives, and my grandparents are buried.

Mumbles Pier – because she had cheery recollections of playing beneath it as a child, though there was also the less cheery recollection of Uncle Clive nearly drowning there. I dunno? I've never fully understood my mother.

And, taking the top spot, Twm Siôn Cati's Cave – the place where we'd deposited the other half of Dad, twenty-four years previously.

So, since Pembroke and Mumbles Pier required the gathering of the family clan, which is a logistical nightmare, I decided to start small and simple with Ystradffin.

The irony is that, in life, Mum wasn't keen on road trips. For her, the purpose of driving was to get from A to B in the shortest, fastest time, whereas Dad and I enjoyed sauntering around country lanes, via the other twenty-four letters of the alphabet.

And wherever we stopped, Dad would always have a story, legend

157

or tale about the place, the people, or the folklore. For me it was magic, for Mum, monotonous.

However, when we'd gone to scatter Dad, Mum and I *had* meandered, ambling along the Tywi to the exact spot below Twm's hideaway where Dad asked to be sprinkled. We'd had a marvellous time visiting the places he, and we, held dear, and that's what I was aiming for today.

It was time to set Mum, and our past pooches, free. But there was another reason, one that's wholly selfish. See, I've been struggling. For months, I've felt down, depressed, and totally lacking my usual vim. Not even upgrading my uke helped – I had to replace my Christmas one because the knobs snarled, and my G-string went saggy – and my mood has continued to sink with every passing day. And I blame Mum.

Because I *still* expect her not to be dead. I *still* reach for the phone to ring her, *still* expect to see her in her riser-recliner when I pop round for a cuppa, *still* send her text messages and expect a reply. Of course, my head knows she's gone but my heart just won't take telling. So, my thinking is that, if we begin dispersing, it might help me start to accept the reality of the here and now, and gee me up a bit. *Fingers crossed.*

Thursday dawned, a dazzling spring day, and Tim made his usual *emergency* flask of coffee, 'in case we break down'. Then we squeezed everything into the car – pups, daffodils, mini Freixenet, plastic cups, one *whole* kitchen roll (Tim likes to take them on journeys for 'possible spillage disasters'. *Sigh.*), Crème Eggs, a couple of photos, three ash-filled Tupperware containers and Trevor, my new tenor uke – and we were good to go.

I navigated, refusing to let Tim use the sat-nav as I wanted to keep some stop-offs secret, and directed him along roads that evoked happy memories and made me smile, despite Tim's frequent exclamations of, 'This isn't even a sodding road, it's a bollocking footpath'. (*Lol!* Okay, so that made me smile too, especially when a padlocked gate meant he had to reverse for half a mile before he could spin round.)

First stop, Carreg Cennen Castle, a jagged black ruin, perched high on a limestone crag. It dominates the skyline and casts dark, looming shadows over the river and surrounding farmland. These days, getting up to the fortress is several steps too far for me, so instead we pulled over on a z-road, shared a beaker of tepid coffee – Note to self: Buy new flask before our next day out – and I told Tim about our family visits, and how we'd creep along the hidden vaulted passage that led to the secret cave.

Next, Llyn y Fan Fach, home of The Lady of the Lake (*possibly*). Each time we would walk around the waters, Dad would tell the same story, making it last the full circumference of the lake. A *very* brief version = Farm boy meets watery fairy princess, woos her with a perfect loaf of bread, they marry, have three sons, princess leaves boy (look it up, she had her reasons), and sons grow up to become the famous Physicians of Myddfai, skilled in the magical healing of the fae.

Annoyingly, the access road that runs from the car park was blocked, so my sneaky plan to drive up and take a few pics was scuppered. But, if you're mobile, it's worth the walk to visit this glacial lake and the craggy cirque that surrounds it.

On to Myddfai, a small village boasting a gift shop which sells paintings by local artists, and a café that makes artisan cakes and 'Hollywood Handshake' bread – *Tee hee*. We were tempted to stop for a cuppa, but we'd already gone off track once, adding fifteen miles to our journey, and Tim was fretting about his fuel gauge. So, we motored on towards the bright lights of Llandovery.

It really is a charming market town. Colourful houses line the entrance from the east, and the main street bustles with interesting independent shops. We parked up and tried the West End Café, Tim hoping for an *extremely* late brekkie, but they'd stopped serving at eleven.

But worry not, because upon seeing Tim's downcast face, they knocked us up three bacon baps – lightly toasted baguettes, crispy bacon, and brown sauce. *Mmm*. And yes, when we'd finished, we both regretted sharing the third between the pups.

One downside of Llandovery was that it cost 20p to use the public loos. Unfortunately, we didn't have even one penny of physical money on us, but fortunately, a lady who was exiting, saw me coming and held the door so I could wee for free. Plus, the car park is genuinely epic, and there's not many car parks you can say that about.

As you drive in, you're greeted by the castle ruins and an impressive

16ft stainless-steel statue of Llywelyn ap Gruffydd Fychan. Embarrassingly, I hadn't heard of him, but a helpful plaque explained that he was a hero of the Welsh resistance, brutally executed in 1401 for his loyalty to Welsh prince, Owain Glyndwr.

A carapace of helmet, cloak, shield, and spear leaves visitors free to fill the void with their own imagined version of the man who would have worn such trappings, and I found it rather moving – this sculpture which commemorated, not only the man himself, but the rebellion, barbarity, and complex historic past of this area of Wales.

Llywelyn ap Gruffydd Fychan Statue

We headed north. But now, en route to our last stop, I felt anxious. Silly, I know, but I wanted this part of the day to go off without a hitch. So, obviously, we got lost, again. However, we happened upon a wonderfully eccentric lady, speeding along in a pony and trap, who gave us detailed directions and waved us off with a strident 'Giddy up, Bess', and a flick of her whip across our back window!

And then, sometime later, on our right was the farmhouse where, the bloody handprint of a maiden, murdered by her brutish father, still appears to this day, no matter how many times it's painted over. Or so Dad said. On our left, the churchyard where, above the grave of a child, stands a stone angel whose blank granite eyes follow those who dare pass by. Or so Dad said.

And ahead, the car park for Twm's cave, now part of the RSPB's Gwenffrwd-dinas nature reserve. We had arrived, and with twenty-five miles left in the tank. The diesel gods were on our side.

It took a while to reach the scatter spot. Tim was, literally, dragged ahead by the pups, and I hobbled along the snaking boardwalk, taking in the mountain air and ancient woodland. The sun was all but hidden behind the Dinas, but the final rays, hitting the gorse and bracken of Craig Clyngwyn, cast a copper glow over the Tywi and turned its clear waters russet.

We set up camp on a mossy bank and got organised. We started with TZ and Barney, sprinkling them into the water, accompanied by our favourite photographs of our much-missed boys, and a couple of Schmackos, their favourite treat. And then it was Mum's turn.

As Tim scattered, I got Trevor out, and we belted out some of her favourite songs to see her on her way – 'Everybody's Talkin'' (loved by us both), 'Sea of Love' (Mum and Dad's wedding song), 'Half a World Away' (only added to the mix because I'd learned it at uke club, but it was fitting nonetheless).

Our special scatter spot

Yes, my renditions were discordant, laboured and littered with expletives, but I persevered, knowing that somewhere in the ether, Mum and Dad were holding their sides and hooting with laughter at my musical homage.

Tim launched the daffodils as far into the river as possible – pups, unaware of the solemnity of the occasion, kept retrieving them – and I continued to, inexpertly, strum a few rock'n'roll crowd pleasers. Then we popped the Prosecco, raised a toast to Mum, Dad, TZ, and Barney,

161

and I embraced the *hiraeth* of this place, and this moment, glad that Tim *had* brought along the *Regina XXL*.

Packing away, we heard distant cheering, and looking up to the mouth of Twm's cave, noticed a youngish couple who had obviously been admiring the view – and had caught the entertainment. But they seemed to have appreciated it, so I guess I've (sort of) done my first public gig.

What a day. I'd reminisced, recalled conversations and details from my childhood that I'd thought long forgotten, and enjoyed hours of laughter, adventure, and gentle grief. And that this also marked the end of my first year of dangerous living seemed a fabulously fitting finale. In the words of Lou Reed, it was, 'Just a perfect day', and I'm so glad I spent it with them.

And I've been thinking that our road trip requires a suitably iconic name. So, if you have a day free and fancy an adventure of your own, consider giving the 'Stephy Sprint' a go. I guarantee you'll love it!

If you'd like to learn more about the people, places, myths, folklore, and history that I touch upon here, the Literature Wales website, www.landoflegends.wales. is an excellent starting point, as is www.visitwales.com.

Hot to Trot

Putting My Best Foot Forward

2nd April 2023

Given that this was to be the inaugural activity for my second year of dangerous living, I'd decided to go all out. Instead of dabbling with the mildly dicey, I wanted to start big, trying something that could, *genuinely*, be classed as hazardous. And I certainly found it – in Lampeter.

This is also the first time I've had to sign a release form, one that emphasises, in bold *and* capitals, that I take part voluntarily, 'as there IS inherent risk involved, and participants agree to hold all parties blameless for any injuries caused'. *Gulp*. Mind, when you consider that tonight promises to 'open the door to a wellspring of endless possibilities, and break through barriers in your life', I suppose it was never going to be easy.

Though what I'd assumed *would* have been, was the short, forty-six-mile drive from Swansea, half of which was M4 and A-roads. But, when the final twenty of those miles twist tortuously through tiny hamlets, and the weather is so extreme that, if Noah was still around, he'd be eyeing up the evergreens and whetting his axe, that's a different story. However, Geoff battled through and got me and Gaynor, to 'Minds Eye Venue' in ample time for the kick off.

It was a peculiar place. Apart from an annoyingly absent apostrophe in the name, it was painted vivid cerise, and had no discernible entrance; we eventually happened upon it at the rear of the building. Here, the stone façade had been left untainted and was framed by a wooden portico, which offered some protection from the elements – and flabby comfort in the form of several leather sofas. If you wanted to do a rustic Welsh mash-up of *Friends* meets *The Wicker Man*, this was the place to come.

Pushing open pea-green timbered doors, we entered a large room that was a muddled mix of spit and sawdust, dive bar, live music club, village hall, and not forgetting, karaoke club. It had a raw, earthy atmosphere, cool and curious artworks adorned the walls and, rather unnervingly, a young woman who appeared to be slicing at someone's ear with a cleaver. Weird wasn't the word.

Cleaving the past

Mind, we must have looked pretty weird too, though by we, I mean me, because even when wet and windswept, Gaynor still oozes county-chic. I was swathed in a waterproof poncho, a grey and Day-Glo gazebo of a garment that could comfortably accommodate an outdoorsy family of four. Yes, I looked a complete tit, but was, without question, the driest person there. I just had to hope it was also flame-proof. (Spoiler: It wasn't. *Sigh.*) Because that's why we were here, honouring Ostara's vernal equinox with a powerful ritual that had the potential to 'unblock our energies and conquer innate fears'. Tonight, we would be firewalking. *Eek!*

Cards on the table, I'm not sure if Gaynor, or I, were *fully* buying into it. I was up for the experience, though couldn't imagine achieving any discernible gains, and Gaynor was yet to be convinced. But, since we'd braved tempests to get there, we pulled up a couple of bar stools – as far from cleaver-girl as possible – and ordered cheesy chips.

Frankly, after the drive we'd had, I'd have killed for an Old Mout, but as the consumption of alcohol before, and during, the event was strictly forbidden, tea it was. And it was cheerily delivered, sometime later, by cleaver-girl herself, minus her chopper. It transpired that she was no random blade-wielding maniac but a member of staff (Lorna) and had actually been cutting a chunk of hair from a willing victim – 'for the burning'. *Phew.* (Though, with hindsight, it showed a somewhat laissez-faire attitude towards health and safety.)

More participants began arriving, and we were soon joined by a lady named Kim, who had done this twenty years earlier and was there to 'burn my ex-husband'. *Uh?* Not literally, though I wouldn't have been overly surprised to find a neatly bundled body, smouldering merrily atop the cinders. Kim explained that when she'd done 'the walk', she'd felt 'very real elysian effects' – and now, with her divorce legally separating her from the ex, this evening was about 'severing the remaining spiritual link'.

And she shared her top tips for getting the most out of our combustible challenge. She used a mantra that was guaranteed to attract favourable outcomes: 'I am the source, I dream the dreams, I am the spark, creation lives in me'. *Hmm?* I'd been hoping for something more rhythmical, but the 'spark' line fitted, so I recited it a couple of times to show willing, then sloped off to the loos.

I returned as Steven, the chillaxed founder of Firewalk Cymru, and a fellow with a comprehensive knowledge of faith, fire, and feet, announced that, while we awaited the arrival of two more brave *soles* (*I'll get my coat*), we'd use the time to sign in and review the disclaimer. As everyone shuffled along to scrawl their signatures, I took the opportunity to pull Steve for a quick chat.

See, when I'd reserved my spot, I'd had to declare my mobility issues, and Steve had phoned for clarification. He'd explained how the evening would unfold, but the key question he had was, 'Can you walk unaided?' *Sigh.* Nope. Clearly my dream of hot footing it into a new era of derring-do was over. *Bummer.*

However, as it turned out, no it wasn't. Apparently, many disabled people have successfully completed the walk, using a friend's arm, or shoulder, for support. Steve said if I was coming alone, he'd be happy to lend me a hand, but as Gaynor had signed up too, she was my prop

165

of choice – plus she's a physio so I'd be hanging onto a medically-capable arm. I'd be getting my blaze of glory moment after all. *Whoop, whoop!*

But, since that conversation, I'd been ruminating, and it came down to this – did I *really* want to stride fiercely into a new empowered epoch, whilst using a human crutch? And my answer was a resounding NO. So, sod it, I'd do it on my own two feet, or not at all. And that's why I'd brought along *Walking Stick #3*.

It was a gift from my mum who, when I began needing ambulant help, thought my hospital crutches and wooden cane weren't 'attractive enough'. *Eyeroll.* Her largesse stretched to a £14.99 foldable floral monstrosity, with a hard plastic ferrule – so hard, that a single drop of H_2O would see it skidding out from beneath me, sending me sprawling across Tesco's, or anywhere with vinyl flooring. Risking its destruction through fire-damage was a no-brainer. Now I simply had to convince Steve.

And that was surprisingly easy. He checked the stick, checked my gait, saw I could manage to cover the short distance alone, and gave me the go-ahead. I signed the release, got handed a large lollipop stick(?) and joined the other walkers for the seminar. *Shit got real!*

I was sitting between Gaynor and Karen, an experienced energy healer who was starting her own business, and it was she who explained that we should write 'what you wish to discard on the stick, then feed it to the fire, with a piece of your hair'. *Ah, I get it now.* (And yes, I did get a blunt cut from Lorna later on.)

Since Gaynor and I hadn't considered intentions in advance, our burn notices were broad-ranging and non-specific. Basically, anything that didn't bring me joy was to be consigned to the flames, and after a brief inner struggle, decided not to add Tim's name to the stick – this time. *Lol.*

Karen murmured that we should write what we hoped to gain too – 'Maybe ask to un-dim your light?' Maybe. But, since starting my life-enrichment regime, I felt 'my light', whatever *that* is, was probably brighter than it used to be, so instead I opted for taking control of my own destiny. It was a biggie, but if you don't ask . . .

All done, we quietened down and Steve launched into his seminar.

He began with a photograph, one he always carries, which showed a slightly younger, considerably larger version of the man in front of us. He explained that he'd suffered from musculoskeletal disorders, putting his transformation down to the breakthrough experienced when he first fire walked. He *knew* it had changed his life for the better, and looking at him, the evidence was quite compelling. Frankly, if all I achieved was the willpower to start, and stick to, a healthy diet, I'd happily take it.

And then we went through a series of exercises, designed to enable us to walk over scorching tinder with minimal discomfort. First, the games. For one, we wrote our biggest fear on a scrap of paper, screwed it up and chucked it into a hat. Then we had to randomly pick one before, 'laughing in the manner of that fear'. *Uh oh.*

Flaming heck - Ouchy!

Honestly, if I'd have realised what we'd be asked to do, I'd probably have binned my 'dying alone' in favour of spiders. Luckily, Gaynor drew mine out, managed a ghostly chortle and everyone applauded her effort; I got 'destruction of the natural world', panicked, thought of birds, and then giggled my way through the intro music to *The Woody*

Woodpecker Show. It wasn't my finest hour.

Then came something that none of us, apart from Karen, had been expecting – 'Walking into our Power' by snapping an arrow with our throats. No, the arrows weren't sharp, but wedging one end against a wall, putting the pointy bit in our 'jugular notch', then stepping forward until it splintered seemed foolish at best, and suicidal at worst. But we all managed it, no one died, and it certainly bonded our 'tribe' together.

Finally came the meditation, where we allowed our minds to visualise 'cool grass and ice-cold flames'. I was nearly napping when we were rowdily interrupted by a loudly discordant rendition of *Sweet Caroline*, which slightly killed our chill. Lorna bustled off to sort out the barmen, who were clearly having a banging time, and soon it became blessedly silent – until somebody, whose repertoire stretched only to *Chopsticks*, discovered the piano. Well, we were probably relaxed enough, so we trooped outside to the bonfire.

Steve's assistant, Becca, who'd been cultivating the conflagration, had got it fired up and burning at a scalding 1300°F! *WTAF?* It wasn't any less alarming when I converted it to Celsius, and so intense was the heat that, even standing some distance from the pyre, my PVC poncho was already losing its stiffness and beginning to sag.

Then suddenly, it was time. With words of encouragement, we got in line, did our utmost to smother any last-minute doubts, and away we went. And it was incredible. Even just watching the other members of our tribe march forth, bare-foot and focused, shoulders set with unwavering determination, was inspirational. But then, once Gaynor had skipped daintily across the red-hot embers, it was my turn. *GULP*.

As I stood facing the fire, I forgot the mantras and intentions, overtaken by an understandable anxiety regarding my pacing. I'm slow, I walk on the toes of my right foot, and carry the bulk of my body weight on my left. Could I do this? Should I? I was on a cleaver-edge, but then encouraging cheers reached me, I dug deep, took a long breath, and set off . . . back to the car park.

Nah, course not. My first paces were tentative, but my sodden feet couldn't detect *any* uncomfortable heat – though there were audible sizzles which I tried to block out, too reminiscent of the sounds from the kitchen whenever Tim cooks steak. Then halfway, I stumbled, saving myself only by plonking my left foot down with far greater force than usual and . . . Yep, it *was* hot. Sodding hot. Hotter than Hades hot. *Abso-bloody-lutely blistering*! But I pressed on, fire-limping my way into the woolly and welcoming arms of Steve, who was tearfully proud of what I'd achieved.

Getting home at midnight, I needed bed, but couldn't think of heading up the wooden hill until I'd soaked my feet, checked for blisters (*unbelievably*, my soles were 100% uncooked!), and come down from my heroic high. So, I poured a restorative Snowball and raised a toast to me, because I'd done it. I'd taken my first flaming steps into a new year of adventure and suffered nothing more than sooty feet, a molten mantle, and distorted ferrule. And, unpacking the mementos of the evening – my broken arrow, a small jar of ash and a certificate bestowing upon me the official title of 'Firewalker' – I confess that I

really did feel pretty damn awesome!

(And, in case you were wondering, I was still feeling awesome the following morning, and motivated enough to start the healthy-eating plan I'd been postponing since 2021. Though only time will tell, I'm

Awesome? Too right I am!

currently eleven days in, still going strong, totally committed and I've even done some gentle pedalling on my static bike. Coincidence? Probably. But maybe there's something in this fire-walking lark after all.)

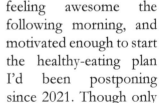

If you'd like to try firewalking for yourself, Firewalk Cymru are on Facebook, or visit firewalkcymru.com where they post all their upcoming events. And, if you want to sample delicious cheesy chips in one of Lampeter's hippest hotspots, search for 'Minds Eye Venue' on Facebook. And yes, leave out that apostrophe.

Whittle While You Work

16th April 2023

If you were a potential serial killer, *this* would be your Shangri-La. It had every implement the modern murderer-about-town could dream of, especially if they were looking to dispatch, and dispose of their targets, with ease, efficiency, and for a *very* reasonable price. And, given that my first instruction was to make a 'stab cut', you might understand why my thoughts were straying towards the macabre.

But, putting aside such morbid musings, it was also a fab place to visit if you fancied learning a new skill – and no, I don't mean *Dissection 101: Avoiding RSI*. So that was why, despite a severe lack of crafting ability, complete ignorance regarding chisels, and with only a vague idea of what 'whittling' *actually* meant, I was at Axminster Tools (Cardiff), attempting to carve a love-spoon.

I was twenty-five minutes into a five-hour workshop and already my scalp was sweating. I was liberally coated with sawdust, was making no discernible headway with my Flexcut carving chisel, and was seriously considering buggering off for a Sausage McMuffin and a sank around St Fagans. After all my recent *branch*-ing out, *wood* wood prove to be my downfall? Maybe I should *leaf* right now? (Sorry, I'll stop. These puns must be driving *yew* crazy. *Lol!*)

But then Derek, master craftsman and 'Wizard of Wood' (a moniker I bestowed upon him because what that man can make from timber is jaw-dropping), sensed my agitation and came over to lend a helping hand. Apparently, two issues were hampering my progress:

1. My stabbing was 'too tentative'.

2. I needed to 'work into the cut' with my blade, rather than prising the loose piece away, 'because that can cause the wood to lift and break'.

Patience itself, he once again demonstrated the correct technique, showing me how to carefully shape the handle, and offered words of encouragement to spur me on; I was doing well, though might do *even* better if I used the correct edge of the chisel. *Doh!* Then, with a paternal twinkle, he padded off to help the twenty other learners who were also chiselling away.

I'd booked today's masterclass via Eventbrite, when I'd stumbled across Axminster Tools and noticed that they offered *free* crafty events in all of their stores. From woodcarving, turning, and blade sharpening, to bandsaw box demos and hosting local artisans, they did it all.

And, as well as that, as I sidled in that Saturday morning, I was made to feel so welcome. The staff, easily identifying a nervous novice

Love-spoon inspiration

who had obviously never been this close to an angle grinder, escorted me to the workshop, where Derek and his team from South Wales Wood Carvers (SWWC), were setting up.

And store manager, Lee, possibly noticing my puffy eyes – a hangover from my night-time Morpheus-meds – brought me a drink from their free Coffee Bar; this is an area where customers can chill out with a cappuccino, have a chinwag about spokeshaves, spindles or slipstones, or even just set the world to rights by chewing over their *knotty* problems. (I *promise* that's the last one.) When it came to customer experience, this store was *tree*-mendous . . . (I lied.)

As was my double shot espresso which caused an instant high octane head rush and ignited a devil-may-care attitude. Frankly, if Derek hadn't kicked off the class when he did, I'd have been haring up those aisles, toying with the orbital sanders and running amok amidst the routers.

Anyway, back to my spoon. Now using the *proper* part of the blade, my snaky stem finally began to take shape. And as it did, all thoughts of pushing off faded, and I started getting into the swing of things. I was making something gorgeous out of *sweet chestnut*, and I was bossing it. (For me, caffeine-overconfidence is deffo a thing.)

I'd also been quite canny when I'd arrived, choosing a small round table that had space for six learners, but which was also shared by Derek, and his two able assistants, Isabel, and Mark. So even when Derek was off circulating, I still had easy access to experts. *Ha!*

They both rapidly realised that my heavy exhalations and throat clearing were codes for 'Help', and seemed happy to put down their own exquisite projects and devote chunks of their time to gently guiding me through whatever problem I was grappling with. That they did this with nary an Eyeroll, gives some idea of how relaxing, and mindful, woodworking can be – though based on my stress levels, that's probably only once you reach a fair level of proficiency.

Saying that, after an hour, I *was* slightly more adept, could go minutes without coughing an SOS, and was so focused on my chisel action that I was oblivious when the most attractive member of SWWC ambled over for a head scratch. Okay, you got me. Who could resist the wavy blonde hair and muddy brown eyes of Summer (Isabel and Derek's golden doodle)? Certainly not me.

And Summer was a fixture, providing a warm and woolly oasis of calm as she snuck around the tables and nudged us with her wet nose. I could feel my stress seeping away as I stroked her soft ears, and after some one-on-one time, returned to my whittling with renewed vigour and purpose.

By now, I'd started work on the bowl section of my spoon, however the hollowing action caused my flabby wrist flexors to twinge with every scoop, leading to incessant ows and ouches. Mark, noticing these subtle signals, lent me a tool called a *scorp*, 'which might make things a bit easier'. And it did, allowing me to gouge away with minimal tendon-tweakage. At this rate, I'd be finished by lunch. *Woohoo!*

Obviously, I wasn't. And lunch was a rather fluid affair anyway. Some of my neighbours headed off for a Maccy D's but, conscious that I still had a *lot* to do if I wanted to take home a finished item, I pressed on. And, conscious of my ongoing healthy eating plan, I didn't even ask them to pick me up a large banana milkshake. (*Polishes halo.*)

Instead, the lovely Lee brought me another cuppa, and I scorp'ed on, until the SWWC gang got up from their seats, a manoeuvre that sent me into panic mode. Surely to God they weren't leaving me alone whilst in charge of a lethal weapon? Luckily, no. 'We're only getting our sandwiches'. And they set their picnic out on the table which meant, not only could I continue with, but I could also watch as Summer circled, finagling the best part of a packet of crisps and several tuna sarnies from her doting fans.

My bowl taking shape

I did take ten minutes out to give my throbbing thumbs a break and took a closer look at the SWWC items that were on display. And wow! I mean, how the hell do you carve a cage, with a moveable ball encased within, out of ONE piece of wood? How does Isabel make those gorgeous leafy bowls? How can Mark – who only started carving last May! – create that beautiful array of pens and spoons? And how can Derek sculpt such detailed relief carvings? Unsurprisingly, the answer from all three was 'practice'. So, using that oft quoted figure of 10,000

173

hours to become an expert at anything, I worked out that, after today, I had 9,995 hours to go. *Sigh.*

By 1pm, I'd finished carving, had a spoon that, to my eye, looked epic, but to Derek's, needed a lot more attention. He passed me over several sheets of sandpaper, told me to start rubbing and I got down to some all-out, abrading action.

It's the sanding phase that brings handmade wooden items to life, smoothing away any hewn-imperfections – of which I had many – and giving a splinter-less sheen. But why *five* separate sandpapers, when surely one would do? Apparently not. For that 'professional finish', you need to work your way down the sandpaper scale, starting with the roughest grain before gradually progressing to the finest. *What?* I'd thought fifteen minutes of solid sanding meant my spoon was ready for waxing, but it appeared I still had another hour ahead. *Argh!*

By quarter to three, I was done. My spoon felt like satin, it looked amazing, and I was ready to add polish. But as I was about to liberally slather a wonderfully aromatic wax into all my nooks and crannies, someone asked about using the pyrograph and my ears pricked up.

Pyrography is the art of decorating wood, or other materials, with burn marks. And Derek said that if any of us wanted to try, he'd show us how to use the machine. *Wowzers!* Grabbing my spoon, I was first in the fire-writing queue.

You'd think that using what is *basically* a pen would be pretty intuitive, but it's not. Derek demonstrated, then told me to practise on the fire-graffitied wood that littered the table-top. And I did, for ten minutes or more, but it ultimately came down to weight – pressing too hard gave a lumpy line, too soft meant no line at all. So, like Goldilocks, I was seeking the 'just right'.

I dithered. Did I risk ruining my marvellous creation for some unnecessary decoration? Time was ticking, the queue building, so . . . *Gulp.* I'm going for it. The outcome was *far* from perfect, but it wasn't dreadful. In fact, I thought it added to the rustic, naive quality of my piece. (Well, that's the line I'm taking and I'm sticking to it.)

And all that was left was waxing on and waxing off – actually, only wax on, because it should be left to 'cure' overnight before buffing. Once well-coated, I washed my greasy hands, wiped the sawdust from my eyes and held the love-spoon out in front of me and . . . it looked incredible!

I was bursting with pride, so much so that I went on a whistle-stop tour of the other carvers, exhorting all and sundry to 'Stroke my spoon'. I got a lot of 'wows' which *maybe* were genuine – or *maybe* they were simply humouring this strange, excitable woman who was childishly delighted with her finished product? *Whatever.* I had made something terrific and felt bloody epic.

Before leaving, I chatted with many of my fellow crafters and heard some quite touching stories. Pete, who had suffered multiple strokes, came along every week 'because it helps me to retain the dexterity in my hands, and I live alone so like the social side of it'. Adrian, a sufferer of PTSD, found it enabled him to 'switch off and focus on one thing, and when I do, it keeps other thoughts away'. And Mike mentioned mindfulness, along with the 'sense of achievement from making beautiful things and sharing that experience with other people'. Yep Mike, I feel you.

It was clear that Derek and his gang weren't only teaching woodworking. They were also giving individuals the opportunity to bond over a shared love of wood, and to join a sociable, and incredibly supportive, community of crafters. It was pretty inspirational stuff.

Back home, I fussed the pups, prepped Tim for the big reveal and then, with a strident 'Ta-da!', set my spoon carefully on the kitchen table. And, though a man of few words, I could tell by his expression that he was quietly, but genuinely, impressed. As I went for a sawdust-removal shower, he headed off to the shed to dig out a hammer and nails so we could get it up on the wall asap. (*Aw.* He can be lush, sometimes.)

However, five short minutes later, I heard a muffled yell, then an ominous silence, and suddenly Tim popped his head around the bathroom door to ask, rather *too* nonchalantly, if I'd taken any pics of my finished spoon yet? *Uh, no. Not yet. Why? WHY?*

Can you guess? In those short, unsupervised seconds, our giant giraffe-necked puppies had swiped my precious spoon and enjoyed a great game of chase with Tim, as he attempted unsuccessfully, to wrest it from their destructive jaws. (It's better if I draw a veil over the subsequent hours but suffice it to say, it's a good job those dogs are sodding cute because I was truly, *truly* heartbroken. *Sob!*)

A week on, and I've pretty much got over it, resigning myself to the fact that my spoon is unsalvageable – though Tim's latest idea of sanding down the rough edges and making it into a salad *spork*, isn't all that bad. And being optimistic, I'm looking forward to Derek's pyrography classes, and the next carving workshop, where I'll be fashioning Spoon V.2, and I'm sure I'll be as proud of it. But this time, it'll be kept well away from two dogs, who at full stretch have a good six-foot reach. *Grr!*

So, whether you're a rookie, an old hand, or anything in between, if you fancy spending some quality time crafting with this skilled and friendly bunch, think about giving woodworking a whirl. As Derek wrote in an email to me:

'Everyone thinks they can't achieve much in the beginning, but if you've got the confidence to have a go, and approach it with enthusiasm, that's what counts. Then you just need to *stick* at it'. (*Lol!* You can't blame *me* for that one!)

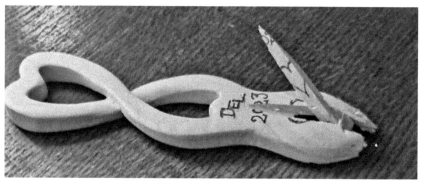

A literal dog's dinner - Sigh!

Derek has been volunteering in Port Talbot's Community Workshops for seventeen years. Now based at Units 10 & 11 Addison Road, details of the courses available can be found on the South Wales Wood Carvers Facebook page.

SWWC also hold weekly meet ups at Axminster Tools (Cardiff), on Wednesdays from 11 – 3, and anyone is welcome to come along. And check out the Axminster Tools (Cardiff) website for details of all their upcoming, free, community events.

A Dead Good Day Out

7th May 2023

It's a splendid Saturday, with empty blue skies, a dazzling sun, and a briny breeze sweeping in from the bay, blending beautifully with the heavy scent of wild garlic. Spring is blooming in glorious technicolour, and banks of crocuses, daffodils, and bluebells soften the rough edges of the gravelled pathways that trail through the avenues of yew.

With birdsong, and the gentle breath of nature, muffling the constant grumble of 21st century living, it's the kind of day that makes you glad to be alive . . . which is somewhat ironic because today I'm at Oystermouth Cemetery, waiting for a guided tour of notable graves, gothic tombs, and the occasional celebrity corpse.

I'm perched on the old stone wall, beneath a seriously impressive cypress tree, and – as I later learned from Bev (our guide) – it was no wonder this bad boy was so imposing because it had a personal history spanning well over a hundred years, and an even more ancient mythology.

Long story short: a teenager named Cyparissus had a pet stag he dearly loved – though not dearly enough to check the surrounding woodland, prior to his daily javelin practise. (*Eyeroll*. But that's kids for you.)

When he found the lifeless body of his antlered pal, Cyparissus' grief was so all-consuming, he prayed to Apollo that he be allowed to mourn forever. Apollo, aware that forever is a *very* long time, and knowing the fickleness of youth, said, 'C'mon kid, think what you're asking for!' But still Cyparissus grieved. So, in my opinion, and going slightly *OTT*, Apollo transformed him into a cypress tree, and that's why it's seen as a classical symbol of mourning.

(Poor Cyp. What he'd really needed was a night out with the lads, a shoulder to cry on, and several bottles of Ouzo, and I'm sure he'd have bounced back, eventually.)

Anyway, as I waited beneath the sad tree for Bev, and our tour group, to arrive, I felt that I could easily be back in 1883 (which is when the cemetery first opened), if I ignored the parked cars, and a charming chap on a scooter, who shot past with a cheery, 'Move, Grandma!' *Sigh*. But, despite such reminders of the here and now, there was a timeless tranquillity that made this a perfect place to rest in peace.

In fact, I was in the process of picking out a theoretical plot for myself and Tim – though it's unlikely he'll stick around in the afterlife because my snoring is, apparently, so loud, he said he 'couldn't put up with that racket for sodding eternity!' – when Bev arrived. I'd guessed it was her because she was clutching a folder of notes and, more of a giveaway, had a smiling skull scarf draped around her neck. She was not at all what I'd imagined.

I'd envisaged her draped in black crêpe, face covered by a mourning veil, with a persona that was sombre, sad, and deathly serious. But Bev was all smiles, very welcoming, and I started thinking that this tour might actually be fun – or at least, less solemn than I'd anticipated. And I was spot on.

Bev kicked things off by telling us a little about her background. As well as a folklorist and researcher of burial customs and superstitions, Bev is also a Master of Death, Religion and Culture, which is without question the most epic academic title I've ever heard. But I wondered aloud what caused her to spend a lifetime investigating such a morbid topic, and she'd laughed. 'Morbid? Not a bit of it'.

Instead, she recalled halcyon days, picnicking in Birmingham's Whitton Green Cemetery, a place that six-year-old Bev felt was made for leisure and enjoyment – and which was exactly what Victorian architects were aiming to achieve with their new, garden 'esque cemeteries.

En route to our first grave, Bev fed us fascinating snippets of folklore and trivia. The difference between cemeteries and graveyards? *Umm?* Basically, if there's an active parish church on site, it's a graveyard, otherwise, a cemetery.

And the small stone mortuary chapel, built to allow relatives to pay their respects prior to burial, is now privately owned, having been sold in 2001 as a 'unique residential opportunity'. Bev had actually put in a bid at the time, it being her dream house, but sadly missed out, and now it's an Airbnb for those looking for a dead quiet holiday let.

We passed through tilting yews, planted by the first caretaker of Oystermouth, Henry Harris. Someone asked why they were so common in burial grounds and Bev explained that they're a regenerative tree; when the branches reach the ground, they can take root and form new trees, and this ongoing cycle of ageing and rebirth came to symbolise death and resurrection.

But folklore also suggested that they kept evil spirits in check, so when Bev said that they're an 'absolute nightmare', I sensed a spooky story was in the offing. 'No, nothing scary. It's because they're difficult to keep them all upright because they're inclined to lean. It costs the council an absolute bomb each year to deal with them'. *Lol!*

As we walked, it became obvious that Oystermouth had a muddled mixture of Victorian gothic memorials, uneasily rubbing shoulders with minimalist, modern neighbours. Bev explained that back then, you could trot along and secure any plot you fancied, anywhere in the cemetery, and the long-term organisation wasn't a particular consideration.

'That's why the earliest graves are randomly dotted throughout the site'. However, that changed in the 1930s when a chronological system was introduced, leading to the more ordered plot layouts you see today.

She told us about other superstitions that often haunt such places. How it was believed that the first person buried in a new cemetery had to remain there, in spirit, to guard it against the Devil. So, in order to prevent a human soul from being forced to perform such a duty, a dog would often be buried in the north part of the churchyard, prior to any human interments. *Eh?*

Though I guess it makes sense – 'Man's Best Friend' would

179

definitely make a most loyal and effective guardian. Bev wasn't sure if Oystermouth had followed this tradition, but one family who probably hoped they had, were the Gelderd's, whose son, Alfred, was the first person buried there in March 1883, aged twenty-three.

Our first stop was at the rather humble grave of one Thomas Harry, a schoolmaster who died in the autumn of 1915. His 'bedstead' plot was quite unremarkable, so it seemed an odd place to begin. But a closer look showed why this was noteworthy – and if any of you chuckled over a news item about a spelling error made by Swansea gas workers (SHCOOL! *Lol!*) – *this* is in a similar vein, though I guess repainting is much easier than doing the carving equivalent of Tipp-Exing a slab of granite.

Mr Harry, 'Shcoolmaster'!

And then we dived into the strange world of Victorian death symbolism. Symbols became popular additions to grave markers during this era, not only from an aesthetical standpoint but also due to widespread illiteracy – symbols made memorials more meaningful for those who weren't able to read the words. And, as might be expected, the most common were crosses, signifying the deceased's faith, love, or goodness. Bev took us past a variety of styles, from the plain to the florid, Celtic to fleur-de-lis.

Then came the host of angels, which to my untrained eye, were much of a muchness. But Bev pointed out their subtle (and not so subtle) differences, explaining that their meaning would alter, depending upon their pose. It was a way in which a family could silently convey characteristics of their deceased loved one.

An angel in flight implied rebirth, bibliophile angels, surveying scroll or book, indicated the deceased had a history of charitable deeds, while praying angels suggested a pious life. My least favoured were the weeping angels who frequently indicated an untimely, or painful, death.

180

Gulp. Doctor Who has a lot to answer for – I didn't blink the whole time I was there!

We stopped at Bev's favourite grave, and I was, initially, a bit disappointed. No urns or angels here, just a carved headstone showing two clasped hands, one a tad bigger than the other. But looking closely, you could see that the cuffs were slightly different – one starkly masculine, the other edged with lace. Such symbology intimated that John, or Archie, would be on hand to guide their sister Effie into the afterlife, where all three siblings would be reunited. *Aww.* It was a lovely sentiment.

And then it was uphill, to visit a grave which attracts people from all over the world, who come to pay homage to a young woman named Morfydd Owen. A Welsh mezzo-soprano, musician, and composer, Morfydd died aged twenty-six.

Supremely talented, she began composing as a young child, and on her passing, left a legacy of some two-hundred-and-fifty scores. Whilst studying at the Royal Academy of Music, she met Dr Ernest Jones, a psychoanalyst of the Freud school, and within three months they were wed.

Unfortunately, the pressures of being a new wife took their toll upon Morfydd, not helped by Ernest's insistence that she manage his professional and social calendars, to the detriment of her own career. But it was when Morfydd was struck with appendicitis, in September 1918, that things took an odd turn.

Though the hospital was barely any distance away, she was operated on at home. Her death was said to be due to delayed chloroform poisoning, though no autopsy took place, and she was buried two weeks before her death certificate had been issued.

And her memorial – a stark sandstone column – bore her incorrect date of birth, her wedding date (which was a *very* uncommon addition), and an engraving taken from Goethe's *Faust*: '*Das Unbeschreibliche, hier ist's getan*', which translates as, 'Here the indescribable has been done/accomplished'.

Hmm? Maybe Ernest wasn't the sentimental type. (And *he* did bounce back one year later – Cyparissus, take note – marrying for a second time. Well, I suppose those calendars aren't going to organise themselves.)

We learned about lead-lined 'chest tombs', where handily marked entrance slabs could be removed, to reveal snaking staircases, leading down to stone shelves where the bodies were laid. We saw memorials to the local lifeboat men who perished in three historic tragedies, and it was terribly touching, looking down on those, still neat and tended graves, whilst Bev described the particulars of each maritime disaster.

On a brighter note, we met William Bancroft (nicknamed 'Billy the Whizz'), a Welsh rugby international and Glamorgan County cricketer, who was memorably described in a newspaper article of the time as, 'ten stones of fencing wire, fitted with the electricity of life'.

There was Harry Parr-Davies, a child prodigy who, as well as writing scores for musicals, collaborated with Gracie Fields, and was her preferred accompanist. 'Wish me Luck as you Wave Me Goodbye' was one of his, and during the war, when he enlisted in the Irish guards, Gracie refused to entertain the troops unless Harry was seconded to ENSA (Entertainments National Service Association). And, as you'd expect, Gracie got her way.

And then we visited the largest tomb in the cemetery, belonging to the colourful Folland family. By all accounts, Henry Folland, was a topping fellow. From humble beginnings, he grew up to be a skilled statistician, eventually working his way from lowly clerk to become company chairman of the largest tinplate factory in Europe.

A keen Egyptophile, he died in 1926, whilst holidaying in Cairo, and it took over four weeks to repatriate his body. You can probably imagine how he must have looked after a month at sea. But if you'd been around back then, you could actually have seen for yourself because, for some unfathomable reason, Henry's coffin of choice was a glass-lidded affair.

However, putting *that* image aside, a more palatable one was conjured by Bev's anecdote about Henry's adored Arabian stallion. Every evening, the beautiful white horse would trot through the cemetery so he and his rider could pay their respects to a master who was, obviously, very well-loved.

Next, after pausing at the unmarked paupers' graves, forgotten by most, excepting Bev, who is passionate about researching these poor unfortunates, we wended our way up to the carbon-neutral Woodland Burial Area.

A recent addition to the cemetery, here mature trees are complimented by new plantings, and you can be laid to rest, content in the knowledge that you are returning to nature, whilst helping to preserve a beautiful woodland. You don't even need a coffin – a shroud is acceptable.

Plus, if you fancy giving your family a bit of a pre-funeral work-out, you can even specify that they dig your grave, which is both a lovely idea, and pretty funny; I could just see Tim sweating over his shovel, and ruing the day he'd ever met me. *Lol!*

And then it was a gentle stroll, back to the sad cypress, passing graves of numerous faiths that share this land. Bev explained Swansea's cosmopolitan approach to interment, and it was genuinely heartening to see that, not only in life, but death too, religious diversity is celebrated and embraced; though the Plosker Memorial Gates of the Hebrew cemetery provided a profoundly poignant reminder of an era that was not so tolerant.

It was a weird, but rather wonderful, afternoon. We'd all enjoyed our symbolic scavenger hunt, and reading the inscriptions gave candid insights into the social history of our city, and its people. Whether that was told by stone angels, marble crosses, or through the absence of all such trappings, when Bev said that 'Everyone here has a tale to tell', she certainly wasn't wrong.

Find Bev at Swansea and Gower Lore, or visit bevrogers.co.uk.

A Murderously Good Weekend, Part 1

28th May 2023

Reception was empty, barring one marvellously colourful lady who provided a blaze of brilliance in the slightly tired magnolia lobby. Attired in a stunning hippy-chic dress, her coarse grey curls cascaded over her shoulders, were held in check by a cerise scarf, edged with tiny, mirrored circles, which framed twinkling eyes, and a lived-in face.

She was propped against the desk, dinging the call bell every few seconds (and with some force), and was evidently impatient for a member of staff to answer its sharp summons. Being fanciful, as I frequently am, if the local am-dram were thinking of staging *Blithe Spirit*, she would have made a terrific Madame Arcati – no costume required. And remarkably, after exchanging smiles, her first words to me underscored her innate suitability for that role.

'Ah, I know why you're here' she murmured, with an eloquent wink. Then she paused, thumped the bell, and whispered one final word, 'Murder!' *Wowzers!*

Right, so she was clearly a bit of a *character*, but as it happens, she was scarily accurate. I was indeed checking into the Four Seasons Hotel – no, not the posh ones – in Aberystwyth, in order to attend the inaugural *Gŵyl Crime Cymru Festival*, where top authors would be giving talks and hosting workshops for whodunnit writer wannabees and crime fiction fans.

It promised to be a weekend filled with good old-fashioned

homicidal high jinks, and Sidonia, Madame Arcati's actual name – 'Call me Sid' – was attending too. (Turned out, she'd spotted the event tickets peeking out of my handbag, which made her initial introduction a lot less impressive, though no less memorable.)

I arranged to meet her later, collected my key from the harried staff member who'd finally appeared, and headed off to my room feeling moderately trepidatious. Why? Well, for some reason, I'd booked *and paid for* the hotel well in advance, without any thought of checking the online reviews first.

See, I tend to rush into things with the fervour of a ball-chasing Labrador, only to frequently rue such haste at a later date. And that's why I was steeling myself for a pretty dismal stay. The reviews for this place, which I perused the previous day, were abysmal to say the least. But I hadn't booked this hotel for its facilities, rather because it was situated an equidistant one-minute amble from the Central Library and Ceredigion Museum, the two locations where *Crime Cymru* would be holding their events. And that made it a perfect location for me.

So, turning the key and entering my 'accessible' room, I was prepared for the worst. But no, I was pleasantly surprised. There was a slight new carpet smell, two beds, a brand-new wet room decked out with helpful grab rails and smart smellies, and a well-stocked tea and coffee tray, with ample milks and biscuits. *Get thee behind me, Bourbon!*

It was clean, fresh and I was delighted. Like Goldilocks, I tried out the beds, settled for the softer of the two, then opened the sash window to let in a cooling breeze, made a strong cuppa, and relaxed for a few hours, in readiness for the intriguingly named 'Dragon Parade'.

Actually, I dozed off for a bit, but it had been a very long day. Yes, the drive from Swansea to Aberystwyth is only a short two-hour, seventy-six-mile hop, but you already know I'm a fan of road-tripping. And this journey was no exception.

Once I'd made my Crime Fest arrangements, I got out my trusty adventure maps and plotted myself a little route that would take in some true Welsh wonders. The outward leg had three stops:

The most isolated phone box in Wales, about which I was extremely excited. And no, I still can't explain why.

Devil's Bridge, a place my parents frequently took me when I was young, and when its very name caused shivers of delightful dread.

The Magic of Life Butterfly House, which sounded pretty amazing, and who doesn't love a flutter-by?

And homeward bound, I'd booked a dolphin spotting boat trip in New Quay. The weekend was going to be epic.

Setting off Friday morning, I waved a cheery goodbye to Tim, kissed the pups, tanked up Geoff, and revved off into an overcast morning with a flask of strong coffee, my Google sat-nav, and a song in my heart. *Woohoo!* Adventure, here I come.

Three hours later, my back was in spasm and a nascent migraine pulsed over my right temple. The grey morning had matured into a murky miasma, and whilst I could barely see the end of Geoff's bonnet, the one positive was that the vertiginous views were also semi-shrouded.

You could say I was regretting heading into the heart of wild Wales, tentatively navigating an infamous road known as The Devil's Staircase, with no more sustenance than a pack of Leerdammer (I'm low-carbing so cheese is my friend), a jar of pickled onions (Onions less so but hey, I was on holiday), and in the company of an increasingly exasperated sat-nav.

This is the road . . . to hell!

Originally an old drover's path, The Devil's Staircase is a single-track road – though calling it 'single track' is tremendously generous – comprising a set of jagged hairpin turns, with a max gradient of 20.1%. It runs the twenty odd miles between Abergwesyn and Tregaron, and it's at the thirteen-mile mark that you'll find the telephone box that was #1 on my 'must see' list.

However, what I hadn't realised was how threadlike, twisty, and truly terrifying those miles would be. My jaw was permanently clenched, my nose was mere inches from the windscreen and the bloody sat-nav insisted on telling me to turn left or right, despite the fact that turning *any* way wasn't an option – not unless I wanted to rock up at one of the Cold Comfort Farms we passed en route.

It was slow going. I stopped several times, to give my eyes, jaw and buttocks a break, leaving Geoff idling in the centre of the road, because there were no other cars, traffic, or people, simply mile upon mile of grubby knitted sheep and springy lambs. Nothing else stirred and, despite sat-nav's propensity for announcing 'unknown' roads with an unseemly degree of relish, I admit I was glad of her company, even if conversation was mainly one-sided.

Only once did headlights appeared in my rear mirror, and soon two bikers barrelled past – though when I say barrelled, I mean they waited for me to pull in as near to the rockface as possible, before squeezing slowly past, then speeding onwards at twenty mph. It seemed that anyone attempting this perfect *Top Gear* road knew caution was key.

We struggled on, and eventually, rounding a sweeping bend, there it was, rising from the mist with a an almost audible *boo!* I had reached my destination. *Praise the Lord.* Honestly, I'm not 100% sure it was actually worth it. It was *just* a telephone box and, though located in magnificently bleak surroundings, I felt a tad underwhelmed.

Still, I parked up, had a fortifying onion and a glug of coffee, then climbed out into the fog, ready to ring Tim from the most remote phone in Wales. Nope, not happening. Why? Because though it really is the most remote telephone box in Wales, the operative word here is *box*; there is no bloody phone, just the cheery red shell containing a multitude of glittery stickers (?) that adorn the back wall. *Sigh.*

Oh well, on to Devil's Bridge. The descent to Tregaron was hair-raising, Geoff's brake warning light began flashing an ABS SOS, and I only fully unclenched when we pulled into a lay-by, where a food van provided a cheeseburger (though no bun for me, thanks), and a very strong cuppa to steady my nerves.

Wales' Most Remote Phone Box

And then, we got lost. Genuinely lost. And sat-nav was clueless too. In fact, she was having such trouble pronouncing Welsh road names, I reckon she'd given up and was sulking, but the fact there was a diversion didn't help proceedings. Four times I tried to follow it, and four times I failed, bouncing around side roads, signs, and sheep. Twenty-five minutes later I was back at the burger van, this time in need of directions, not protein.

Back on course, things started looking up. The cloud lifted, Devil's Bridge lay ahead, beckoning with cloven hooves, and Geoff was purring along, all warning lights dimmed, for now. And, dropping down into the wooded valley, there it was. Or rather, there it wasn't. *Bummer.*

See, the last time I'd visited was over thirty years ago, and time had wiped away the memories of steep slippery descents, and the need for healthy legs. Instead, I ordered a coffee in the fancy Hafod Hotel, sat out in their alfresco area, and listened to the rushing waters of the falls. Of course, it wasn't the same as seeing them, so I bought a postcard, and ten minutes later was back on the road. Next stop, butterfly central.

On The Magic of Life website, they give directions on how best to reach their location: 'Please plan to come via Capel Bangor, unless you like adventure'. *Hell yeah, I do!* Challenge accepted. I checked the map, switched off sat-nav and followed the A4120 to the sneaky right turn and . . . Yep, should have gone to Specsavers, and via Capel Bangor.

Geoff's wing mirrors brushed the fences on both sides, and the overhanging hedgerows frequently blocked views of the way ahead. This route was, potentially, an adventure too far.

So, I caved, switched sat-nav back on, begged her forgiveness, and with an audible sigh, she advised me to turn around and head back to the A4120. Unhelpful. I'd already gone too far to contemplate a U-turn, but more importantly, there was nowhere to exact that manoeuvre. *Sigh.*

I struggled on, and after many alarming miles, arrived at The Magic of Life Butterfly House – a giant polytunnel on the banks of the Rheidol.

Trotting in, I was cheerfully greeted by two lovely young men (Chris and Max), who did their utmost to make my visit as unforgettable, and well-informed, as possible. However, we got off to a sticky start when I couldn't figure out why I qualified for discounted admission. After confusion on both sides, we resolved the situation amicably – or as amicably as was possible, given that I was being charged the concessionary OAPs price, and at fifty-three, I *definitely* didn't want it.

Fool that I am, I insisted on paying in full, joked about grey hair being deceptive, and though it didn't do much for my self-esteem, consoled myself with the knowledge that, when you're a teenager, everyone over thirty looks ancient. Well, that's what I told myself.

Then I gently pushed through the heavy strips of plastic that masked the entrance/exit – used to ensure no morphos, malachites or common Mormons make a bid for freedom (or possibly Utah) – and carefully stepped inside. Chris had suggested leaving my fuzzy shacket in reception, but it was a cool day, and I didn't want my elderly bones catching a chill. *Lol!*

However, as I should have realised, these sustainably farmed pupae and butterflies hail from sultry climes, and their living environment was kept at a steamy 24 – 28°C, with a humidity of 60-80%. Immediately, my menopausal temperature gauge spiked, and my shacket was consigned to a nearby bench.

And then I saw the inmates. The air was filled with flapping wings, and in such an enclosed area, it took a little getting used to. It was like a scene from The Birds, though less intimidating, and certainly more colourful. But soon, I was dipping my fingers into the little jars of sweetened water, using this syrupy solution to tempt the lively Lepidoptera into landing on me. Initially they didn't, fluttering around my head and hands, before flitting unconcernedly away, to perch on someone else. *Pfft!*

But as I was taking a snap of a green glass wing (?), I felt a tickle on my hand and saw I had a visitor. It was a large, mothy specimen and, as butterflies go, was probably the least eye-catching of the lot, but it was on me and that warranted a photo. And thank goodness I bothered, because as I clicked, its wings briefly opened to reveal the glorious glowing sapphire of a blue morpho. *Wow!* It was a real beauty.

But life gives, and it takes. It remained on my hand for some time, and when cramp set in, I placed it gently on a palm tree. The wings parted, giving one final cobalt flash, and then it fell to the floor. *Shit!* I'd killed it!

I called the staff to help, but nothing could be done. Max bore it solemnly away to the chapel of rest, or whatever the bug equivalent is, and Chris explained butterflies live for only two to three weeks. For my blue morpho, this was day nineteen. *Aw.*

After that, I wasn't bothered about getting up close and personal with the others – just in case – and was happy to head back to the seasonal chill of reception.

But as I was buying the obligatory fridge magnet, Chris mentioned stick insects, and suggested I might want to '. . . have a photo taken with one?' *Hmm?* Though insect-averse, this type of bug holds no fear for me. They're basically twiglets with legs. So yeah, let's do this.

THAT is NO stick insect! EEK!

Okay, what he placed on my arm was like no stick insect I'd ever seen and thank God I'd already donned my shacket. As I urged Chris to 'Hurry up and take the sodding photo', he, with a breathtaking inability to read the room, or my facial expressions, suggested I might want to try smiling. *Grrr!*

And that was Day One of my mini-break, apart from the evening's bizarre, but strangely enjoyable, Dragon Parade – think Rio, then replace scantily-clad dancers with dragon-wielding-Birkenstock-wearing individuals. Afterwards, Sid and I agreed that alcohol was a necessity.

However long later, as Sid debated a flaming sambuca, and explained that her tolerance for liquor came from 'eighty-four years of practice' – *Drunken Lol!* – I, lightweight that I am, excused myself and trundled merrily, and vastly more unsteadily than usual, off to bed.

Overall, I'd had a splendid, if sometimes stressful day, but with a funicular railway, dolphins and a large dose of crime lined up, maybe the best was still to come? (Spoiler alert – it certainly was.)

Visit magicoflife.org for visitor information.

Visit the crime.cymru website for news about the annual Gŵyl Crime Cymru Festival.

And though I missed the signs, Devil's Bridge does have a viewing platform suitable for people with mobility issues. Details are available at devilsbridgefalls.co.uk.

A Murderously Good Weekend, Part 2

29th May 2023

Day Two dawned bright and clear, with a sun that, even when blocked by thick curtains, was still too intense for my thumping hangover. It took a lengthy shower, three strong cuppas, and several Co-codamol before I was fit to leave my room – and even then, if my stomach hadn't been grumbling for scrambled eggs and sausages, I might have gone back to bed.

But the pills soon kicked in, a tasty mound of protein set me right, and two cups of black coffee had me feeling as normal as was possible, given the amount of booze Sid and I had shipped the night before.

Actually, I saw Sid outside the breakfast room, and what a woman she is. Swathed in vibrant scarves, today she was a vision in shades of pink – rather like a bohemian Barbara Cartland. She was also pink-cheeked and surprisingly perky, and if I hadn't known better, would've thought that nary a drop of the hard stuff had ever passed her lips. Though, she was getting a tad testy waiting for a table, and I noticed a waitress surreptitiously removing the call bell from reception.

Back in my room, I dug out my tickets and got organised. My day looked like this:

10:15 – Trade Secrets and Twisted Identities

11:30 – Archives for Authors

12:30 – Writing Crime Fiction

14:45 – Historical Noir – Writing in the Past

20:30 – An Evening with Clare Mackintosh and Philip Gwynne Jones

Phew. It was a lot to fit in, but at least it didn't necessitate too early a start, and for that I was profoundly grateful. So, given that I had around forty-five minutes before Twisted Identities, I celebrated feeling partially human again by wolfing a few slices of Leerdammer, and heading to the prom for a takeout latte and some bracing sea air.

As I lounged, uncomfortably, on a bench overlooking North Beach, I was joined by Sid, and a young man she'd picked up outside Siop Inc, a pop-up bookshop that was hosting signings by some of the festival's authors.

Apparently, Sid had thought that Lawrence 'looked rather lost', so decided to take him under her, quite considerable, crimson batwings. Lawrence later told me that he'd been leaving one of the festival's bilingual events, had bumped into Sid in the doorway, had briefly chatted – which made him wonder if she was 'quite with it?' – and decided to escort her to wherever she needed to be. *Aw.*

Fortuitously, where we *all* needed to be, was the library (Lawrence to *The Effects of Crime*, and Sid to *Is Wales becoming Sexy?*), so we set off at a leisurely pace, and arrived with time to spare.

As the day unfolded, and temperatures climbed swiftly from mild to unseasonably roasting, my iPad and I both began to flag. It was like being back in the tropics of the butterfly house, so I made copious use of my emergency fans, but iPad, with an already sluggish, six-year-old processor, lagged well behind my typing speed.

And just like sat-nav, it eventually gave up the ghost, no doubt knowing that, if it withdrew labour, I'd stow it in my cool shady bag where it could enjoy a restorative reboot. Which is exactly what happened, and left me recording heaps of helpful advice using a borrowed fountain pen (that leaked), and some scrappy sheets of A4. *Eyeroll.*

Whilst all the sessions were interesting and useful, the most beneficial – speaking as someone who is currently attempting, and spectacularly failing, to plot a coherent whodunnit – was the *Writing*

Crime Fiction Workshop.

Bestselling author, Katherine Stansfield, guided us through two hours of tips on developing our sleuths, upping both the stakes, and the jeopardy, and explained how to write a twist in the tale that would, hopefully, leave readers eager for more. I left feeling buoyed up, bursting with ideas, and raring to revisit my plot.

Murder in the Past was my last session of the day, and by the time the panellists had finished debating various approaches to historically set novels, I was ready to get outside, grab some grub, and explore. And I knew exactly where to start.

See, *many* years ago, I'd done my teacher training in Aberystwyth. Back then, with no Costas, KFCs, or McDonalds, and half the number of students, it was a much quieter town than today – and the current one-way system (*almost* as stressful to negotiate as The Devil's Staircase), was probably nothing but a twinkle in a young sadist's eye.

And during those halcyon months of study, under the gothic arches of the Old College, we'd invariably catch sight of two tiny carriages, crawling up and down Constitution Hill, and vowed to visit the 'longest electric funicular cliff railway in Britain', before beginning our careers at the chalkface.

We never got round to it, distracted by lesson planning, behaviour management, and kids whose raison d'être appeared to be the moderate, low-level persecution of student teachers. So today was the day I would take that train.

The Cliff Railway and wonderful Aberystwyth views

And I'm so glad I did, because not only were the views of Aberystwyth, Cardigan Bay, and the surrounding mountains staggeringly beautiful, but I also got a little boost to my self-confidence which, after yesterday's OAP debacle, was very welcome indeed.

(There was a lovely old gent in the ticket booth who, when filling in my gift aid details and learning that I was a 'Miss', responded with 'Never! What's wrong with men today, that a gorgeous girl like you is single?' *Lol!*)

Anyway, I had a lovely sedate ride up the cliff-face, and on reaching the top, found other delights to enjoy, in addition to the vistas; one of the world's largest Camera Obscuras, a children's play area, miniature golf course, gift shop, café, and even an indoor games room, for when the weather isn't as fabulous as toda— *Uh-oh!* Spoke too soon.

As the sky rapidly darkened to a heavy solid grey, I took the next carriage back down, and my stroll to the hotel was a damp, drizzly affair. But, if you're ever in Aberystwyth, riding the cliff railway is a definite must-do.

As is catching the daily murmuration extravaganza, which occurs at dusk, mainly through the winter months. Of course, this evening's sunset would clash with listening to a couple of crime-writing behemoths, but with the feeling that last night's imbibing session was catching up with me, I decided to swerve the social.

Instead, I stopped at Istanbul Kebabs – the lowest-carb takeaway I could find – then ambled along to the pier and worked my way steadily through a large lamb doner, whilst enjoying this stunning natural phenomenon.

Though the setting sun was hidden by a bank of thick cloud, and though many of the non-resident birds had flown home to warmer climes, it was still as remarkable as I remembered. As one, the starlings swooped and spun, in a brief balletic aerial display, before dipping low beneath the pier, and roosting for the night.

Back at the hotel, I found Sid and Lawrence working their way through the cocktail menu, but since tomorrow meant an early start, I ignored their squiffy solicitations to join them in an espresso martini, settled my – somewhat excessive – bar bill, and took myself off to bed.

After a solid night's sleep, I was up with the lark, bags packed, and toiletries snaffled. Bidding farewell to Aber, I pointed Geoff south, towards home, but not before one last stop on our road-trip. We took the charming A-road through pastel-painted villages, and forty minutes later, I was parking up in the seaside town of New Quay.

Bright cottages edged the road that led down to the curving harbour, and fishing boats rocked beneath the sullen sky. The village was a veritable visual treat, and since I'd arrived well in advance of my boat trip, I popped into The Bluebell Deli, grabbed a take-out, and sat on the harbour wall, drinking in the views, and a marvellous macchiato.

Next to me sat a lovely couple, juggling – not literally – newborn twins, and their chunky boxer named Billie. Her eyes had locked on to my complimentary Lotus biscuit with an intensity I well recognised – I'm exactly the same whenever I'm near banoffee pie.

And I'd have given her the treat, but apparently, she, like me, was on a diet. *Aw Billie, I feel your pain.* Talking to her *parents*, I learned they had a caravan nearby, and had been visiting this beautiful seaside village for years, 'because it's much quieter than other places, and has a really chilled vibe', which, based on my thirty minutes experience thus far, I would certainly second.

And then it was time to climb aboard. Giving Billie a final pat, I walked the length of the harbour to where Captain Andy was waiting. He was a slightly gruff chap, but I guess crusty seadogs always have a bit of bark, and when the tour got going, he loosened up and became an animated fount of knowledge on everything nautical.

Once we were all present and correct, he launched into a safety lecture, emphasised *many* times that dolphin spotting was a 'hit-or-miss affair', then retreated to the wheelhouse, and we were away.

I'd booked this trip because I've actually never seen a dolphin in real-life, but ever since I was a kid, and saw a film called *Day of the Dolphin,* I've loved those shiny, fat-nosed mammals. I don't know if, in reality, they can be taught rudimentary language, but in the film they could, and my seven-year-old self wept buckets at the end when Fa (the star dolphin), was forced to bid goodbye to his human dad (George C. Scott), with a sorrowful, 'Fa love Pa'. *Sob!*

Obviously, I wasn't expecting to converse with any that might pop up today, but given that the stunning coastline of Cardigan Bay boasts the largest population of bottle-nosed dolphins in Europe, at around two hundred and eighty, I was confident we'd see at least one, despite Andy's pessimistic heads-up.

As we followed a figure of eight course around the coast, Andy taught us all about the flora and fauna, gave facts about the passing kittiwakes, razorbills, and guillemots, and waxed lyrical about the local whelk factory which clung to the side of a cliff, and frankly looked like one gentle splash would see it consigned to Davy Jones' Locker.

But he was doing a sterling job, attempting to hold our interest when he clearly knew that everyone there only had eyes for the sea, and those, currently imperceptible, mini-whales. But I did learn a lot.

At over four metres, bottle-nose males are bigger here than in any other location worldwide, mainly due to the excellent feeding conditions. Like me, they're not fussy eaters, going for anything that they can swallow, but unlike me, they don't get fat, just big, which helps keep their bodies insulated. (Yeah, that's my excuse for over-indulgence too.)

Lone dolphins, adolescents, and both bachelor and maternity pods all favour Cardigan Bay, because it's shallow, and that offers them protection from the Atlantic swell. But the sweetest fact I learned was that, because baby dolphins don't understand that they need to come up for air, their mums have to push them to the surface until they learn how to breathe. So, this sheltered spot was the equivalent of a dolphin Early Learning Centre. *Bless.*

Andy's informative lectures were occasionally interrupted by someone shouting an excitable 'Dolphin!' and we'd all crane to follow the pointing fingers – but disappointingly these *always* turned out to be false alarms, and were either cormorants, oyster catchers, or in the case of my potential sighting, a buoy. *Oops.*

Heading back to shore, I think we were all feeling a little deflated. Yes, it had been a fascinating trip, but the stars of the show had chosen not to appear. Seemed like this wasn't going to be the climax to my trip that I'd been hoping for. *Sigh.*

That is, until Andy suddenly hollered 'Dolphin!' and there, cutting through the water, was a silvered adolescent, who dived, then surfaced twice more, before disappearing into the depths. And then another came scooting through the waves, smiling that dolphin smile, and we all rushed to record these momentous seconds.

(My visual mementos of Flipper 1 and 2 weren't great, and I'm clearly no cinematographer, but in my defence, if the people port side had sat down, I might have got better footage. *Pfft!*)

Back ashore, I dropped change into a lifeboat bucket, grabbed another takeout, and because the clouds had cleared to reveal scorching sunshine, copped a squat in the terrace gardens that overlook the waterfront and beach. Here, there was a memorial fence of sorts, festooned with padlocks, their heartfelt messages written in Sharpie, or engraved. And sitting there, watching as a small pod of dolphins began frolicking in the bay below, I couldn't think of a nicer spot to sit and reminisce.

Beautiful New Quay

So, I've fallen in love with mid Wales, and New Quay in particular. I'd live here in a breath; in fact, I was scanning Rightmove before I'd even sipped my cortado. But some quick mental calculations, and a frank assessment of our (lack of) assets, mean that this was another pipe dream to add to a growing list. *Sigh.*

But it's no wonder Dylan Thomas liked the place – he used some of the buildings, pubs, and people, as inspiration for *Under Milk Wood* – though these days, it deffo doesn't suit his humorous Llareggub moniker. Now, with a bustling community, and buzzing tourist trade, this place is a world away from the New Quay Thomas would have known. Mind, that 'fishingboat bobbing sea' remains the same – and my trip on it was truly the most tremendous end to a wonderful weekend.

SeaMor Dolphin watching trips are bookable at the harbour offices, or online. And Aberystwyth Cliff Railway info can be found online too.

Err on the G String

11th June 2023

It's been almost six months since I began the affair, and to say that Tim is cheesed off with the strident noises issuing from our bedroom (when Trev and I are going at it full throttle), is an understatement.

Of course, I'm not cheating on Tim, and we haven't had a mid-life crisis and suddenly decided to become a throuple – though if we happened upon a professional dog-trainer, who enjoys housework, can knock up a meal in minutes, and has an NVQ in garden design, I think we'd seriously consider it.

But there's no denying I have developed an unexpected, all-consuming passion for Trevor, my twenty-six-inch, mahogany beau, who's blessed with smooth good looks, a rich vibrant voice and, to me, is the finest tenor ukulele in all the land.

Yep, he has been the cause of a few minor disagreements on the domestic front, but chiefly they're due to my lack of musical ability, coupled with a keen determination to practice every day. Not that Tim wasn't initially encouraging of my new hobby, and strict melodic regime, but after he complained that I'd been 'twanging Take Me Home, Country Roads for bloody hours, and it's doing my head in', his interest waned. *Lol!*

(But he did have a point. So, I have subsequently varied my repertoire – though I couldn't help but be thrilled that he'd *finally* recognised the song I'd been grappling with for eight days. Was this progress? Too right it was.)

But while I *am*, slowly, improving, two obstacles still remain, which have the very real potential to hinder my playing prowess, and it's strange because they're rarely ever mentioned.

Despite numerous internet searches – with some quite eye-watering results – it seems that I'm the only woman who struggles with the logistics involved in making sweet, sweet music, whilst cushioning a small stringed instrument against a pair of aging, flabby knockers.

I've previously mentioned that during lockdown, I revelled in consigning my upper-topper-flopper-stoppers to the back of the wardrobe, and instead embraced the unfettered joy of allowing my ladies to just chillax and hang loose. And I've never looked back.

Naturally, there have been occasions over the last couple of years – four birthday dos, numerous funerals, W.I. Meetings – where I've had to dig one out and, resentfully, strap myself in. And this was especially necessary during the six-week puppy training course, which involved a lot of bending, because I didn't fancy chancing my baps against a roomful of rollicking pups who had reached the ball-obsessed stage of development.

But mostly, my boobs have been allowed to run wild, tumbling downhill until, depending on my position, they'll either settle comfortably under each armpit, or come to rest somewhere a smidge north of my waist.

However, in my experience, it seems that free-range breasts are incompatible with ukulele musical proficiency. My right one impacts upon my strumming arm, the left hinders my ability to reach higher frets, and attempting the Fmajor7 requires concentration so great, I can't simultaneously juggle either of my nomadic norks.

And once, whilst playing with wild abandon (think Animal from The Muppet Show, if he swapped drums for a uke), a stray nipple encroached on the G string, which resulted in mild friction burns. It was nothing a spot of Germolene couldn't handle, but the reason I'm mentioning these mammary mishaps is because, if I wanted my music-making odyssey to continue, it was either submit to the bra, or take up a less intimate instrument, like a kazoo, or finger cymbals.

Thus, it's an indication of my love for Trevor, that I have, albeit reluctantly, fallen back into the reinforced, restrictive cups of an M&S Flexifit™ Wired Minimiser. *Sigh.*

But it's a good job I have, because it would be rather unseemly, not to mention distracting, playing a gig, only for my melons to romp around with every rigorous chord change. And yeah, you read that right – I am actually going on my first ever gig with the Swansea Ukulele Club (SUC) and will be playing in front of *real* people. *Gulp!*

I mean, obviously I've played for people before, but only my completely biased family, who, like the Flexifit™, are super supportive of my musical endeavours, and have schooled themselves to rarely wince. (I'm excluding Tim though, because he's a man of forthright opinions, gives candid feedback, and can't master the slight eye twitch, which coincides with every bum note and missed chord. *Eyeroll.*)

So, first gig, and I was 90% nervous, 10% excited, and knowing my playing needed *a lot* of work, I booked in for some emergency uke lessons at the Music Factory in Llanelli. And that's where I found Aled.

I could immediately tell I was in expert hands. He was one cool dude, sported a wide-brimmed Fedora, and had a beard that, if it wasn't a prime example of *the hipster*, I don't know what would be. The walls were a gallery of guitars, a large screen displayed menacing musical notation, and there were two green velvet sofas which, to normal people, probably looked comfortably sumptuous, but to my eyes, was an upholstered trauma waiting to happen.

(I have a thing about velvet, in that I abhor it. Maybe this stems from my Sidonglobophobia – my number one bête noire is cotton wool, the balls in particular. But both textures set my teeth on edge, and even worse are the penetrating squeaks they emit when they're touched, squeezed, or stroked. *Ick!*)

Sadly, there was nowhere else to sit, so I perched precariously on the edge of the couch, crossed my arms to avoid tactile entanglements (*Shudder!* Note to self: long sleeves next time) and prepared for my first official ukulele lesson.

Actually, I'd initially tried another chap, but that lesson had mainly consisted of me sitting in silence while he played Trevor, and was a demonstration of the skills I could aspire to achieve – after twenty or so years of practise, and a financial investment on a par with the price of a small semi in Mumbles. *Humph.* Somewhat deflated, I sloped off, and started my search for another tutor who could possibly turn my ham-fisted playing into something more melodic – and do it a bit quicker.

So, though Aled embodied the term 'musician' and, on paper, was hugely talented, did that indicate he could actually teach? And by that, I mean, could he teach someone as talentless as me?

Amazingly, he could. He turned out to be blinking brilliant. In the few weeks I've been going, we've worked on chords, strum patterns, tempos, and he's managed to locate my sense of rhythm, which I honestly thought I'd lost long ago.

Plus, he's got me to release my stranglehold on Trevor's neck and start playing with a 'more relaxed hand'. This has led to clearer chords, a freer movement on the fretboard, and I don't get those painful grooves on my fingertips anymore, or cramp. *Result!*

Imbued with marginally more confidence, the next step in my gig-preparedness was shopping. SUC's unofficial dress code seemed to be Hawaiian shirts or fancy florals, both of which bring a splash of sunshine to any venue. And whilst my favoured palette is mainly uninspiring shades of blue, this was for a good cause, and I wanted to look the part.

I picked up a pair of rainbow-striped daps, a pink, smocky number in a cool cotton, and a small-but-mighty fan; understandably, nursing homes run hot, as do I, so guarding against potential flushes was essential. I bought a microphone stand, with iPad attachment (for my music and lyrics), and a Kinsman Clamp Hangar for Trev to chillax in.

Though most of our group stand up when performing, I needed to explore seating options, and this triggered a frantic spiral of buying and trying, before one of our club members gave me a medium height, low-backed stool which was lightweight and pretty comfortable. Right, I was ready to rock'n'roll. *Double gulp!*

22nd May, Grovesend, Swansca. 3:30pm start, 1 hour set. I was there by two-fifteen, my phobia of tardiness forcing me to arrive at the care home stupidly early. Still, it gave me time to sit in Geoff, and quietly panic. What if I forgot my chords? What if I broke a string? And, heaven forbid, what if I played a loudly discordant note at the exact time the rest of the band fell silent?

But my major concern was how I'd react in front of an audience, because for no good reason, I've recently begun suffering from stage-fright – and that I first discovered this during two agonising minutes at the mike, midway through a poetry slam, still causes cold sweats. And the symptoms are extreme – my voice ricochets through a panoply of pitch, and I experience full-body tremors that would rate a strong 6.9 on the Richter Scale. If that happened today, forgetting chords would be the least of my worries.

It was a scorching afternoon, so staff had taken the residents outside, and we were going to perform *al fresco*. Great news, because the breeze would help keep my hormonal fever spikes at bay, but it did mean I had to keep a wary eye on my floaty top. Even though my bazookas were safely locked and loaded, who knows what impact a flash of a nude balconette might have on an OAP?

After setting up mikes, cables, keyboards, and other unidentifiable techie stuff, at last we were good to go. Leading on vocals were Dawn (glorious in a rockabilly dress and red sneakers), Lynsey (pretty in polka dots), and Phill (peerless in a confection of palm trees). John (sharp in waistcoat and kepi hat), was revving up his electric guitar, Ian was expertly tickling his ivories, and Chris, Teresa, Josie, and Maggie (all veteran giggers), provided harmonious backing. Which left me, Vicki, and Laura – relative newbies and gig virgins – lurking at the back.

I had a gulp of Um Bongo – my mouth was so dry, I had to physically peel my lips away from my teeth – and took some deep breaths, praying I could face the onlookers with a smile, and a voice steady enough to carry a tune. Then John counted us in with, 'And a one, two, three, four', and away we went. And it was absolutely marvellous.

There was energetic bopping from the more mobile residents, animated applause and occasional whooping, and the exhilarating atmosphere, combined with playing as part of a group, meant I felt nary a tremble as I smiled, sang, and strummed my heart out.

We brought the house down, quite literally, when a freak gust of wind during 'Great Balls of Fire', caused one of the hefty sun umbrellas to lift off and head for the bright lights of Gorseinon. It took out a glass-topped patio table, and a small planter, before landing on a couple of the, thankfully, sturdier residents.

But even as disaster played out before us, we played on, a bit like the band on the Titanic, and thus our 'Johnny B. Goode' finale was punctuated by the rapid removal of broken glass, and the administration of some mild first aid. But still, we got that nursing home rocking, big style.

Everyone at SUC had said that, once I'd taken the plunge, I'd want to do more, and boy, they weren't wrong. In fact, I've played another two since – both of which were blooming epic – and I'm merrily filling in my calendar with as many as possible.

However, I should confess that my desire to gig didn't *wholly* spring from a place of altruism and philanthropy. In truth, I'd already been searching for more opportunities for synchronised strumming, because those few hours on a Tuesday evening with SUC aren't enough.

Me with the other gig-virgins, Vic & Laura

But last Wednesday, we played at a local dementia support café, and it was a turning point for me. There were many highlights, much boogeying, enthusiastic audience participation, and delight on some faces (alright, mainly mine), when we played 'Take Me Home, Country Roads'.

But afterwards, when I'd packed up all my gear and was heading out to the car, an elderly lady unsteadily approached me, took my hand, and said, 'Thank you, you were wonderful'. (*Sniff. I'm not crying! Damn that grass pollen.*)

Okay, so she *probably* meant 'you' plural, and I had no right *at all* to start channelling Beyoncé. But as well as feeling like a rock star, it made me realise that, in a tiny way, I had been *instrumental* (*teehee*) in brightening someone's day, and that felt fantastic, and totally worth the restrictions imposed by my M&S *mammo*-flague.

So, it matters not a jot where my initial motivation came from. No, what matters is getting out there, having a cracking time with my uke pals, and sharing joyous music with anyone who cares to listen – and to echo the great Willie Nelson, when it comes to gigging, I 'can't wait to get on the road again'.

There are several Forget-Me-Not Dementia Cafés in Swansea and the surrounding areas. Find out more information by visiting their website.

Support is also available on the Dementia Friendly Swansea website which gives details of clubs, activities, and services available.

And Swansea Ukulele Club meet every Tuesday evening from 7:15pm at Dunvant Rugby Club. All uke players are welcome, from absolute beginners upwards. Visit their Facebook page for details.

At Music Factory, Llanelli, Aled is one of the talented teachers, and between them, they can pretty much teach any instrument you fancy – possibly barring the bagpipes. So, if you're looking to learn or improve, visit musicfactory.wales or find them on Facebook.

On the Bright Side

2nd July 2023

It's been some time since I've explored the pagan side of life, so with June's Solstice on the horizon, I'd decided to attend a *Celebration of Light*. And that's why I was sitting on an arse-numbing upright, in a chintzy community hall, surrounded by sixteen women, a lone man, a box of bodhráns, and a large wooden gorilla, adorned with floral wreath.

The walls were plastered with an array of spiritual iconography, navigating a haphazard pilgrimage through Christianity, Hinduism, Buddhism, Paganism, Wiccan, and any others you fancied throwing in the mix.

A hefty oak table held dragons, crystals, chalice water, corn dollies (*Shudder!* Stephen King has a *lot* to answer for), and what I think might have been a Knight's Templar ashtray. The room was definitely a visual feast, but the kind liable to cause heartburn, if not acid reflux.

And that's not even taking the *altar* into account – a frothy confection that resembled the aftermath of a toddler's sleepover, if you held it in Hobbycraft, and served alcopops. The flowers looked nice though, if slightly limp.

But back to the solstice, and if ever a day heralded the official start of summer, this was it. At 7pm it was still sweltering, so I bagged a spot near an open window, which luckily, offered a gentle breath of blessed breeze, and slightly dispersed the heavy scents of excessive incense. (I also got an occasional hit of Old Spice from Rupe, the music guy, which though retro, was a distinctly better olfactory experience than patchouli, sandalwood, and vanilla. *Ugh*.)

However, unluckily, it also meant that the M4 (two-hundred-yards away, as the crow flies), made its presence continually felt, with the relentless rumble of tyres on hot tarmac, or zealous horn action, frequently disrupting the sacred vibes. As far as locations for communing with nature went, I knew I should have gone to sodding Stonehenge.

But that would have necessitated camping, coping with a crowd of around eight thousand people, and at least two tanks of petrol. So, I'd binned the most revered solstice site in the UK, in favour of a cheap, twenty-minute hop, arriving and ready to get my pagan groove on . . . in Port Talbot. Yeah, I know it seems like an odd location, but I was up for giving it a go. And actually, the view of the steelworks from the car park, was really quite a sight.

I'd booked through Eventbrite, where I was sucked in by the reference to cake, fire, and the possibility of some (seated) ecstatic dancing:

'The Wheel turns, and we enter a time of energy and light. We reflect on our purposes and motivations as we journey from spring, and into the summer element of fire. So, find your passion, and your heart-felt path, and join Geri and Rupe for meditation, sacred fire, drum circle, music-making, free dance, and singing. (Food to share most welcome.)'

Sounded fab, eh? Undoubtedly, I needed help locating my 'passion', which has been AWOL for at least ten years, and though I was clueless about where my 'heart-felt path' might lead, I definitely wanted an opportunity to find out. So, I bought two tickets (£10 each), and started prepping.

Initially, my mate Gaynor was coming too, as she wanted to experience a drum circle. But last-minute baby-sitting duties meant she had to bow out, so Cath stepped into the breach, eager to take her first tentative steps along a pagan pathway.

Next, we organised supplies. To be honest, 'food to share' was a little woolly. Should we take crisps and dips, or a couple of sandwich platters? Cath suggested something to cook, but we were going to a solstice ceremony, not a bloody BBQ, and I didn't think Geri would approve of us contaminating her sacred fire with 'chicken kebabs, burgers, or marshmallows'.

I did a bit of research, and because I wasn't invested enough to attempt brewing 'Midsummer Mead', or baking a 'Sunshine Loaf', I popped to Nisa and bought a large bag of Onion Rings, and a box of Mr Kipling's Lemon Slices. Yes, it was the easy option, but in my defence, I did consider the sunshiny theme, and deliberately picked yellow foodstuffs.

But the day before our adventure, Cath cancelled too, a virus laying her low. *Bummer!* As a *very* last resort, I asked Tim if he'd come along, but as you can probably guess, his response was negative, and unprintable.

Solstice Provisions

So, it was me, Geoff, and Trevor (my uke, 'cause if there's going to be music, we're there for it), who revved off to the sunlit lowlands of Port Talbot, for an evening of hotly anticipated, fiery fun.

After a series of wrong turns, we finally pulled up to a stone farmhouse, flanked by a couple of large barns, and a lake filled with heritage fowl. It was a tranquil spot, or would have been, if you were hermetically sealed inside a triple-glazed box, with added acoustic caulk. But I parked, left Trevor belted in the passenger seat (for now) and headed off to join the throng.

It was immediately clear that my double denim getup wasn't fit for purpose. There were *lots* of florals on display – clothing, cranium-crowning circlets of sunflowers and gyp, and even a couple of floor-length cloaks. And I've got to say, they all looked brilliant. Bizarre, bonkers, but brilliant.

And they were so welcoming too. Many of them were regular attendees at Geri's 'moots', and while we waited, I learned *a lot* about tonight's festivities from a delightful pagan named Gwen. A free spirit, with silver hair, purple cloak, fishnets, and Doc Martens, she talked me through some of the customs and beliefs that were popular around *Lithia*, the pagan name for this solstice.

Symbolic of fertility, abundance, and prosperity, and tied closely to bountiful harvests, people of pagan Europe would light fires, often accompanied by druidic rituals. Customs included bonfire-jumping, with the highest believed to predict the height of the year's coming crop. Large wooden wheels were often set alight, before being rolled down a hill and into the nearest body of water. It was something to do with 'balancing the elements', and whilst *that* would be an epic spectacle, I didn't think the rare-breed ducks would be overly impressed.

When our hosts appeared, we were ushered into the 'sacred space', and everyone, bar me, unrolled yoga mats and made themselves comfy. I chose a chair because, yes, it was by the open window, but also, if I'd descended to floor level, I'd still be down there come the winter solstice.

And then Geri uttered those hellish words, the bane of team building exercises the world over – 'Let's introduce ourselves to the group and give an interesting fact about yourself'. *Uh-oh*. But it soon became clear that I wasn't alone in dreading this sort of thing because, by the time my turn came around, names were being quietly mumbled, and interesting facts were wholly inaudible. *Phew*.

Next came meditation, but the fact that Rupe was scrupulously polishing metal bowls made me think he had a part to play, and I was right. Seriously, if I'd known in advance, I wouldn't have come, because I've experienced a sound/gong bath once before, and it was the polar opposite of relaxing – the rattle of sharp sounding plinky-plonky seashells still haunt my dreams. But maybe Rupe was the fella who could turn my frown upside down. So, I closed my eyes, and embraced it.

That this was *guided* meditation had also come as a surprise, and not a welcome one. See, I've got Aphantasia, which means that I can't picture images in my head, at all.

(Side note: It was actually Lizzie who, unofficially, diagnosed this after seeing a test on Twitter. She asked me to imagine an apple, I did, and when I pointed to image 5 = a dark square with no discernible apple, she was amazed, and so was I. That people can actually *see* pictures in their heads was mind-blowing for me, because all that happens when I close my eyes is blackness.)

Anyway, the reason I'm mentioning this is because Geri was going to 'unleash our imaginations by telling a story'. Rupe would accompany on gongs (*humph!*), and we were going to take a 'visual stroll through a fairy-tale forest'.

And it was dreadful. Obviously, I *saw* nothing, which left the sound of the gongs as my only focus – and given that our woodland walk was meant to be magical, with 'trickling streams and gently swaying branches', the sounds issuing from Rupe's side of the hall were menacing, panic-inducing, and made my fillings ache.

If I could have done so without disturbing the others – who were spread eagled, with beatific smiles on their faces – I would have snuck away. But later, when I listened to the ladies wax lyrical about their *journeys*, and how breathtaking it had been, I realised that it was only me who'd loathed it, and I admit to feeling slightly envious of their spiritual sojourns.

The next activity was the drum circle, and *this* I was looking forward to it – 'Let there Be Drums' by Sandy Nelson is a favourite toe-tapper of mine. Rupe handed out dhols, Idakkas, and bongos – I got a small bodhrán – and we trooped outside to get our first glimpse of the solstice bonfire, which was massive . . .

. . . in terms of disappointment. If you'd stuck a metal grill on the top, you could have *maybe* cooked a couple of rib-eyes and a string of chipolatas, but it would have been a squeeze. We were all rather underwhelmed, but when Geri launched into a song about oak trees (which had a Native-American-meets-Outkast feel), with every 'Haaaaay Ya', we swallowed our disappointment, hammered hell out of our instruments, and focused on the tiny flames.

It wasn't great. Some of us were attempting to thump with the beat, some were striking random blows, and some gave up after the first verse. And the noise – because it wasn't music in *any* sense of the word – left many of us looking rather more pained than empowered. Plus, my puny biceps were killing me.

Geri clocked it, brought the song to a hasty end, and gave us a mini-lecture about things we could do to attract luck, and dispel negativity, on this auspicious day. Now, *this* was more like it. Bring on the good fortune, because God/Goddess knows, I could certainly do with some.

Geri's frosted tisty-tosty

She handed round 'magic' pine cones, which were clearly Christmas leftovers – their ersatz iciness was a dead giveaway. (And that she didn't call them *tisty-tostys* earned her a black mark in my book!) She explained that they were 'spiritual, seed-bearing organs, which represent enlightenment and can banish bad energies'.

So, while Rupe and Geri worked themselves up into a rhythmic frenzy, us ladies considered what we wanted to manifest, and what we wanted to banish. I asked the sun for mastery over Trevor, control over our two pups, and some much-needed self-confidence, while ridding my life of any bad shit. I realise it was a lot to expect, but it was worth a shot.

One by one, we solemnly placed our tisty-tostys in the fire, and poked them vigorously with sticks of mugwort, because according to Geri, today was also 'Mugwort Day', though she didn't explain the significance. But we ran with it anyway.

And once everyone's cone had burned, it was time for audience participation, where we could recite poetry or sing songs, written for the occasion. *Eek!* Was this Trevor's moment to shine? No, it wasn't. Geri didn't feel that playing 'Take Me Home, Country Roads' – the only song whose chords I know off by heart – was 'in keeping with the sacred ethos'. *Sniff.*

Thus, my only nod to involvement was listening, with an encouraging smile, as I applauded every contribution. And so it went on, and on, and on – until it was rudely (and fortuitously), interrupted by a speedy sheepdog who cavorted into our circle, woofing at all and sundry, but especially those still drumming. He (Scout) belonged to the farmer, and I watched him caper about, before he darted around the unkempt privet, back from whence he'd come. *Hmm?*

As Geri headed inside to make tea, and the rest of the group stood rapt by Rupe's tympanic talents, I activated ninja mode. I casually meandered across the patio, ostensibly admiring the herbaceous borders, and on reaching the hedge (aka Vanishing Point), rounded the corner and trotted away as fast as my limpy legs could carry me.

Then Geoff burned rubber up the gravel drive, shot through the open gateway, and headed west, leaving nothing but the squeal of tyres, and a cloud of dust, in our wake. *Liberty! Freedom! Woohoo!*

So no, that particular event hadn't been my cup of camomile. During the evening, I'd felt nothing, spiritual or otherwise, apart from increasing irritation, and an intensifying desire to do a runner, asap.

But that's why I mentioned my blind mind's eye, because I reckon it was my stupid, empty aphantasic head that was at the root my apathetic response. Everyone else seemed to have an absolute ball, so if you're toying with trying something like this, I'd really urge you to give it a go.

But it wasn't all bad. On the way home, as the sun touched the distant horizon, I pulled off the M4, found an elevated vantage point, and snapped a few pics. Because, it might not be part of the *natural world*, but seeing the steelworks bathed in the fading rays of the solstice sun, was 100% worth the journey.

N.B. When I was writing up this article, I messaged my friendly neighbourhood Chaos Witch, to find out a bit about mugwort. It's classed as a 'dream herb' because it has *a lot* of beneficial uses. And solstice day is recommended for picking most herbs, because they are more 'charged' due to extra sunshine.

But she also happened to mention that the most propitious time for affirming manifestations would be at sunrise on the 21st, not sunset.

Yeah, looks way better in colour.

Sigh. Deffo should have gone to Stonehenge.

Eventbrite has hundreds of 'alternative', and unusual, events. Local moots can be found on Facebook, or by visiting the Pagan Federation online for more information.

Finding Judas at the Ministry of Minchin

24th September 2023

So, this summer, my dangerous living programme of fun, fear, and frolics, screeched to a shuddering halt, along with my PhD progress, and any capacity for creativity. My head was overloaded, I felt rough as buggery, and I barely stepped outside the house – no, not even to attend Uke Club! Instead, I skulked around in a dressing gown and fluffy mules, like a less sociable Eleanor Rigby, wholly submerged in the dark waters of a big fat blue funk.

It started with cold sores – truly the Devil's work – and though age has lessened their aesthetic impact, blisters up both nostrils, with a hefty propagation across my philtrum, wasn't a great look. Plus the associated nerve pain's a bitch. Add in a stomach bug, toothache, and screaming sciatica, and I hope you'll appreciate why I maintained article silence for a few weeks.

Tim reckons stress was at the root of it all, and he was probably right. House renovations were causing metaphorical, and literal, headaches, with the work still grumbling on, months after we should've been the proud owners of a shiny new bathroom, and a flat roof that could successfully withstand anything our wonderful weather chucks at it.

We're also still sorting out Mum's deathbed demands, re: desirable ash-scattering locations. Most of her is still sitting in her Moët bottle on the hearth, and whenever I pass by, I just know she's glaring accusingly through the green glass, and muttering, 'Get your arse in gear, book that ferry to Ireland, a weekend in Padstow, and don't forget about the Ardèche Gorge'. *Sigh.*

Then, to *cap* it all, I had to fork out £595 for a new crown. *WTAF?* For that price you might well assume I'd procured something on a par with Camilla's coronation headwear. But no, merely one bog-standard, fake tooth, and that didn't even include the £157 I paid to join the dental practice for one year, OR the £60 to see the hygienist. *Grr!*

Anyway, suffice it to say, for the last few months, navigating *normal* life has been more than dangerous enough. However, there were some highlights, the most notable of which was finding Jesus, or more accurately Judas, on YouTube.

I'm not religious. I only ever skimmed my junior Bible – it had great pictures, especially the ones of a flaxen-haired Jesus prepping a fish supper for 5,000 covers – but I can still recall when the Gideon Brigade came into school, distributing their burgundy books with an eager enthusiasm that was compelling to a swarm of suggestible ten-year-olds. That day, my pals and I became extremely virtuous, spending lunchtime pretending to read the good book and thinking godly thoughts. It didn't last; twenty-four-hours later we'd reverted to our usual, unsaintly selves, much to the disappointment of our teachers.

And even though I've previously written that I'm always up for a wedding, or funeral – both great opportunities to dust off the old pipes and belt out a few hymns – I've never discovered anything, in any church, chapel or otherwise *sacred* space, that has made me want to become a regular. Frankly, religion of whatever persuasion, seems to cause nothing but trouble, and thus is best avoided.

My family were eclectic when it came to their beliefs. One set of grandparents were strict chapel, and on those few occasions when I accompanied them, found the fanatical fire and brimstone alarming. Even though it was delivered in deafening Welsh, I didn't need to understand the language to know that the minister, and *his* God, were certainly not the forgiving types.

My other grandparents were Church of Wales, and I liked that vicar, who was comfortably in his eighties, rosy-cheeked, with a halo of white hair and a shy smile. But his oratory skills in the pulpit – reading verbatim in a voice that barely carried past the first two pews – didn't set the congregation alight. In fact, the acoustics frequently picked up hissed whispers, and the occasional 'Ow', indicating that someone had dozed off and received a sharp poke in the ribs from their mortified spouse.

Dad fancied the idea of reincarnation, preferring to 'keep busy' rather than kicking his heels in either Heaven or Hell for an eternity, and Mum would pop to our local for the odd harvest festival or Christmas service, but she didn't seem bothered about weekly attendance. And me? I guess pragmatic-atheist-with-shades-of-optimistic-agnosticism probably fits the bill.

So no, I don't buy into the big beardy in the sky, but I'd actually quite like to believe. It would make the bummer of dying so much more palatable if I *honestly* thought I'd be greeted with a pearlescent balloon arch, unlimited wine (*obvs*), and a throng of family, friends, and best of all, pets. How splendid to have a knees-up and paint the town – or clouds – red. (*Ooh.* Maybe that's what sunsets are – welcoming parties for new admittees?) But, after some consideration, even if I *am* judged virtuous enough to make it up the stairway to Heaven, that, in itself, might cause problems.

See, last year, in one of the trippiest experiences of my life, I spent an unforgettable hour, Vaseline-smeared, sweating and starkers, bobbing about in a sensory deprivation tank. Memorable for *many* reasons – not least being the total absence of pain for the first time since 2015 – during those sixty minutes, my consciousness dipped in and out, before finally settling into a spiral of increasingly bizarre hypotheticals. As an aide-memoire:

If I had sex with a car, which would be the tenderest lover? An Austin-Healey 'Frogeye' Sprite. He's 100% the man for the job.

Would Tim stay with me if I morphed into a dog, but could still talk? Happily, yes, but only if I was a Golden Retriever, and definitely *couldn't* talk! (*Eyeroll*)

Can you sin in Heaven?

And it's this last one that bothered me most, because if, as you'd expect, there's a pious party-line up there that you probably have to toe, I'd be in trouble. Tim (Catholic – lapsed) thinks it's all bollocks, but hypothetically, says he'd hate to be plonked for perpetuity in a place where you can't smoke, gamble, or have no-strings-attached sex. And that's the key issue I have with the idea of an angelic afterlife, because though I'm not majorly depraved, I'd definitely want to sate some minor lustful, gluttonous, and slothful tendencies.

I mean, what if I ran into Alan Rickman, togged up in his *Sense and Sensibility* military garb (*swoon*), and fancied a quickie? Would that be allowed, or is marriage mandatory before indulging in the sins of the flesh? (Saying that, if there happened to be a celestial Ann Sommers – unlikely I know but go with it – I'd probably pick up a cherubic rampant rabbit, and matrimony be damned.)

I'd also need regular Hawaiian hedonism (extra pineapple, extra cheese, added anchovies – I'm hoping incorporeal weight gain isn't a thing), along with extended sessions of cider-induced indolence, a weekly delivery of Golden Virginia, and some quality iPad time. The point being, if you *can't* indulge your vices up there, I'd be picking the locks on those pearly gates, and hot footing it south asap, where such behaviour might not only be tolerated, but I suspect, actively encouraged.

Anyway, back to YouTube and the audiovisual highlight of my two months of misery. Now, I love a good musical, and there's no doubt that Andrew Lloyd Webber and Tim Rice are one heck of a team, but this one had completely passed me by. The 1973 film version pops up on telly occasionally, mainly at Easter, but I'd usually swerve it, settling down to watch something less secular, and much less psychedelic, like *Death on the Nile*, or *Ben-Hur*.

But *this* version, filmed during the 2012 live arena tour, showcased a grittier, contemporary production which, if you swapped out Jesus (a brooding Ben Forster who's tastier than the massive French Fancy of my dreams), for Jeremy Corbyn, would have proved terrifyingly prescient, especially viewing the crucifixion scene through allegorically-tinted specs.

And it was when Tim Minchin (Judas) sang the opening number – with a voice that would surely make the rock opera gods exhale in orgasmic delight – his kohl-rimmed eyes brimming with tears of exasperation and anguish – that I was hooked. Add in Sporty Spice as the plucky, lovesick Mary Magdalene, and the holy trinity of *Jesus Christ Superstar*(s) was complete.

That weekend, I obsessively played, and replayed it, watching the narrative unfold from this unusual perspective – despite its title, this is Judas' story. And whilst all the cast shone, Minchin was phenomenal. His every scene was mesmerising, filled with tortured emotion and incredible rapid-fire vocals. But when he finally realised *exactly* what his actions had triggered, and how he'd been 'Damned for All Time'? Well, he certainly left his heart and soul out on that stage for all to see.

His scenes with Jesus were testosterone-fuelled voice-offs, and in a finale rammed with corseted, frilly-knickered angels, frenzied flashbulbs, and a bemused and beaten Jesus, Minchin was magnificently mental, blowing the press a traitorous kiss, before going all out on a tambourine. Utterly bonkers, but abso-bloody-lutely brilliant.

Soon *my* Tim was begging me to either 'turn it down or turn it off, 'because I can't take any more of that bloody caterwauling'. *Lol!* I dug out some old headphones because he did have a point. But things didn't end there.

Along with a major ROMI (Rapid Onset Minchin Infatuation – seriously, that guy's eyes are something else. *Longing sigh*), I was also filled with a hitherto unsuspected thirst for theological knowledge. But it was

And even more gorgeous in colour – swoon!

Judas who'd bewitched me. Was he as treacherous as the good book painted him, or merely a disposable pawn in God's ineffable – and it has to be said, rather unreasonable – plan? I needed answers, and in the absence of a family bible, I visited the wellspring of all wisdom – Wikipedia.

I read *a lot* of bible passages, studied *many* scholarly interpretations, and ended up swirling down a frightening number of holy wormholes (Batman!). I dived into religious Twitter – no matter what Elon says, I'll never warm to X – where the gospels were rich fodder for numerous 'experts' to engage in highfaluting arguments, and where one of them was helpful enough to direct me to 'BBC Bitesize, which has the basics explained in a way *even you'll* understand'. *Hmpf. Rude!*

Anyway, it was noticeable that even in Christian doctrine, the versions of events, and Judas' death, differed significantly, and it seemed that reaching any definitive conclusions was as likely as me turning a two-litre bottle of Evian into a fruity little Merlot. But it was fascinating all the same, though not convincing enough for a heathen like me, who is clearly missing that *je ne sais quoi* which true believers of any denomination have – faith.

I'll admit that I'm a bit envious (*Oops*, another deadly sin), of those people who do have it; those who require no evidence or proof, but nurture an unshakeable certainty regarding the existence of the Big Man/Woman/Man-lion/Bull etc. But sadly, since I'd need some tangible substantiation before committing, that'll never be me.

Mind, Dad once told me about a medical experiment in which a doctor placed dying patients on a weighing scale – *WTH?* Guess medical ethics weren't a thing back then – and was ultimately able to hypothesise that the twenty-one grams (approx.) lost at the *exact* moment of death, was the weight of a human soul leaving the body. *Wow.* Now if that could be fact-checked and validated then I might be up for boarding the soul train, last stop Paradise Central, but until then . . . nope.

But in what could be classed as a modern-day miracle, I did subsequently emerge from my doom-scrolling, ditched the dressing gown, and made a tentative return to my dangerous living regime, and ukulele club.

It was a 'Strange Thing, Mystifying'. Had I been infused by the Holy Spirit and was getting a crafty, celestial helping hand? Or was it that *JCS* had acted as a type of televisual tonic, causing me to not only contemplate my religious convictions, but by default, my own mortality? I dunno. *Shrug.* I'd certainly had an epiphany of sorts, coming to the realisation that life is much too short to waste weeks of it, hosting pyjama-clad, table for one, pity parties.

But what I do know is that twenty-three banging songs, extraordinary acting, and sheer musical genius has certainly ensured that 'Everything's Alright' in my little world right now, and that's despite a water-logged bathroom ceiling which is bowing quite alarmingly. Well, we have had some semi-biblical downpours of late.

But now you'll have to excuse me, because I've got a date with YouTube, and where Heaven, in the form of the aqua-eyed Mr Minchin, will most definitely be on my mind. And amen to that.

Fear Factor 4, Part 1

'Bloody hell, Del!'

7th October 2023

Okay, so to say I'm operating *well* outside my comfort zone is severely understating the gravity of my situation. In fact, to say I'm 'operating' at all, is a stretch. I'm wedged into a velour bucket chair (*Shudder!* Not velvet, but near enough), my face is sporting a rictus grin, and I've just realised that arse cheeks, genuinely, have the ability to sweat.

In fact, my whole body is awash with a clammy panic that, for once, is nothing to do with the menopause, and everything to do with a 100,000-lumen beast of a lamp, which isn't only pushing temperatures up to Saharan levels, but is also accentuating my every facial blemish – whilst ensuring that each bead of perspiration on my upper lip is captured, on camera, and in ultra-HD. As I wait for the interviewer's next question, all I'm thinking is, 'Stupid bloody London, and stupid bloody me!'

So, you already know that I'm on a *dangerous living* program (where 'dangerous' = mildly dicey, occasionally), the aim being to embrace opportunities and start living, rather than relaxing in my riser-recliner as life passes me by. I've dabbled with arts and crafts, explored the arcane and the odd, and met amazing characters along the way.

But, to maximise the positive impact of my regime meant facing up to some lifelong fears and phobias. Hands down, the worst thus far was getting up close and personal with Dylan, a curly-haired tarantula, which makes him sound *way* cuter than his squat and menacing reality. But today outstrips even Dylan, because *this* is truly terror-inducing, and I'm utterly regretting allowing an eleven-year-old to convince me that it would be, in any way, shape or form, a good idea.

See, back when the weather was great, and my mood was too, I was enjoying a languid afternoon in my pal, Sarah's, lush and leafy garden, getting quietly hammered on G&Ts, whilst eating my bodyweight in her homegrown, homemade fare. (Sarah's a marvellous mix of Domestic Goddess – though nowhere near as loquacious as Nigella – and Mother Earth, with a dirty laugh and a penchant for Pinot, and planting.)

Anyway, talk somehow turned to spooks, and I was *relaxed* enough – my Mum's euphemism for pissed – to share my, one and only, 'ghost' story. It took around an hour to spill my supernatural skeletons into Sarah's sceptical ears, but when I'd finished, she nodded sagely and pronounced it one of the 'more compelling ghost stories' she'd ever heard. And that was that. We forgot about spirits (well, apart from the gin, *obvs*), and got roundly bladdered, while indulging in a cathartic moaning sesh about our other halves.

The following day, as I lay prostrate on the sofa, nursing a well-deserved hangover, I was tentatively scrolling through Twitter, when I noticed a shoutout for ghostly experiences for Series 3 of *Uncanny*. *Hmm?* I'd actually written about this seriously scary podcast, created by award-winning writer, Danny Robins, in my Nation Cymru Cultural Roundup for Christmas 2022, and had recommended having a listen, if you like spine-chilling stories, or want to find out why the phrase 'Bloody hell, Ken!' keeps trending on Twitter.

I admit, I was tempted. They probably wouldn't be interested in hearing about it but several hours, several edits, and several paracetamols later, I'd finished. I dithered, but after such an extraordinary effort – I'd written a behemoth of an email whilst totally hanging – I had to, and with a gentle whoosh, it was done.

And wouldn't you know it, but apart from a standard, *don't call us* email, I heard nothing, and being entirely honest, I was massively relieved. Because I *really* hate putting myself out there, being more of a lurk-in-the-shadows kinda gal. Imagine if they *had* wanted to use it for the podcast?

With mortifying memories of *that* poetry slam – where I discovered, in the most public and humiliating way possible, that my voice is not my own when I get nervous, and in fact, belongs to a pubescent boy whose larynx is rapidly evolving – I realised that being interviewed would have triggered that same irrepressible response. So, I cheerfully forgot all about it.

Until last week, when an email arrived, asking if I could Zoom with Simon (*Uncanny* co-producer), to discuss using my story for their podcast. *Eek!* Bad enough you might think, but oh no. This was quickly followed by another email, asking if I'd mind being interviewed – ON CAMERA – to be used for the *Uncanny: I Know What I Saw,* live tour. *EEK!*

Epic timing! *Eyeroll.* Why now, when four weeks prior, a Joe's Coffee Sundae (large), had knocked me off my low-carb bandwagon, leading to my current, more-chunky-than-curvy corpulency? (And isn't the camera meant to add ten pounds too? *Wail!*)

Why now, when my fifty-three-year-old, poker-straight hair had suddenly, and dramatically, morphed into a frizzy, wiry mop? (Envisage an elderly Little Orphan Annie and you won't be far off.)

And why now, when it's obviously too late to learn the mysterious complexities of 'contouring' and I knew that my usual, low-key, mascara and lippy look simply wouldn't cut it on screen.

I imagined a packed theatre, my massive messy head, projected on the back wall, and then the swell of laughter as the audience clocked my triple chins, unhinged hair, and sallow, *au naturel*, visage.

Nope. I couldn't do it. I typed a brief *thanks but no thanks* email and was about to hit send, when Thomas (Grandson #2), stepped in, and gave me a pep talk to rival Michael Sheen's 'Welsh sugar' call to arms, and argued me to a standstill.

No, apparently, I'm not fat, 'only a bit, sort of, soft'. *Lol!*

No, my hair isn't a disaster because, 'frizzy hair is dope'. *LOL!*

And no, I don't need extra make-up, because 'you look like you'. (*Sigh.* That's exactly what I was afraid of.)

Honestly, I wasn't 100% swayed at this juncture, but I was vacillating, and Thomas, sensing this, pushed home his advantage. 'What's the worst that can happen? Nowt! And who cares what other people think? It's not like you'll ever know, is it? So do it!'

I zoomed with Simon. He batted away my self-conscious concerns with the consummate ease of a pro – he'd clearly convinced many a camera-shy person to face their fears and appear on film. And, of course, the minute *THAT* thought entered my head, I knew I'd have to say yes, because *this* was probably the biggest fear I'd ever have to face. *Shit!* I was doing this.

Then, things moved fast. Wednesday saw us on a train to London, me wondering if a G&T at 8am is acceptable, or whether I should drop a Diazepam, to take the edge off my growing anxiety. Sarah was with me, acting as my *dame de compagnie*, because I need a bit of help when I travel.

And she was as excited as I *would* have been, if I could simply meet Danny Robins, maybe snag a signed book and a few free tour tickets, all whilst staying safely behind the bright lights of camera-land. (*Sigh.* Diazepam it is.)

Our train got into Paddington fifteen minutes late, and we hustled to the taxi rank to meet our Uber. Then we had a sixty-minute ride in a stuffy Kia E-Nero, with the taciturn Rashid, who gloomily navigated the 4.3 miles across a muggy, manic London, destination, Shoreditch.

According to TripSavvy, Shoreditch is a 'progressive's paradise', renowned for street art and trendy bars. But we were heading to an old tea factory – recently repurposed into a collaborative, work-spacey nightmare, with industrial lifts, and biscuit-themed lounges, where 'businesses and creative thinkers can come together and share ideas'. *Hard Eyeroll!*

We were met at reception by Sam, the theatre producer, who steered us through labyrinthine corridors and open-plan offices, crammed with hot-desking hipsters, before finally arriving at the studio. Inside, you could barely move for the black backdrop screens, and colossal light, so I was delighted to discover aircon humming happily away in the background. And then Danny appeared, and the moment I heard his distinctive soft northern tones, I felt my agitation, and vocal quavering, subside, and I was ready to rock'n'roll, *Uncanny*-style.

Okay, so *that* upsurge of confidence didn't last long. Telling my story, interspersed with forensic questioning from Danny, was unexpectedly knackering. My nerves kicked back in, I sporadically forgot how to speak – grappling unsuccessfully with the pronunciation of 'auntie' (*WTH?*) – and no matter how much water I drank, my lips kept sticking to my teeth with an annoying regularity.

Plus, the aircon had to be knocked off because it was interfering with the sound, so my hair was wilting, my under-boobs were broiling, and whenever I tried shifting in my seat, I got rather intimate electrostatic shocks from the flocked fabric.

Del and Danny, mid-interview

Sarah, noting my obvious discomfort, and in her official 'Keep Del Calm, Cool, and Make Her Carry On' capacity, hastily unwrapped several elements of the cold collation she'd prepared for the train ride home, and stuffed the melting ice packs down my back. *Ahh, bliss.*

Three hours later, we were done. Following a flurry of farewells, we *finally* managed to exit the 'creative space', after a wrong turn through 'Bourbon', and then 'Garibaldi', had us traversing 'Custard Cream' enough times to raise some perfectly plucked eyebrows.

Outside, we waited for the Uber which Sam had ordered, and waited, and waited . . . and waited some more. Alexander (BMW 5-series) never turned up, and Steffan (Honda Accord), did arrive, but he had a customer already in the back who, despite marginally heated remonstrations, refused to just bugger off.

But our luck changed with the traffic lights. A black cab rumbled round the corner, I waved my stick wildly, and we enjoyed an extremely comfortable, air-conditioned drive back to the station, in the company of Nick, a cockney charmer, who had *a lot* to say about Ubers, and even more about the new ULEZ regulations.

We missed our train, and the next, so while I cooled my heels, Sarah undertook a cider-quest, and I kept a close eye on departures. Train #3 was so overcrowded, the Tannoy lady had to threaten travellers with the transport police, if they didn't voluntarily get off, and it seemed to me that, if you're not capable of qualifying for an Olympic 100m final, catching a train in London during rush hour(s) is a complete no go. Even Usain would struggle.

Eventually, train #4 arrived, we scrambled into the nearest carriage, and that it was first class didn't deter us. When the ticket guy came a-calling, we willingly paid the extra because there was no way I could stand all the way to Cardiff. And we got a table too, which was fortuitous, because Sarah's 'picnic' certainly required one.

You know that scene in *Mary Poppins* when she unpacks her carpet bag? Well, Sarah might not have had a hatstand in there, but everything else you'd need for a substantial banquet magically appeared.

Plates, cutlery, condiments, plus potato salad, stuffed vine leaves, honey-roasted root veg, coleslaw, cheese, ham, quiche, chutney, and salsa. And napkins. It was certainly a first-class feast, and as we toasted our grand day out with Kopparberg, it was no wonder that the rest of our carriage were casting covetous glances and muttering darkly, as they nibbled on their wilting M&S sarnies.

Back in Swansea, Tim was idling impatiently in the taxi rank, and on the drive home, I babbled away, in the manner of someone who's experienced, and survived, a traumatic life event. Though, he wouldn't believe I'd hated being filmed, 'because in that menopause article, you said you didn't give a stuff what people thought of you'. And he was right because I had written those very words.

But, when it comes to taking centre stage, I realised that I had a whole host of hidden neuroses and insecurities, waiting to creep out and erode what little confidence I have. And they tried, damn hard, to sabotage any enjoyment I might have derived from my day out in the Big Smoke. However, they'd ultimately failed, because I'd had fun, in part.

I'd met some smashing people, had a two-hour taxi tour of the East End, and, for better or worse, had become an integral part of a show which plumbs paranormal waters, explores the eerie, and which I absolutely love.

But, without question, the pinnacle of the whole experience occurred towards the end of my interview, when I'd covered the part of my narrative which, even now, brings me out in goose bumps. As I took a welcome glug of water, Danny leaned back in his chair, slowly shook his head, then uttered the three-word, esoteric equivalent of a Hollywood handshake . . . 'Bloody hell, Del!' *BOOM!*

Fear Factor 4, Part 2

'Bloody hell, Dave!'

22nd October 2023

I've packed an overnight bag, Geoff is fuelled up, and we're both eager to take to the open road. Tim posits I'm off for a 'sneaky night away with your fancy man'. *Lol!* But he's not 100% wrong because, though I will be seeing someone who I'd like to consider my beau, it'll be alongside several hundred others, so it won't be the intimate seduction scenario Tim might imagine. And being totally honest, even if it was, I certainly wouldn't choose the Tiverton Travelodge for a night of unbridled passion.

But now, my pedal's hard to the metal, and Geoff is gasping as we slog up the 18% incline that marks the point where Risca becomes Pontywaun. We've chugged past an inordinate amount of Baptist chapels, Methodist meeting houses, C of E (or W) churches, and what can only be described as a tin shed, but that's spiritualists for you – no need of pesky, or pricey, religious trappings in their houses of worship, and fair play to them for that.

However, after passing a chantry, sporting the ever cheery, 'The End is Nigh', it proved swiftly prophetic, and before sat-nav lady could even attempt to wrap her tongue around Gelli-Unig Place, I pulled over, parked up, and heard her sigh of relief as she chirpily intoned, 'You have reached your destination'. Geoff breathed a sigh of relief too, though that was his radiator overheating. *Sod's bloody law.*

We're en route to Exeter – more on that later – but since we've got some time to kill, I decided to take a detour and stop off at a museum I've wanted to visit for some years. I actually stumbled across it during a 'weird stuff in Wales' Google search, and already I can tell that, boyo-oh-boyo, this place is weird, with a capital, and bold, **W.**

Outside, faux cobwebs and gigantic fluffy spiders add a touch of eerie to this traditional miner's house, as does the setting. Though the cottage itself is cosily cwtched between the steep greenwood peaks of Mynydd y Lan and Twmbarlwm, the cool mist that's coiling along the valley floor definitely brings a creepy chill to this bright, autumnal day.

But if more evidence were required, regarding the strangeness of this unassuming stone semi, the two willow wreaths which adorn the front doors provide some visible clues; one featuring a pentagram, which exudes strong *Blair Witch* vibes, whilst the other, rather disturbingly, contains various decapitated dolls' heads – well, I hope they're dolls. *Eek!*

The Morbitorium

So, I'm at The Morbitorium, which contains 'Curios for the curious, and oddities for the odd', and since I'm both, I can't wait to get inside and have a root around. But I've just noticed that it doesn't open until 11:00am, and it's currently half ten. *Bummer.*

Still, you can book online, so to bypass any potential queues, I filled in the form, grabbed the first slot of the day, and settled in for a thirty-minute wait. But the instant the transaction completed, the sage green door swung open, and I was greeted by Dave. *Spooky.* Dave grinned and shattered my sibylline illusions. 'Nah. The booking page beeped, so I thought I'd let you in early'.

Dave is the owner, and custodian, of this cottage of curiosities. He's bearded, with long hair, and has a touch of the Gandalf about him, though the nose ring, circular specs, and fancy hat (embroidered with golden swirls and small fragments of mirrored glass), make him look less bewitching, and slightly more beatnik. But, as I soon discovered, Dave is a keeper of considerable kooky knowledge.

We began our tour in the front room, which was a true freaky feast for the eyes. There were stuffed animals everywhere, and I don't mean the cuddly toy variety (though there was an original Bagpuss which I'd snaffle in a second). But no, here bright-eyed squirrels rub shoulders with seagulls, pheasants face-off against ducks, ravens sport tiny top hats and monocles, and ferrets are twisted into all manner of improbable poses.

There were even a couple of taxidermised cats on the windowsill; one ginger, curled up as if asleep, whilst the black puss was so realistic, you could almost expect it to start grooming its whiskers – which it did, causing me to literally yelp in fright, and Dave to enjoy a hearty chuckle at my expense.

There were beautifully lit cabinets filled with all manner of Victorian 'remedies' – heavy on the cocaine – whilst another held hundreds of porcelain gnashers, and a selection of glass eyes. Created in the 1930s, they made for a surprisingly colourful display, though the eye-extractor will forever haunt my nightmares.

And then we moved to the back room which housed the more arcane and esoteric artifacts. As you enter, you're confronted by a huge display of ouija boards, and Dave pointed out his favourite which was an understated sepia original.

But I was drawn to the gaudy – a cerise Mystifying Oracle Board, and a rather incongruous one, featuring Scooby Doo and the gang, haring away from a 'ghost', with psychedelic flowers and strategically placed 'Jeepers', 'Jinkies', and the iconic 'Zoinks'. That was another item I'd have liked to filch – and I'd have gotten away with it, if it hadn't been for those meddling kids – well, Dave.

Where had they all come from? Dave pulled out a folder, containing papers and letters, all of which related surprisingly similar events, hinting at dark doings, and even darker disturbances after the boards had been used. It seemed that The Morbitorium drew those who had (possibly) been touched by the paranormal, thus acting as an unofficial supernatural surrender zone.

Dave's ouija wall

But this room also contained the most bizarre items in Dave's collection. We started with shrunken heads. At my look of horror, Dave hastened to reassure, 'They're copies, and this one is made from alpaca skin'. Frankly, despite the silky facial hair, and the humanoid features, it wasn't a curio I'd fancy displaying on my mantlepiece, but Dave was fond of it, 'even though it took around a week to settle in'. *Uh, what now?*

For several nights after the head entered the museum, Dave and his partner had heard loud bangs and crashes, but then would wake to an undamaged and pristine museum. Dave reckoned it was the head, ironically, finding its feet. *Lol!*

But next came my favourite piece, as I beheld the beauty of an honest-to-God, vampire hunting kit. The craftsmanship was outstanding, and when Dave opened the lid, and I peered inside, it was blooming extraordinary. Lined with violet velvet – *Shudder!* – the bottles of holy water, crushed garlic, plus a variety of other pointy-toothed-terror deterrents, glowed richly against the polished copper straps that held them snugly in place. Along with a dagger, there was even a Victorian pistol, complete with those essential silver-tipped bullets.

A massive mallet was hidden beneath, to ensure that stakes are fully driven home – you'd need arms like Schwarzenegger, or Buffy, to thrust a stick through a sternum, so a hefty hammer is a vamp-hunting necessity. And those stakes were sharp enough to make mincemeat of any children of the night – though, much as I might be tempted, I don't mean those hoodie-wearing youths who loiter outside the local Spar.

(Side note: I was harassed by a small band of teenage rascals, some months back. On my way to grab milk and bread, they first wanted money. But when I refused, they then asked if I could 'pick up a packet of Reece's Pieces, please?' *LOL!* I didn't, but as a lifelong peanut butter fanatic, I felt for them, plus, as hustling goes, they deffo get 10/10 for sass, and for giving me a bloody good laugh too.)

Honestly, the place was a veritable treasure trove. The occultist, Aleister Crowley's death mask (repro), was set beside an artist's naïve rendition of Boleskine House. And then I discovered the 'witch nails'. At one time, they would have been square-headed coffin nails, but with our modern 'MDF and glue approach to casket building', it's difficult to source proper, rusted originals these days.

Dave, who I'm rapidly discovering has excellent attention to detail, now simply takes them to the local cemetery, buries them, and waits awhile until they become sufficiently corroded. Then he bundles them up, ready for any passing witch, or wizard, to purchase for binding, casting, bewitching, or conjuring spell work.

And this same meticulousness is applied to his wands, which he cuts every solstice, dries, and then carves, thereby ensuring the wood is imbued with magical equinox energy. Obviously, I had a go, but my attempt at 'Wingardium Leviosa' garnered no miraculous results, floating or otherwise. (*Harry Potter*, be damned!)

But thinking about floating brings us nicely onto what Dave calls his 'wet specimens'. I didn't inspect every jar, in which all manner of miscellanea were submerged, but he ran me through some of the scraps of fur and tissue he had on show. There were mice, lambs' brains, scores of organs, medical samples, and veterinary odds and ends. But once he mentioned puppies – even though they'd been stillborn – I wasn't keen to probe further.

Anything human? 'No, I don't have the licenses for that'. *Phew!* 'Though I once had some items from a chap who collected freak show stuff from the 1850s, and he had a genuine two-headed baby'. *No way, Jose!*

Apparently, it's common for 'suspending solutions to cloud over time', and Dave's the man who can change your fluids, like a sort of mystical mechanic. It starts with formaldehyde, which 'fixes the specimen in place, stiffening and preserving, and then they're put into isopropyl alcohol for the long term'. It was fascinating, fairly macabre, but I guess that's what passes for a normal day at The Morbitorium.

And then came the most absorbing part of the tour – the gift shop! After extensive browsing, I bought an enamel feminist cauldron pin, a massive 'Witches Aperitif' mug (which I later discovered can hold a Travelodge's kettle-worth of coffee), and an epic, 'I heart Weird Shit' badge! Perfect.

But on the way out, I started noticing all I'd missed on the way in. The ventriloquist dummy gave me the shivers, and a few medical gadgets took me down the (rampant) rabbit-hole of Victorian 'blood circulators'. (Yep, we're talking vibrators!)

Victorian 'massager'!

Bloody hell, Dave! This was heavy-duty machinery! And God help the lady who fancied getting her juices flowing, because you'd need a fair pair of biceps to get that device ricking. Dave obligingly demonstrated, but after a few cranks of the handle, even he was struggling. Then his partner appeared with a plate of scrambled eggs, so it seemed as good a time as any to push off.

Ninety-three hassle-free miles later, I was happily ensconced in my basic, but comfortable, room in the Tiverton Travelodge, my fluid-filled legs r upraised up on four pillows. (My medication means that I sometimes retain water, and today was one of those days. (*Ah, joy.*)

I had hoped my ankles might miraculously reappear before my big night out, but alas . . . Footwear that evening, to accommodate my elephantine feet, were ancient, beribboned moccasins. Yep, I was going *out out* in slippers. *Sigh.*

At sixish, Geoff and I set off on the last leg of our trip, destination Northcott Theatre. And sat-nav certainly earned her keep; we breezed through Exeter, bypassed the rush hour traffic, and arrived at the car park at 6:35pm. Perfect timing for a pre-show drink to calm my nerves because my stomach was churning something rotten. (I put it down to tension, but it *might* have been the large Maccy D's shake I'd slurped earlier – despite lactose intolerance, sometimes I have to get my fix of banana milk!)

But it *was* more likely stress, because I was there to watch *Uncanny: I Know What I Saw*. You've already read how I became involved with this show, and I'd been given four free tickets to watch it at my nearest theatre (Cardiff), on 12th November. But I couldn't wait that long, and no, it wasn't because I was excited to see myself on screen. Nope, it was actually because I was absolutely dreading it. And so, I'd come along, alone, to watch from the shadows in order to assess how unpleasant it was going to be when I took the family with me to Cardiff.

As I walked the few steps from the carpark to the theatre, the weather closed in, storm clouds gathered, and it made the whole set-up ominously ill-omened. Mind, that was probably simply my mood. Did I mention I was bloody terrified? So, I messaged Tim for some much-needed support at 7:06pm:

Me: Okay, am going in. Wish me, and my mental hair, luck.

Me: Am REALLY nervous!

Me: Like proper worried I'll look weird.

Me: Say something soothing!

And he did, even if it was a somewhat facetious response, and didn't arrive until the interval at 8:31pm! *Eyeroll.* But it made me laugh:

Tim: You'll look great.

Tim: It'll be a triumph daaarling!

Tim: A tour de force!

Once inside, I grabbed a bottle of water, necked a diazepam, and took a look at the merch available; #TeamSceptic and #TeamBeliever t-shirts, Danny's book (which btw, is a great read), along with mugs, mags, and posters. But I didn't want any mementoes of tonight – seeing myself on screen would be traumatic reminder enough. Now shush, it's starting!

Interval, and I haven't appeared yet. Hopefully, my interview's been consigned to the cutting room floor, and another's taken my place. But nope. In Danny's shed (which has been emulated on stage), I spot a teddy bear lamp and know I'll be up next. Wish me luck guys.

Okay, so yes, it was dreadful initially – and I mean me (not the show – *that* was amazing). I looked pretty chunky, but since the camera adds ten pounds, and there had been *two* cameras on me, maybe I'm not quite as weighty in the flesh? But my face was flushed, and my hair was, as feared, mildly crazy.

Danny's shed, recreated on stage

However, there was no huge screen, with me looming above the audience in ultra-HD. Instead, I was displayed on the side flats of the shed, which meant the wooden slats softened my face, and made me much more tolerable to watch. *Yay!*

And no one laughed, at least, not *at* me, so that was another fear unfounded – though I seemed to talk for an inordinate amount of time about bears. And no, I still dunno why. But the important bit was that my story went down well, with believers and sceptics alike.

And I think *that's* the aspect of Uncanny that makes it such a success

– those debates between the audience and experts. Tonight, Chris French was the opposition, with Evelyn Hollow, her of the high cheekbones and doe eyes, batting for the believers. And though their input was intriguing, Chris won't ever manage to convince me that what I experienced wasn't 100% real.

And I also got a tiny taste of celebrity afterwards, with numerous people approaching me to say thanks for sharing my story. It was lovely, and it seems that the #uncannycommunity really has created a safe space for believers, sceptics, and those on the fence, to come together and discuss the paranormal in an open and respectful way –

and which, in our frightening and increasingly fragmented world, makes it an exceedingly rare beast indeed.

Before I left, I had a brief chat with Danny and the team, thanking them for doing my story justice. And I'm actually looking forward to Cardiff, because who cares what I look like? All that matters is, to coin a phrase, I know what I saw, and now I'm more than happy for others to share my experience too.

Visit The Morbitorium website www.morbitorium.co.uk for details of opening hours, taxidermy courses, and witchcraft/magic workshops run by Delphi Nile.

Though the live show has now finished the 2023 run, tickets for the 2024 live tour will be available from spring onwards. Keep an eye on the Twitter page @uncannypodlive for future dates. And remember that, if you haven't yet joined in with the whole Uncanny experience, the TV series is available on BBC iPlayer, Danny's book, 'Into the Uncanny', is available at all good bookshops, and all series of the Uncanny podcasts are available on BBC Sounds.

Death & Chassés:

Plié-ing Through an En Pointe Evening

19th November 2023

I'm not so keen on November. I should be because it's my birthday month, and yes, I know I'm an adult, but even at fifty-four, I still experience that childlike fizz of excitement, the eager anticipation of a stack of thick envelopes littering the doormat, and the delivery of flowers that Tim, probably, won't send. *Longing sigh.*

But no, it's because it's a bit of a death month. This November 1st marked twenty-five-years since Dad shuffled off his mortal coil, and November 2nd was two years since Mum popped her Jimmy Choos. And, as I acknowledged their passings, it naturally dredged up memories of my childhood, and the life we'd shared.

Growing up, a weekend wouldn't pass without us going somewhere. Dad's mystery tours were firm favourites – discovering castles, caves, and countryside – and he'd always have a spooky story, or fascinating fragment of folklore, to keep me entertained. Even in winter, we'd bundle up in our sheepskin coats – they were a *thing* back then – and barrel along the backroads of wild Wales, with the MG's roof down and ABBA blasting out of the tape deck.

There'd be scavenger hunts, day trips to Hay-on-Wye (returning with armfuls of books), and thrilling nights when, for a reason I didn't understand at the time, we wouldn't watch telly, the lights would stay off, and we'd sit at the dining table, bathed in candlelight, playing cards, Scrabble, or KerPlunk.

(Side note: It seems we're worryingly close to those National Grid shutdowns again, with warnings that blackouts could become common in winter 2023, and the future. But happily, the government has said that it's working to secure supplies, which has certainly put my mind at rest. *Hard Eyeroll!* Adds candles to shopping list.)

Rare holidays abroad were planned so that Mum, who wanted a fortnight floating on an airbed in the sun, could do so, while Dad and I explored, poking through dusty old ruins, climbing mountains, and taking wobbly photos with our Kodak Instamatic.

Top – our first holiday abroad
Bottom – glorious Gower

As a family, we were always doing, and it made for a terrific childhood. But whilst there were a vast number of activities and outings which I loved, there were also those that I very much didn't.

I was forced to attend Brownies, and rather than skipping merrily about with my fellow Kelpies, I'd trudge gloomily in their wake. So, I wasn't at all unhappy when I was eventually ejected from the troop, leaving under a bit of a cloud, due to a tombola incident at the 'Joy & Jumble Sale'.

(In my defence, Brown Owl should have kept a closer eye on proceedings, because how was I to realise that the 2p payment meant you were allowed just the one rummage? *Teehee!*)

I had elocution lessons because my parents were considering sending me to a private school. These were dreadfully dull, and that I was never once asked to sing 'The Rain in Spain' with a mouthful of marbles, made it all the more so.

And they didn't eradicate my normal accent, though I can speak proper posh if the situation demands it – generally when dealing with telephone scammers, or G.P. receptionists (who frequently have the interrogation skills of the Stasi).

I had piano lessons but displayed not a smidge of musicality. I joined a marching band – 'The Tycoch Silver Spurs' – but my lack of rhythm, and inability to differentiate between left and right, meant that, after a summer of chaotic displays, it was suggested that I might be better suited to a different pastime. As I solemnly returned my Stetson, spurs, and Kazoo, I admit to having no regrets whatsoever.

Then I started horse-riding, and I finally found my niche. This was what I was made for. Sam was a 15.3hh Welsh cob, with a good turn of speed, and the sweetest nature. In fact, my parents had been about to buy him for me, when Dad was made redundant. *Aww!* My dreams of Sam being mine were shattered, but so were theirs – no private school for Del. *Yippee!*

So, given I was a chunky child, whose only talent emerged when my feet were off the floor and secured in stirrups, I can't for the life of me understand why Mum thought ballet lessons might suit. *WTH?* She later told me she thought it would help with my posture and 'elegance, because you were quite an ungainly child'. *Humpf!*

But those Saturday mornings were torture, as was getting in and out of the pale green leotard, with a small frill at the waist that did nothing to conceal my lack of one. Mum would scrape my hair into a brutal bun, tie on those stupid ribbony shoes, then drive me to the YMCA, where I'd endure three hours of torment.

Me and a monkey?? Yes, it's real and nope, I dunno where it came from

Compared to the other little girls, who flounced 'like softly drifting snowflakes', I was an avalanche. Taller, bigger, and much bulkier than them, my steps were clumsy, and 'très, très fortissimo', as our ballet Mademoiselle complained to Mum. (Basically, if you've seen that Vicar of Dibley episode with Darcey Bussell, that's almost exactly how it went for me, but worse.)

After too many months, Mum (and Mademoiselle), finally accepted that I'd never morph into anything more graceful than the hefty-footed tomboy I was and consigned my leotard and slippers to the bin. *Woohoo!* And soon after, when Mum caught Dad teaching me a fab – if not particularly feminine – party piece, she didn't even bother objecting.

I showcased *that* new talent at the next family gathering, when the calls invariably came from some elderly relative for us kids to 'do a turn'. My female cousins did a dainty dance, my male cousin sang 'Calon Lân', and me? Well, I tore a phonebook in half! And yes, I'm serious.

We went through a phenomenal amount of telephone directories, Yellow Pages, plus a few Argos catalogues, with the knack being, to crack the spine first before tearing widthways. But the point I'm, somewhat laboriously, trying to make here is that girlie stuff, and ballet in particular, was emphatically, not my bag.

Which was why, despite Mum's pleas to accompany her to various performances, I never did. Psychologically scarred by that formative foray into the world of dance, I could imagine nothing worse than watching people cavort and caper around on stage. And when Mum mentioned that they 'act with movement and facial expressions', that added an extra nightmarish layer of, what sounded suspiciously like mime. So, it was a decisive no from me.

But tonight, I'm at Swansea's Grand Theatre to give it a go. No, with the state of my spine, I won't be attempting an arabesque any time soon, but I can manage the *petit plié*, which'll allow my *derrière* to sink into my (velvet. FFS!) seat, Row F16.

I'd asked Tim if he wanted to join me on my cultural expedition, but he'd stared at me with horror and said, 'Sometimes, I wonder if you know me at all'. *LOL!* And when he followed up with, 'And stop trying to drag me into your adventure crap!', I knew I'd be flying solo.

So, I'd forked out £35 to endure that perennial festive favourite, Tchaikovsky's, *The Nutcracker*, and was filled with not one whit of enthusiasm or crumb of Christmas cheer. Frankly, I was mad as hell at Mum for dragging me here – though as she's dead, I've only got myself and my conscience to blame, for what I intended to be a mini-tribute

241

to her.

The Grand Circle was rather like being inside an ornate wedding cake. Ivory balconettes, swathed with garlands of golden curlicues, and the gilt pillars – one of which was included with my 'restricted view' ticket. *Sigh.* – were embellished with intricate scrollwork. It was florid, but fantastic.

The house soon filled with a wide mix of generations – ranging from cute littlies in tutus, up to those, like me, in the silver-haired society. But there was a preponderance of teenage girls, all frighteningly lithe, and probably ballerinas in training. (Well, either that, or they didn't get the excessive nutritional spoiling I had as a kid.)

However, what did give me a frisson was the small-but-perfectly-formed orchestra, because like the teens in Row E, I also think classical music is 'sick'. (I'm not including Wagner here, as Ride of the Valkyries can make ears bleed, and I feel for the string section who constantly seem to be scampering behind the horns.)

I got chatting to my seat neighbour, Sam, who had been bringing daughter Emily to see this ballet, 'for fourteen years, and counting'. Apparently, whatever date they came, would also be the day they'd put up their tree. It was a lovely tradition, and I felt a fleeting sadness that I'd denied Mum the opportunity to do the same with me. But then Sam mentioned that on one occasion, they could only book a mid-October showing, 'So we had to get a plastic one that year'. *Lol!*

If, like me, you haven't seen this ballet before, there was a helpful summary in the programme (£7!). Basically, it tells the story of Marie, a girl whose godfather, Drosselmeyer, gives her a nutcracker doll as a present on Christmas Eve. When the evil Mouse King, and minions, invade the house, the nutcracker comes miraculously to life, and with the help of some toy soldiers, manages to defeat the malevolent meeces. *Huzzah!*

But when midnight strikes, the nutcracker, somehow, becomes a real boy – and a prince no less – who whisks Marie off to the Land of Sweets, where they are entertained with dances from all corners of the world, culminating in the famous Dance of the Sugar Plum Fairy.

Aw, bollocks! This was full-on fairytale stuff, clearly for kids, and I was seriously considering doing one when, with a smart rap of the baton, we were off.

And straight into a scene with three chirpy couples chucking imaginary snowballs, and grappling with, what appeared to be, a metallic, inflatable alien! *Huh?* But it must have been an in-joke, as there was widespread tittering, and in that moment, I knew this was going to be a tedious two hours. *Yawn.*

Ten minutes later, I was becoming increasingly more restive than festive, and the mannered Christmas party unfolding on stage was not the 'enthralling extravaganza' advertised. But then Drosselmeyer appeared, eye-catchingly adorned in sequinned waistcoat and cloak, and brandishing, fairly menacingly, his magic wand. *Hmm?* Right, I'll give it another five mins.

He made partygoers do cartwheels, forced them to act like dolls, and though it smacked of coercive control, as the story was nearly two hundred years old, I decided to overlook such pesky modern values. Then, probably in an attempt to make up for his earlier, non-consensual hypnotism schtick, he gave everyone presents, and the celebrations began in earnest. And, surprisingly, I started enjoying myself.

Real Snowflakes

Because it wasn't the snoozefest I'd imagined, and I genuinely got swept along on an enchanted excursion that was, quite simply, lovely. Okay, so without getting too carried away, there were a few niggles, but it says something that, instead of sloping off during the interval, I stayed until the curtain fell.

Beginning with the downsides, the biggest disappointment was the staging, or more accurately, the scenery. I'd looked at, what I'd assumed were, the official pics on the production company's website, and unfortunately, these backdrops weren't a patch on them. So, I'd advise lowering your expectations, because you won't see anything that spectacular on a stage near you.

Another was the non-emergence of the 'real' Sugar Plum Fairy, and her Cavalier. That was a bummer because, even though I hadn't been aflame with anticipation, I'd once caught a snippet of the Royal Ballet's *Nutcracker* on TV, and boy, did those plums sparkle!

However, this was a much smaller company, they had to work with what they had – so it was Marie (in a shimmering tutu), and the prince, who danced, what Emily whispered, 'is the most challenging pas de deux in ballet'. And though I'm obviously no judge, they were pretty mesmerising.

And also, according to Emily, the Russian Cossack dance was missing too, which might have been due to the current political climate, but was a shame, as she said it was her 'favourite bit'.

But no matter, because the upsides far outnumbered my little grumbles. And the most mind-blowing aspect of the show, and one that I'd stupidly never even considered, was the sound of the dance – and I don't mean the music.

No, I mean that after each lissom leap, you heard the thud of the landing; when the twinkling ensemble of snowflakes drifted past, you heard the tips of their slippers skittering against the stage, and rather than interrupting the flow of the performance, it actually added to its charm.

These guys weren't the bounding buffoons in tutus and tights that I'd expected. They were gymnasts, athletes, thoroughbreds, with a hard-core physicality, and exceptional stamina, strength, and musculature. And my initial thoughts that ballet would be svelte individuals, fluttering flimsily across the stage, was far, far removed from the reality.

And, it wasn't only a visual spectacle, but an audio one too. My car radio is always tuned to ClassicFM, and I've heard Tchaikovsky's *Nutcracker* score many times – remember those Cadbury ads of the 70s ('Everyone's a fruit and nut case')? But in that theatre, watching that ballet, it was as if I'd never heard the music properly before, and that the dance, somehow, made it sound all the sweeter. It was truly astonishing.

So, yep, you've guessed it, I'm honestly amazed to declare myself a ballet convert. And that *The Nutcracker* is about the magic of childhood meant it was the ideal ballet to honour Mum, who had made mine so wonderful. It really couldn't have been any more marvellous.

No, scrap that. Mum being with me would have made it an absolutely en pointe evening, so, it's a good job I decanted a fair amount of her ashes into an empty quart bottle of Freixenet, and tucked her in my handbag, with one of her 'death party' beermats! Okay, it wasn't the ideal scenario, but I can tell you, without a shadow of a doubt, that she'd loved our night out. But next time, we'll deffo be avoiding that bloody pillar.

And now, I'm off to get our tree up – though how Tim will feel, buggering about in the attic at this time of night, I really can't imagine. *LMAO!*

If you'd like to experience ballet for yourself, visit the Classical Ballet & Opera House website for details of forthcoming dates and venues, or see their Facebook Page which gives details of this, and other ballets, which they will be performing over the coming months.

Four Santas and an Exorcist:

Getting Frighteningly Festive

10th December 2023

Since booking, the venue had changed twice, with the final destination (*gulp!*) sent through mere hours before the kick-off. I'd also received strict instructions regarding the 'total ban' on recording any video, audio, or even taking a few snaps. *Hmm?* It seemed curiously clandestine and somewhat *OTT*, but I guess that's exorcists for you – wary, watchful, and constantly cognisant of those furtive forces of evil.

Though, if your day job involves dealing with real-life Linda Blairs, it undoubtedly pays to take precautions – even if that's purely packing a brolly, to deflect possible pea-soup emissions. (I've got Tim's Callaway Classic Golf Master, just in case. *Eek!*)

I'd mentioned it to my mates who remained unyielding in the face of my entreaties to, 'Come on, it'll be fun', but were happy to speculate on what they considered, the 'shady nature' of the event. They favoured cults, stepdad (ex-VATman), plumped for a pyramid scheme (?), and Tim's contribution boiled down to a blunt, 'It'll be bloody muckment and I'd have nowt to do with it! *Sigh.*

However, their comments did give me, brief, pause for thought. Maybe, when it comes to my dangerous living regime, I should 'exorcise' (*sorry – couldn't resist*), more caution, rather than bounding into each activity with the naïve enthusiasm of an over-caffeinated cockerpoo?

But answer me this – how often do you get an opportunity to learn effective ways to 'safeguard yourself against the dark arts, possession, and more'? Not blooming often enough, I'll wager. So, pour me a coffee, scratch my belly, and call me Fido, because this sounded epic, and there was no way in hell (*oops!*) I was gonna miss it.

But before that, my week was filled with the festive, starting with the annual Killay Community Council's 'Santa Parade'. Heavy on the fairy lights, his faux reindeer might have been static, but were life-sized and glowing, as were the kids (and me), who could barely contain ourselves when his sleigh came into sight. That it was being towed by a truck didn't mar the magic, and the Christmas carols issuing from hidden speakers, plus a fair dusting of snow, had us all entranced.

When he'd switched on the tree lights in the precinct, I headed home to consult my SAC (Santa Assessment Criteria), derived from the classic 'A Visit from St. Nicholas' poem (aka 'T'was the Night Before Christmas'), with marks available for: Appearance, Character, Ho-Ho-Knowhow, and Overall Impact.

Santa #1 lost marks for the lack of Ho-Ho-Hos, but despite limited vocal interaction, the kids were starry-eyed, his reindeer were radiant – the addition of a red nose on one being a lovely touch – and the man himself did a lot of enthusiastic waving and seemed exceptionally jolly. Santa #1 = a solid 7.5/10.

Santa #2 took me to Margam Park, early on Saturday morning. I'd asked if Tim fancied coming too, but his response was, 'Who's child are we taking, coz I wouldn't go unless we had a five-year-old with us'. Heavy sigh.

But, as I lurched from the car park towards the entrance, a passing 'Rudolph' (aka Dennis), offered me a furry arm (leg?) and escorted me into the castle. It was like a scene from Frozen, which was fitting because it was freezing AF. (Thank God for the coffee and mince pies included in the ticket price!)

Dennis introduced me to Doreen, another member of Margam Park's Friends, and co-ordinator of the free activities on offer to visitors. And it was Doreen's colleagues who were outside, in all weathers, posing patiently as parents took pics of their littlies (and not so littlies), with the usual yuletide suspects.

I took myself off to the terrace, eyed up the best spot for Santa's 11am arrival, and was soon surrounded by hundreds of hyperactive kids. And it was fab. Their excitement was infectious, as was their collective moaning – Santa was running late, and a host of small, disgruntled voices complained incessantly. But I loved the excuses parents were making – everything from 'finishing his porridge', to 'road works on the M4', and my personal favourite, 'defrosting his joy-ometer'. *Aw*!

Me with the Margam Massiv!

But the instant his tractor rolled into view, trailed by a hefty herd of reindeer, a ripple of genuine delight flowed through the crowd, and the kids were thrilled, me less so. (I have an irrational fear of reindeer – those gummy biting plates they have instead of teeth freak me out. Shudder! But these were safely below the viewing area, and were actually quite cute, as was Santa.)

His Ho-Ho-Hoing was admirable, he wished us 'Merry Christmas' and 'Nadolig Llawen', his wave was outstanding – more so, considering he was alternating between that, and scattering reindeer food – and his appearance was all a Santa should be. There was even evidence of a 'little round belly/That shook, when he laughed like a bowlful of jelly!' Santa #2 = an impressive 8/10.

Santa #3 was at the St Paul's Christmas Fayre in Sketty, where our uke club were booked to play a set. After we'd finished strumming (and very successfully too, if I do say so myself), I had a quick sank around the stalls, before joining the kids in the queue for Santa's Grotto.

And for a paltry £1, I got to spend five minutes with Mr Claus, including an unofficial photo shoot and a brief cwtch. And he did well on the SAC scale too. Whilst there was no Ho-Ho-Hoing or waving, I noted that his beard was authentic. And 'His eyes—how they twinkled! his dimples, how merry! /His cheeks were like roses, his nose like a cherry!'

Marks were lost due to the absence of reindeer, but I appreciated it was a small church hall and reindeer are large and a bit 'fighty', so fair play. However, the backdrop of Santa's Sitting Room was smashing, and I was going to award a well-deserved 8/10.

But, as I was leaving, he squeezed my hand and said, 'It's so lovely to meet those who still believe', and in that instant, I truly still did! Santa #3 = 9/10, for not breaking character when confronted by a fifty-four-year-old woman, and for bringing the magic.

My final Santa (#4) saw me at the Gower Fresh Christmas Tree Farm. I'd chosen a Monday so I could be, relatively sure, I wouldn't need to elbow many kids out of the way in order to spend quality time with the big guy. And it was a fantastic experience.

Entering through a beautifully carved wooden door, leading into a snowy tunnel, you strolled past numerous animatronic plushies, all belting out festive faves, and there were real reindeer in there too. Eep! And then you reached Santa's house.

It was like walking into an actual Christmas card, and looked superb, but I was focused on the man himself, and he didn't disappoint. So, despite there being no jelly belly on show, the beard was real, the eyes sparkled behind grandad glasses, and after a brief photo op, he was happy to answer a few quick questions:

Me: Hi Santa, great to meet you. How are preparations going for Christmas Eve?

Santa: Oh, very well indeed. I've nearly finished reading all the letters that the children sent to me, and my elves are working extra hard to make sure that everyone will get what they want on Christmas Day.

Me: Excellent. And how are the reindeer shaping up for the big night?

Santa: Ah, my team are doing very well. They're experienced fliers, but to give them an extra dash of speed, I feed them a top-secret boost food, which ensures they're tanked up for take-off.

Me: Brilliant. Is there anything you'd like for Christmas, Santa?

Santa: (Long pause) Uh, well, I'd have to say world peace, as we currently seem to be making rather a hash of things regarding that.

Me: (Nodding) Mmhmm, you're not wrong.

Santa: But failing that, I'd like everyone to be kind to one another. Not only at Christmas, but every day throughout the year. Oh, and remember to recycle.

Me: That's a great message. And what do you do on Boxing Day? Sleep, I suppose?

Santa: Ho-Ho, yes, but there's always time for a sherry and some picky bits with Mrs Claus.

Me: Of course, and I totally agree about picky bits. So, my last question, Santa, is this – am I on your 'Naughty or Nice' List?

Santa: Ho-Ho, oh, you're unquestionably in the nice column.

Me: Yay! And how about my other half, Tim?

Santa: Hmm? Now, let me check. (*Long pause.*) Oh dear, he's very definitely borderline.

Me: Hah! I bloody knew it!

Santa #4 = an almost faultless 9/10. Wonderful from beginning to end.

And so, filled with an over-abundance of Christmas cheer, it felt slightly bizarre to be barrelling along the M4, heading towards a potential, occult nexus. But I was up for it and had armed myself with what I felt were necessary accoutrements – bell, book, and candle (obvs), along with a box of Frosty Fancies, and a six-pack of Frazzles (in case deliverance from demons took a while).

After grabbing a latte at Pont Abraham, thirty minutes later I arrived. Gulp. No, not gulp – at all! I'd been expecting, if not a gothic pile, something with a turret or two, or an Amityville Dutch colonial. But even a new-build semi would've been preferable to the prefab village hall that had seen better days. No, scratch that – better decades! Maybe Tim's 'muckment' prediction wasn't that far off the mark. Damn and blast!

I probably should've turned tail there and then, but curiosity is one of my besetting sins, so, attempting to ignore its idiomatic effect on cats, I shouldered the door open and tentatively stepped inside . . . And was greeted by a trestle table, heaving with an array of pick 'n' mix that would've rivalled Woolies. WTH?

Exorcism essentials

This was way stranger than feared. Still, I'm a bugger for cola bottles, so I filled a bag and bought a bottle of (non-holy) Highland Spring, for the very reasonable price of £2.80. Right, whatever came next, I was ready for it.

And 'it' was a gathering of around thirty silver surfers who, like me, had doubtless come along due to a morbid sense of adventure, and possibly because they recalled the terror of watching The Exorcist on Betamax in the 70s. At the centre of a semi-circle of chairs stood Ben (mid-40s, plaid shirt, jeans), and who, given I'd been expecting a Max von Sydow type, was a bit of a letdown. But then he got going, and I perked up, but not for long.

Ben was clearly knowledgeable on possession but was also clearly terrible at presenting. In fact, Ben was a little boring, and there was a distinct increase in pick 'n' mix rustling/consumption, whilst he attempted to dispel misconceptions about demonic possession. We'd all been hoping for some hair-raising tales, so his lecture on mental health issues – though 100% valid, and the no 1 consideration in 'current exorcism guidelines' – was a tad dull.

Neighbour on my left (Barry) tutted, neighbour on my right (Joyce), tittered, and there was obvious Eyerolling and whispered giggles, which Ben clocked. *Aw.* Poor Ben. I willed him on. C'mon Ben, get to the good stuff.

But no. Next came Harry Potter. Yep, really. Obviously, anyone who's ever read it/watched the films, would consider that Harry's on the side of angels, while Voldemort's a depraved, flat-faced psycho. But Ben posited that 'these books plant the idea of two types of magic, good and bad. But actually, all magic must be termed evil!' Hmm? (This was more book club than anything malevolently meaty, and I was beginning to think Ben's exorcism credentials were either wildly exaggerated, or purely academic.)

In fairness, Rowling's books did prompt some semi-animated discussion, until Sandra – one of the local W.I. group of eight – informed us, somewhat stridently, that she'd bought the books for her grandkids, 'and they love them!' This led to an accusation, from a bloke at the front, of 'sowing the seeds of witchcraft!' LOL! Ben, aware things were turning ugly, moved swiftly on.

And we, finally, got to the good stuff – the symptoms of possession. Wicked! Ben said there were 'many signs of demonic possession', so count yourselves lucky because I'm going to share them with you. Right, here goes:

Pain in lower back, heaviness in shoulders and/or neck, headaches, blurry eyesight, thickness in the throat, chest pain, stomach-ache, bloating, excessive wind, indigestion, constipation/diarrhoea, pain in womb/groin, hip/knee ache, insomnia/hypersomnia, overheating, and frequently irritable/argumentative. Oh, and feeling disappointed with life. Hard Eyeroll!

Frankly, most of the audience looked like they were feeling

disappointed with life right about then, but shelving that, given that the bulk of us were in the 50+ age bracket, it seemed we might all be ripe for exorcising. As one, the W.I. rose, leaving in a flurry of huffing, but the rest of us stayed put, mainly because we felt a little bad for Ben – but, from a less altruistic perspective, in the unlikely event that my spine, and Barry's knees, were cursed by hellish hitchhikers, we were keen to find out how to banish these malignant menaces.

And Ben's advice was twofold. Firstly, visit your doctor and get the full raft of tests done, to rule out any medical conditions. WTAF? You can barely get an appointment these days, let alone inform your G.P. you'd like a top-to-toe MRI to rule out demonic possession.

But, he continued, if tests are negative then yes, you 'might be possessed'. Barry, who'd reached the end of his, fairly long and relatively relaxed tether, rapped out a brisk, 'And then what?', which led to a smatter of applause (and a flirtatious glance from Joyce, who whispered, 'Now, there's a man who knows how to take charge', before helping herself to another packet of Frazzles).

And the answer, if you've stuck with it thus far, and fear you might have something more sinister than the menopause or arthritis, is . . . drumroll please . . . Be happy, no matter what, and read whatever your faith uses as their Good Book. Un-bollocking-believable! We'd gotten sod all from the evening – apart from a marked increase in bloating and

Tim thanking the REAL Santa, Christmas Day, 2022

wind, no doubt due to an excess of gelatine goodies rather than possession. Harumph!

But I felt sorry for Ben who, in the face of a lacklustre audience reaction, heeded his own advice, and remained upbeat. Poor Ben. I left him my last Fancy as consolation. Mind, I reckon he was dead wrong about magic. I mean, I don't really believe in maledictions and hexes, but thinking of my Santa sorties, you only had to see those spellbound little faces (and big ones), to realise that Mr Claus has an enchantment all of his own. And that is magic, of the very nicest kind.

If you'd like to see Santa feed his reindeer, visit the margamcountrypark.co.uk, for details and availability. Visit gowerfreshchristmastrees.co.uk to book their Winter Wonderland & Santa's Grotto. And if you're interested in learning more about exorcism, you can find details of various events and seminars on Eventbrite – but you probably won't be needing that brolly!

Un-cultural Highlights of 2023

Obviously, I understand why 'impulse control' and 'delayed gratification' are lauded as positive traits that we should all aspire to. But my restraint has always, at best, been patchy – a Joe's Hazelnut Sundae can knock me off the healthy eating bandwagon for months – and these days, middle-aged and with a hastening sense of my own mortality, I'm hesitant to delay anything, pleasure in particular.

Which is why I rarely explore a new (to me) author, if they don't have at least a couple more books in their locker, my logic being, if I love it, I'll want to devour the rest of their canon post-haste.

So, it was doubly lucky that I stumbled upon C. K. McDonnell's, *The Stranger Times*. Not only were there another two books in the series (with the fourth due in January 2024 – *huzzah!*), but a quick internet search uncovered that, under his Caimh McDonnell moniker, there's a hefty lump of delightfully surreal crime fiction to enjoy too. This includes the, paradoxically named, *Dublin Trilogy* (which currently comprises seven books), along with various spin-offs. And yep, I've ploughed through them all, and they're darkly comical, have delightfully drawn characters, and are brilliant.

The Stranger Times series is a quirky urban fantasy/whodunnit, set in the Manchester offices of a Fortean'esque newspaper. The editor, a hard-drinking, foul-mouthed, ex-Fleet Street hack (who subtly uses a shotgun to scare away humanity), oversees a motley crew of loveable misfits, including a naked Rastafarian, a God-fearing secretary, and a sentient printing press. It's a madcap and genuinely *LOL*-inducing read, combining the paranormal with proper investigative journalism – a first for *that* newspaper! So, even if you're not normally a fan of this genre, I'd deffo say give it – and Mr McDonnell's other books – a go.

And as Christmas rapidly approaches, there's one favourite which I always return to in the run up to the big day – the BBC's adaptation of John Masefield's fantasy adventure novel, *The Box of Delights.*

First broadcast back in the dark ages of winter 1984 (when you had to wait a whole week between episodes!), I was a pain-in-the-arse, fifteen-year-old, with an affected air of perpetual boredom. But, catching that first instalment, with its eerily beautiful title sequence and haunting, unsettling music, I dropped the 'much too cool to watch kids TV' act, and revelled in the fairy tale unfolding on screen.

Telling the story of orphan, Kay Harker, it begins with a train journey, two sinister vicars, and a card trick, and basically gets weirder from there. There are magical dealings with the mysterious 'Punch and Judy Man', and his adorable Barney Dog (*great name*), and that most of the series is shot in a snowy, Christmas-card landscape, simply adds to the festive enchantment. And I promise that when you hear the words, 'The wolves are running', you'll shiver with a creepy anticipation of the delights to come.

Watch it for free on Internet Archive, where the full series is available, or you can buy the DVD from various high street or online retailers.

And my final offering is a little gem of a series that will be ending forever with one last festive finale. (*Sob! Pass me the Kleenex.*) I'm talking about BBC's *Ghosts.*

Created by the same fantastic team who brought *Horrible Histories* to the telly, *Ghosts* is about a young, cash-strapped couple who inherit a decrepit mansion, only to discover that it's chock full of some very needy – well, you can guess – ghosts.

Those who have died within the boundaries of Button House cover a range of eras, extending from the first ghost, caveman Robin (killed by lightning), all the way up to 80's Scout leader Pat (killed by a scout's stray archery arrow, with a penchant for Scotch Eggs), and 90's Julian (trouser-less corrupt MP, suspected heart attack when cheating on wife, Sam Fox fetish).

The whole cast are wonderful, but my fave has to be the WWII Captain who, despite being a stickler for routine, and assuming the bossy mantle of group leader, was the most perfect fairy godmother in the last Christmas special, and in the history of pantomime. I could say more, but I don't want to give away any major spoilers, so if I've piqued your interest, give it a watch.

As this disparate group of spooks face up to the boredom of eternal purgatory, endure various existential crises, and grapple with twenty-first century 'living', this ultimate in house-share sitcoms follows their hilarious, and oftentimes poignant, wait to finally make it to the, hopefully, heavenly afterlife.

So, if this has passed you by, you're in for a real treat. All five series are now available on iPlayer which, I guess, is the one upside of saying farewell to the Button House gang. But even if you're already a fan, why not have a binge in readiness for the climax? Mind, I think we'll need to keep those tissues handy, 'cause I'm betting quite a few will be getting 'sucked off' this Christmas Day!

Good Goddess!

2nd February 2024

When your body has the contours and consistency of an uncooked cottage loaf, scrutinising your – completely starkers – self in a full-length mirror, was never going to be the most enjoyable experience. Okay, so technically I'm not *totally* in the buff – though my new pair of specs, whilst endowing me with a welcome façade of wisdom and gravitas, also bring my numerous knots of cellulite into startling, crêpey clarity. *Sigh.*

But this sharp-eyed evaluation of my pudgy physique isn't the worst of it. Not by a long shot. Because the next step, as advised by Bex – 'healing guide' and facilitator of the *7 Days to Release Your Inner Goddess* plan – is to 'touch yourself!' *Oo-er missus!* Bet you didn't think you'd be spiralling down that raunchy rabbit hole, but in fairness, neither did I. And it's only Day 2!

No, what I'd scheduled for January was a marvellous month of llamas, spell bottles, seated tai chi, and getting my first ever tattoo. But those delights had to be bumped because, for the last six weeks, I've not moved from the house, and I won't be first-footing it anywhere for the foreseeable.

Instead, due to a stupid spinal flare-up, I've spent the whole festive season (and still counting), swaddled in dressing gown, slippers, and a serious heft of self-pity – whilst doing hourly rotations of two TENS machines, a spongy neck collar, and various hot water bottles.

As a 'glass half full' kinda gal, the upside of being housebound means I don't need to faff with hair, make-up, bra, or pants (and thus making Bex's Day 2 call to action that much quicker to achieve). But the downside is that Christmas was a washout and, as my days drift by in a drug-fuelled, nerve-blocked fog of pain, tears, and irrational arguments, I'm starting to go stir crazy. I can't even go to Uke Club because my left arm doesn't work and I can't make chords – though, as Tim helpfully pointed out, 'Bet no one would notice'. *Eye-roll.*

However, despite this enforced health hiatus, I still wanted to do *something* to officially mark the start of a shiny new year, so I signed up for this Goddess online workshop. Advertised on my go-to site for the weird and/or wonderful (Eventbrite), this was *guaranteed* to unleash the 'divine' me in only one week. *Terrific, eh?* And, though I wasn't entirely convinced it would achieve all, or any, of the promised outcomes, it was free. So, with nothing to lose, and possibly *everything* to gain, I registered and waited impatiently for the link to land in my inbox.

I could envisage myself, reborn as a more beautiful, confident, and hopefully, slimmer Del, emerging from the chaotic waters of my past like Charlize Theron in that perfume ad. When I mentioned it to Tim, he tutted, shook his head, and said, 'More muckment, and it can't work miracles'. (He's *very* lucky that I find his straight-talking and Yorkshire common sense amusing, most of the time. *Lol.*)

Six hours later, I was good to go, diving straight in to Bex's introduction, and . . . *Damn it!* It didn't engender confidence. Much was made of her being an 'ancient soul', who has had many 'forms in alternate universes'. *Hmm?* Should probably have left reading about Bex until after I'd done the course.

Still, the fact that her lifetimes on Earth had been, 'as shaman, medicine woman and witch', gave me a smidge of hope that I *might* be in the right (*healing?*) hands. She'd also added – in a random though laudable aside – that, 'over the centuries I led slaves to freedom' – so I guess if anyone could liberate my sacred feminine, it would be her. Righto, let's go girl.

Day 1 gave an overview of the week ahead, with the overarching focus being to, 'access energy that brings out the confident you, the you that experiences pleasure on a daily basis'. *Wow!* Strong start, because I can't recall the last time I felt *proper* pleasure – apart from Uke Club, which is totally jolly and uplifting, and I'm missing it dreadfully. *Sob.*

But Bex did warn that the process, 'can bring up painful emotions, troubled thoughts, and new fears'. *Uh-oh!* However, with the carrot being a, '100% *assurance* that, on the other side, is the divine feminine you deserve'. *Bugger it!* It was worth the risk.

Each day was structured in a similar fashion, with questions followed by action points. Seemed straightforward enough, but that soon changed. For example, 'Do you enjoy being a woman?' *WTH!* Couldn't say I'd ever considered it. And what was the alternative? I suppose I could dabble with non-binary, but I find all that a bit of a minefield, and though I envy blokes for their low maintenance ablutions (Tim in particular – being bald's a gift), I simply wouldn't know how to embrace masculinity at my age.

Next, what did I love about being a woman? Blinking heck, I dunno. I'm starting to come round to grey hair, my eyes are okay, and I suppose my legs are alright – though my aunt once described them as, 'excellent for rugby', which didn't help with the whole self-love schtick. But I knew that Bex was expecting me to plumb emotional depths, and I felt thoroughly uncomfortable trying.

So, the 'action point' was a welcome distraction from my introspective and inadequate navel-gazing – though I hoped it wouldn't be too active, given my current stasis state. It wasn't. In fact, all I had to do was shout a positive affirmation, ten times in quick succession, repeating the process hourly: 'I love being a woman and goddess, each and every day'. Apparently, the greater the volume, the more beneficial the effects. *Okey dokey.* Here goes nothing . . .

Loud and proud, I did it. I felt a bit of a fool at first, but by my third iteration, I was roaring myself hoarse, and the dogs were onboard too. On my fourth, Tim donned earbuds, and before I'd finished my tenth, he'd vacated the property in favour of the shed. *Lol!* Day 1 – done.

Day 2 and 'Welcome to the Pleasure Dome'. Bex prompted us to consider if, reading that, we 'immediately thought of physical pleasure?' Yep, I sure did – banoffee pie, pizza, and banana milkshakes. *Lush!* But, when Bex mentioned 'coming together, physically, in a joyful union with your significant other', I realised I'd misinterpreted the brief.

She asked us to think of times when 'you shared juicy moments with a lover'. *Steady the Buffs!* I mean, Tim and I have been known to *Netflix and Chill*, more literally these days, but honestly, our juiciest moments are sharing a Sunday lunch at the Plough & Harrow in Murton. (Side note: Sod ambrosia, because their roasts are nothing short of divine!) And it's only Uke Club that leaves me with a satisfied glow. Anyway, moving swiftly on, the focus turned to the 'body', and that's when we *really* got personal! *Eek!*

Initially, it was interesting. Bex supplied a potted history of the female body, how it was once worshipped, with ladies treated like idols. But pesky patriarchal societies soon took over, feared the divine power of women, and were the reason today's woman 'struggles with disliking ourselves, and our vessels'. She had a point, though I think social media and reality TV should take a chunk of blame too. But reclaiming 'our magic' was going to take work. So, saddle up ladies, we've got power to salvage.

Unbelievably, Bex did today's action point with *four* of her friends, finding it 'scary but completely freeing, as we cried, raged, and screamed away the pain of suppression'. *What now?* Look, I've got some great mates, but if I invited them to pop over and share a nude bonding session, whilst shrieking about male dominance, they'd either ghost me, or ring to check I'm not midway through a psychotic break – and to be fair, I wouldn't blame them.

But I did try it – alone, *obvs* – awkwardly checking myself out, whilst wishing I'd put the heating on. And I categorically didn't catch the feels Bex had experienced when gazing at herself in the buff: 'As I saw my true me, the more I wanted to touch myself. So bring your hands to your body, touch between your thighs, caress your hips, and waist. How do your breasts feel?' *Klaxon Alert!* I'll gloss over this, but suffice it to say, I certainly felt a tit – though definitely not in the way Bex had hoped.

Next, Bex outlined her, 'pathways to pleasure', none of which particularly floated my boat: Take a bath (*Meh*), stretch in the morning (*Obvs*), buy your favourite flowers (*Okay - tick*), oils (*?*), face masks (*Nah*) etc. Yeah, I enjoy a bubble bath, and a hand-tied bouquet never goes amiss, but oils and face masks don't cut it for me.

'So,' asks Bex, 'what does?' And I was mildly disturbed to discover that I honestly couldn't say. We were seeking out, 'soul-level pleasures', and I was clueless. *Hmm?* Though this whole course was, likely, absolute bunkum, Bex was undoubtedly making me probe my psyche.

And so the week continued. I did affirmations each day, Haydn (next-door down), dropped in to ask what was up with the dogs (whose melodious howling now accompanied every affirmation sesh), Tim kept to himself, and his shed, and I happily followed Bex's syllabus, glad that the discomfort of Day 2 was behind me . . . Until Day 7 dawned, and we launched into 'The Cycle and the Womb Space'. *Sigh.*

According to Bex, 'our periods are a built in form of detoxification that men don't have, hahahhhaha suckers, so let's start healing it'. And her top tips were to 'switch to organic tampons/pads' and to recognise that 'bad periods are a sign that you are denying your female power, you're not secure in your feminine essence, or there's trauma that says it's not safe to be a woman'. *Hard eye roll!*

Twenty plus years back, when I suffered 'bad' periods, it wasn't because of inorganic products, an uncertain essence, or the risk of potential anti-feminine peril. It was simply due to a couple of melon-sized tumours, *down there* (Honeydew and Galia). So I thought that Bex's action points were going to prove *fruitless* (*teehee*) for me, much as I'd lovingly embrace a miracle cure for the menopause.

'Bring awareness to your womb space. Put your hands on it. Feel it. What's in there . . . mystically?' *Aw, bollocks!* My radical hysterectomy whisked womb (and *all* accessories), away, so there's nothing at all lurking near my lady parts, physically, spiritually, or otherwise.

But then she recommended 'V-steaming', which I hadn't heard of, and was initially intrigued by – until she explained it involved, 'squatting over a bowl of boiling water, infused with curative herbs; turmeric for healing, sage for cleansing, and cinnamon for its anti-fungal qualities'. And I'm done. Yep, call me old-fashioned, but crouching over an odorous bain-marie and broiling my *hoo-ha* like a fillet of hake, is deffo not up my alley, and healing properties be damned.

A week on, and I'm not any more divine, but I did learn from the process. What I found interesting were the levels of discomfort I'd experienced throughout. Yes, some of the 'action points' *were* a little alarming, but it was actually the daily reflective questions that gave me pause. Because, now I've stopped to consider it, I rarely psychoanalyse myself, and actively avoid excavating my emotions – especially those of sadness, heartache, and grief.

Don't get me wrong, I'm not some reserved robot, in fact quite the opposite, but I don't like being *forced* into feeling . . . well, feelings. Like, I can't watch *Watership Down* or *ET,* and steer clear of films classed as tear-jerkers, or feature a dog, because I don't want to find myself a mess of snot and sorrow.

It's the unsuppressed ferocity of misery and melancholy that bothers me, combined with an embarrassment to fully let myself go, and it was thanks to Bex's bizarre programme, that I became self-aware enough to realise it.

And though it's been easier, and habitual, for me to incarcerate all sombre sensibilities in my personal prison, maybe the time has come for me to unfasten the fetters, ignore the inhibitions, and let loose the real me? There's certainly an insistent, deific voice shouting, 'Do it Del!' . . . and, good goddess, I think I bloody well will.

But first, I've got a date with a hot bath and pan scourer because, though Helen at Holland & Barrett said 'don't worry, it *will* fade', you try *not* panicking when your bush is bright orange, and your mons pubis resembles Donald Trump – but with better hair. Knew I should've swerved the sodding V-steam. *Sigh.*

NB: And if, for some unfathomable reason, you decide to give your *foof* a facial and want turmeric in the mix, Helen suggests purchasing the 'organic varieties, which don't contain colourants and don't stain skin, but avoid the supermarket stuff because they're filled with dyes that do'. You have been warned!

If you've been inspired to try Bex's Goddess programme, you can find it, and numerous others, on Eventbrite – check out the Spiritual, Mind & Body section.

ACKNOWLEDGEMENTS

If I hadn't done an MA at Swansea Uni, I'd never have had the opportunity to write for the best news outlet in Wales, *Nation.Cymru*. So I'd like to give a big shout-out to Fran Rhydderch, Alan Bilton, and Dai George, for all their help and support. A special mention goes to Gilly Adams because it was during her 'Writing the Self' workshop that I penned, what was to become, my first ever article. So huge thanks Gilly, for the fun, the feedback, and the very sage advice.

But 'Naked Attraction' would never have escaped its dusty folder if I hadn't met Sarah Morgan Jones (weekend editor and fellow alumni), and if it hadn't been a *really* slow news day. After mentioning that she needed some newspaper appropriate articles, I tentatively mentioned my art piece and, with trembling fingers, emailed it across. Only then did I dip into *Nation.Cymru*, realising with horror that my memoir was 100% unsuitable for the 'Culture' section. *Bollocks!*

But astonishingly, it was published (Did I mention it was a slow news day?), and that was the beginning of my first regular writing gig. So massive thank yous to Mark Mansfield and Jon Gower, for taking such a gamble on an untested writer and sticking with me for the long haul. And huge love and endless thanks to Sarah, an inspirational writer, who has championed and encouraged me every step of the way. She's coped with my crippling impostor syndrome, skilfully managed my meltdowns, and corrected my many typos, all whilst, somehow, imbuing me with the confidence to finally think of myself as a writer. Sar, you are the Gandalf to my Bilbo, and an absolute bloody star!

To Chris Jones at Cambria Books, thank you for your kindness, unlimited patience, and for turning my pipe dream of having a 'proper paper book' into a reality. And thanks to Josh (aka Sketchy Welsh), for encapsulating my adventures so perfectly and for making my book look utterly epic.

Thanks also go to *all* my stalwart supporters, but special mentions to Lizzie, Ian, Derks, Cath, and Gaynor, for the critiques, the comments, the reposts, and retweets. And to Tim, for supplying the doughnuts, but mainly for being *so* Yorkshire that his character writes itself. (Though, believe me when I say he's *much* more entertaining to read about than to live with. *Sigh.*)

And lastly, to those I've met along the way. Without you, I would never have (*deep breath*): flown an owl, dabbled with witchery, discovered natural poisons, freed my inner stag, enjoyed sublime sensory deprivation, tried taphophilia, starred in a smash hit stage show, walked on fire, faced down serious fears, chased phantoms, bathed in sound, communed with cacao and experienced terpsichorean thrills, become semi-proficient on a ukulele, handled my haystack of heartache, dined with the dead, toured the wildlands of Wales, written a book, found a diverse and wonderful group of new pals, and be living my best life for the first time in fifty-four years. And for that, I truly thank you all. *Diolch yn fawr iawn.* #YOLO

Milton Keynes UK
Ingram Content Group UK Ltd.
UKHW022310020424
440481UK00014B/487